ATHINA: THE LAST ONASSIS

Other books by Chris Hutchins and Peter Thompson

Sarah's Story: The Duchess Who Defied the House of Windsor
Elvis and Lennon: The Untold Story of their Deadly Feud

ATHINA

THE LAST ONASSIS

CHRIS HUTCHINS AND PETER THOMPSON

SMITH GRYPHON
PUBLISHERS

First published in Great Britain in 1996 by
SMITH GRYPHON LIMITED
Swallow House, 11–21 Northdown Street
London N1 9BN

A CIP catalogue record for this book is available from the British Library

ISBN 1 85685 108 7

Typeset by Computerset, Harmondsworth
Printed and bound in Great Britain by Butler and Tanner Ltd, Frome

Jacket photograph acknowledgements

Front Jacket: ©Associated Press
Athina clutches the hand of her father, Thierry Roussel,
at his wedding to Gaby Landhage at Villeny, central France.

Back Jacket: ©Alpha
Golden Girl Athina chose a white bikini for a set of magazine
pictures taken in Ibiza in July 1995.

CONTENTS

PART TWO

THE LEGACY

HEIDI WITH SHOULDER HOLSTERS

I N A HEAVILY GUARDED Swiss mansion, an 11-year-old girl is growing up amid all the normality great wealth can buy. Despite the efforts of her father to give her a healthy, stable life, Athina Onassis Roussel cannot help but feel different from other children of her age. Although she would prefer to ride ponies or play in the enchanted forest at the bottom of her garden like a storybook Heidi, Athina knows only too well that the security systems, armed bodyguards and bullet-proofed limousines are there for her protection. 'How can she not know,' asked her father, Thierry Roussel, 'when she already has people requesting her autograph in the streets?'

Athina is the last Onassis, sole survivor of the dynasty founded by the fabled Golden Greek shipping magnate Aristotle Onassis and heiress to an estate approaching $10 billion. As might be expected from the immensity of the wealth involved, her passage towards full inheritance at the age of 18 is neither smooth nor conventional. Overshadowing her life is a legal battle between her father and a group of distinguished Greek trustees, known because of their collective longevity as 'the greybeards', for control of the Onassis estate. Every passing year, Athina's worth in cash terms increases by at least $100 million from bank interest and from dividends on low-risk investments made in her name. The value of her assets in bonds and property continues to soar. No little girl on earth is richer or more sheltered, yet none will become more famous than Athina when she takes centre stage in the high drama that accompanies her birthright.

This is Heidi with Shoulder Holsters, a thriller played out against a backdrop of snow-capped Alpine peaks, ski resorts and golden Mediterranean beaches; of kidnap threats, rowdy newspaper headlines and courtroom battles; of dashes through hordes of photographers at airports and sudden departures in private jets to secret destinations. And surrounding the whole scenario is the spectre of an immense and heart-breaking grief.

On a winter's day in 1995, the blonde streaks dyed into her naturally jet-black hair showed that although Athina was becoming more adult, she was not growing up as the Greek she had been born. Instead, her French father and Swedish step-mother, the former Gaby Landhage, were raising the Onassis heiress in the style of their own three blonde children, Erik, Sandrine and Johanne.

However, Athina's conversion into a proper little French schoolgirl – *une jeune fille de bonne famille* – had been only partially successful. No amount of chic French styling could disguise the likeness to Athina's natural mother, Christina Onassis, who lay buried near Christina's father, Aristotle, and Christina's brother, Alexander, in a white-walled annexe attached to the Chapel of the Little Virgin on the Greek island of Skórpios.

Wearing a selection of their northern European clothes, the Roussel family were photographed at Thierry's hunting lodge in the Sologne region of central France during a New Year holiday for a series of articles to be published in a number of European magazines to promote his newly created association, Action for Childhood. Some of the photographs would show all four Roussel children sitting with their father in the lodge's living room and studying a film of him doing the humanitarian work that, he said, was essential in the modern world. Rather in the manner of the Duchess of York, the photo spreads were to include snaps of Thierry distributing gifts to children on one of his many charity trips to Asia. 'What I am doing is not exceptional,' Roussel informed us. 'I only try to put into practice certain ideas dear to my heart.'

Nevertheless Roussel clung to the belief that his abilities as an entrepreneur were considerable and his contribution to both business and international aid relief deserved to bring him recognition in his own right. Although Athina's fortune carried the unmistakable Onassis imprint, her father hated few things more than the role of walking in the shadow of his first wife's famous name.

One of the magazines on Roussel's list of approved publications was *Paris-Match*, whose executive editor, Chris Lafaille, said: 'It was a condition of us publishing these pictures that we did not mention the name of Onassis – only Roussel.' Twice a year, the French magazine paid a sizeable fee for similar picture spreads showing how well the Roussel family functioned and how admirably Thierry worked for those children less privileged than his own. 'It was necessary for him to project these images in the eyes of the Greeks,' explained Lafaille, referring to the four Athenian keepers of the late Christina's estate who are also directors of the Alexander S. Onassis Public Benefit Foundation, a philanthropic organization set up by Onassis in remembrance of his son.

Apart from the foundation, Christina had been the chief beneficiary of her father's will, and she, in turn, had left her fortune to Athina when she reaches the age of 18 in January 2003. In the intervening years, Roussel has been entrusted by his late wife with the task of bringing up the child for a generous annual stipend of $1.42 million, plus expenses. At the time of Christina's funeral, his weeping was considered less than genuine. 'He has set out to rehabilitate himself, not just with the press but especially in the eyes of those Greeks,' said Lafaille.

'It was very important that they had respect for him, which they never did have because as soon as Christina died he started using her private plane. The Greeks had to confiscate it, and a number of clashes followed. They wanted Athina to come to Athens, but he wouldn't have that. Then he did a stupid thing: he tried to claim control of all of Athina's fortune. In addition to the rest of the estate, she had a billion dollars in the bank – in cash.'

In November 1993, Roussel had applied to the Swiss courts in the Canton of Grisons for the right to administer his daughter's inheritance until she comes of age. He claimed that, as her guardian, this was his entitlement under French law. The four Greek trustees, who had worked for Aristotle since they were young men and whom

Christina had regarded as honorary uncles, strongly resisted Roussel's takeover bid in the courts. They also complained vocally and publicly that he was trying to steer Athina away from her Greek heritage. 'She is living in Switzerland, far from Greek culture,' said one source in Athens. 'The trustees think that Mr Roussel is weaning his daughter from all things Greek to ensure he is the main influence in her life.'

To counteract these charges, Roussel encouraged Christina's long-time friend and former maid, Eleni Syros, to keep in touch with his daughter. 'Mr Thierry gives me permission to go to Switzerland to see Athina two or three times a year,' she told us at her home in Athens. 'I see all of the Roussel children and accompany them to school. Athina is very busy with her studies, but she is a very happy child. She likes horseriding and skiing – she goes to Villars and St Moritz every year.'

One of Roussel's closest friends said: 'No matter what the trustees think, Thierry loves his little girl and wants only to do what is best for her.'

The great imponderable as far as her father and the trustees are concerned is what Athina will do once she has full access to her fortune. According to Roussel's former mistress Kirsten Gille, it is clear that 'he adores his daughter and would never harm her. Obviously, if anything terrible happened to her, then he would get everything, but he's not a mean person.'

There is always the possibility that Athina might follow the path of other heiresses through the ages and elope with an entirely unsuitable lover, perhaps even a fortune hunter. At the age of 20, Athina's mother Christina had married a man whom Aristotle had heartily despised, her grandmother Tina had wed against her parents' wishes when she was 17, and her great-grandmother Arietta had been a child bride of just 15 summers. Only time could establish whether such romantic inclinations ran in Athina's genes, and Roussel was subscribing to the theory that environment would, in his daughter's case, override heredity.

According to those closest to the Roussel household, he could console himself about the strength of his daughter's feelings towards him. 'Athina loves her father,' said one of Christina's best friends. 'She has the same way of looking at Thierry as Christina used to do when he walked into the room. Christina would be there talking, Thierry would come in, and she would get all excited. It was like a god coming in, and Athina has the same thing about her father.'

'Thierry is a great father to all his children, and he tries to raise Athina as best he can and give her the most love he can,' his friend Paul Hagnoer said in Paris. 'It's difficult when you have the daughter of a mother like Christina, and it isn't easy when everybody knows she's the heiress to a very big fortune. That is why she has to be protected and very well educated, and Thierry does that extremely well. He is a public person, and, of course, everybody tries to find out the worst about him. What I read in the press and what I hear is always bad, but I say he is a great person, a wonderful person. He is extremely generous and someone who has a great sense of friendship.'

However, Roussel's critics claimed that not even reckless generosity could account for his track record in business before and after his marriage to Christina. Florence Grinda, Christina's friend who had married into the Roussel family, said, 'He's got charm, he's good looking, and luckily he had Christina at one point, but he doesn't have her now.'

Naturally enough, Roussel was aware of the suspicions about his motives towards Athina's money. He stated his position in words that no one could possibly misunderstand. 'Athina is mine,' he insisted. 'She does not belong to the Onassis fortune.'

At the same time as the little heiress to $10 billion was posing for those family portraits, the Greek millionaire Alexander 'Alecko' Papamarkou talked about the tragedies that have haunted the Onassis family through four generations. An international financier renowned for his influence from Wall Street to the City of London, Papamarkou was also a member of the prize-giving committee of the Onassis Foundation. As a long-standing friend of the Onassis family, he cared very much about what had happened to Christina Onassis – and what was happening now to her daughter Athina.

'When I saw Christina in St Moritz in the eighties, I was impressed by how wise she had become,' he told us in New York. 'Her father was dead, and the buck stopped with her. She was looking back on her life and making some very grown-up conclusions. She was full of life and spirit – but I have to say she was also so bloody arbitrary!'

Then he gave voice to the question that has angered and

perplexed many Greeks ever since Christina's mysterious death in Argentina in November 1988: 'Why did she change her will at the last minute? Hand-written instructions about the girl who was her everything? Giving Thierry Roussel power over her child? Why did she do it? Why . . .?'

To seek out the answer, we travelled 25,000 miles around the world until we came at last to a village in the Swiss countryside not far from the border with France. With an air of tense anticipation, we entered through the electronically controlled gates into the grounds of a villa called Boislande. This was the place at which Christina's life had reached a crossroads; the point of departure between the playgirl who had squandered her youth and wealth on worldly pursuits and the mother who had found a new beginning through the birth of her only child. Many of the secrets of her tormented life were waiting to be uncovered in the only house Christina Onassis ever called home.

PART ONE

THE LEGEND

ONE WIFE AND THREE LOVERS

A COCKEREL CROWED AT the far end of the Rue de Derrier as a navy-blue Mercedes limousine carrying Christina Onassis and her four-month-old daughter Athina swept into the centre of an unpretentious Swiss village hemmed in by farms in the foothills overlooking Lac Léman. Some of the village's 500 inhabitants glanced up to watch the vehicle's progress past the bank, the general store, the Auberge de la Poste and the score of stone houses with green shuttered windows and tiled rooftops. Even though Christina wasn't visible through the car's smoked-glass windows, they knew she was returning to their midst with her longed-for child. The baby was swaddled safely in a crib, which was belted to the rear passenger seat between Christina and Eleni Syros, the Greek woman who was more family than servant to her 34-year-old mistress.

This was the homecoming that the people of Gingins had eagerly awaited, but after that single glance and a friendly wave or two, they had gone about their own business. Christina Onassis had come among them the previous year very much in the manner of a refugee in search of sanctuary, and they had welcomed her with open arms, not because of her vast wealth from the estate of her father, the shipping magnate Aristotle Onassis, but because she was a human being in distress. The villagers had decided at the outset that she should be accepted as one of their own and, against any instincts to the contrary, treated her privacy with admirable respect. 'We were very pleased she had chosen our village to make her home,' said Tina Schneider, *patronne* of the Auberge de la Poste. 'But no one here likes gossip, and we agreed she was entitled to the same consideration – perhaps even more so because she was famous.'

The Mercedes veered left at the Hôtel de la Croix Blanche and the Norman church, and disappeared in the direction of cowbells, which tinkled round the necks of dairy cattle in the surrounding meadows. Apart from the cockerel, the cowbells and the occasional barking of a dog, the only sound to be heard was the noise of streams running down from the looming mountains into granite horse troughs in farmyards as neat as only the Swiss could make them. On this spring day in 1985, little Gingins was an island of tranquillity in a sea of leafy green.

At a bend on the Route de St Cergue, electronically operated gates marked La Boislande swung open, and the car headed down a semi-circular drive, past lush thickets of rhododendrons and a stone fountain dated 1828, and drew to a halt on the paved courtyard outside the front door of the house. Now answering to the fourth of her married names, Madame Thierry Roussel, Christina had bought this gracious, 18-room villa from the German industrialist Gunther Sachs for $4 million soon after her wedding on 17 March 1984. The place had been a hive of building activity ever since and, although she had spent much of her pregnancy in a hotel suite for fear of a miscarriage, Christina had been kept up to date with the renovations by scanning photographs of the work, which had been brought to her bedside.

Had Athina been old enough to take in the detail of that short drive inside the high wooden gates she would have noticed two security guards, discreetly armed, patrolling the tree-lined perimeter of the relatively compact three-acre garden. Four other men also trained by the British SAS had been hired to work later shifts and three more to act as her bodyguards, never straying far from her cot with their guns. Waiting inside were a team of nurses engaged by Christina to work round-the-clock shifts, ready to attend to the precious infant's every need. Indeed, the watch on Athina would become smothering because of her mother's fear that she might fall and injure herself. 'At the age of three,' said Thierry Roussel, 'she didn't know how to run.'

The cost of this protection would amount to a million dollars a year on top of the $2.5 million Christina had lavished on converting Boislande into a luxurious fortress equipped with surveillance cameras in every room, electronic detectors and every other anti-kidnapping, child-minding gadget on the market. In her sleepy-eyed innocence, Athina took in nothing of her mother's elaborate interior decorating, which had turned the sprawling villa into a palace worthy of its new-born princess. A sunken swimming pool had already been erected in the living room and, before Athina was six months old, there would be a zoo with lambs and deer in the grounds – and a qualified animal trainer to tame even the wildest Bambi.

Christina's chauffeur had driven the Mercedes to Geneva airport to collect mother and daughter after they arrived in her private jet from Paris. Mercedes-Benz was the only make of car in Christina's personal fleet. 'She believed they were safe,' a close friend told us. 'She wouldn't even drive in a Rolls-Royce.' Nor was the driver permitted to accelerate above 30 miles an hour on the homeward journey to keep the risks of a traffic accident down to a minimum. Athina was far too precious to leave anything to chance.

The baby had been delivered prematurely by Caesarian section at the American Hospital of Paris on 29 January 1985. This was the same hospital in which Athina's grandfather, Aristotle, had died 10 years previously at the age of 75, having completed a life that still ranked as one of the most buccaneering of the twentieth century. However, the ruthlessness he had displayed with bewildering effect in the marketplace had not been confined to his business rivals. Aristotle had tried to prevent Christina's birth by beating up her mother, the former Tina Livanos, after failing to persuade her to have an abortion. He already had a son and heir, Alexander, and claimed that more than one child 'only clouds the issue'. It was not until after Alexander had died from injuries he had received in a suspicious air crash when Christina was 23 years old that Onassis had come to appreciate the daughter he had subjected to a lifetime of opulent neglect and emotional cruelty.

Finally certain of his need for her, if not exactly his love, Christina had wept night after night at his bedside as he had slowly wasted away, and there had been more tears at his funeral on the Onassis island of Skórpios until, free of any controls whatsoever and richer than any royal princess, she had embarked on a career of marriage and divorce, intermingled with numerous affairs, that had been the despair of those few people who truly loved her.

But that was in the rapidly vanishing past as Christina supervised Eleni in bringing Athina into the house and placing her in a bedroom that included a full wardrobe of miniature Dior originals. Even among the most sceptical of her friends, there was no doubt that the only male who mattered to the Onassis heiress was her husband Thierry Roussel, the man who had succeeded in making her pregnant after she had undergone expensive fertility treatments during the first three months of their married life. After at least three abortions – two of them while she was married to previous husbands – Christina knew that pregnancy would be a problematical endeavour, but she had been determined to bear Roussel's child and thus bind him to her not only by holy matrimony but through parenthood as well.

With his boyish, sunburned good looks, strapping physique and lively, enquiring mind, Thierry was held far higher in Christina's esteem than any of the three other spouses who had borne the title of 'Mr Christina Onassis': the Californian real-estate millionaire Joseph Bolker, the Greek banker Alexander Andreadis and the Russian shipping agent Sergei Kausov. However, it was part of Christina's tragedy that no matter how unsuitable she might have found her previous husbands for a variety of reasons, Roussel would create more emotional havoc in her life than all the others put together.

'I simply hope to make Thierry happy,' Christina had said just before their wedding. 'We will try to be together as much as possible – in Paris, in St Moritz, in Greece. I want to look after my house and start a family. I think I deserve to be happy.'

There was not the slightest reservation in any of her friends' minds that these were fine objectives, but they doubted that Thierry Roussel was the man with whom she was likely to achieve them. One of her closest friends, Florence Grinda, warned Christina that Thierry was a free-spending playboy with a poor performance in key areas of fidelity and money management. As she had once been Thierry's aunt by marriage, she spoke with some authority, but Christina had charged on regardless. This time, she told everyone, it would be different.

Learning of the hostility towards him, Roussel had counter-attacked by claiming that Christina's friends were the chief cause of the trouble between them. Picking up her address book, he had scored out dozens of names and extracted a promise from his wife that she would carry out his wish to exclude these people from her life. Friends said that only a week after the wedding Christina was talking about getting a separation. Instead, she had tearfully agreed to Thierry's terms. He also insisted that the couple should have a Swiss home other than the Villa Crystal, which Christina had inherited in St Moritz. He argued that this was Onassis territory, where friends of her family past and present had enjoyed the late Greek tycoon's largesse (even if he had rarely ventured there in person) as well as, in a number of cases, his daughter's favours. Roussel shared his dead father-in-law's contempt for the fur-clad poseurs and town-and-country types who swarmed into the ski resort for the season.

Christina had conceded Thierry's point about St Moritz, but she had been faced with a huge disadvantage in trying to select a suitable location for them to put down roots. She had never had a settled home during her parents' long-distance marriage, having been shunted from the Plaza in New York to Claridge's in London, or from a penthouse apartment on Avenue Foch in Paris to her bedroom in the Onassis yacht *Christina* at Monte Carlo. Intermittently, she had been raised by her childless aunt, Artimus Garafalides, at the villa near Athens that Onassis had bought for his natural sister. With much heart-rending indecision, Christina had chosen Gingins, one of the prettiest backwaters in the lakeside canton of Vaud, because it was close to her mother's tomb in the Livanos family vault at Bois de Vaux, Lausanne. She knew the area from her time at St George's, a French-speaking boarding school further along the shore to which her father had sent her as a teenager. She had hated the school but spent hours gazing at the breathtaking countryside that swept down to the placid waters at Montreux.

As well as its picturesque surroundings, Gingins had resounding appeal to someone who was trying to start life over again. Although only a 15-minute drive from Geneva airport along Switzerland's main road, Route Nationale 1, there was a noticeable absence of any representatives of the fabled jet set in the region. Even before she had been old enough to fasten her own seat belt, Christina had been initiated into the jet set by her father. Onassis had founded this informal society of fast-moving high fliers in the fifties to achieve his overwhelming ambition of being in several places at the same time.

Here in Gingins, apart from the widow of the hamlet's benefactor, a Venezuelan millionaire called Neumann, the local population were mostly farmers and land owners who cared more about wheat crops than the night clubs of Paris, London and Rome that had hitherto been Christina's natural habitat. Here, you were more likely to encounter a tractor hauling a trailerload of fresh cowdung than a Ferrari or a Porsche.

From Boislande, Christina would be able to stroll down country lanes with her baby and husband like any other young married woman, even though there would be a bodyguard somewhere up front and another man covering the rear. In winter, she could travel along a scenic railroad with traditional rolling stock, which wound its way from the lakeside Roman settlement of Nyon to Gingins and then up through the hills to the charming little resort of St Cergue, which was noted for the good skiing facilities it provided for children. In summer, showjumping was held in a large, freshly mown field with spacious stables and a tented grandstand, where enthusiasts drank champagne and the only sound was a polite ripple of applause for a clear round or the clunk of horses' hooves hitting wooden crossbars. Christina had been ecstatic when Thierry had approved of her choice. Within days, great pantechnicons had swayed through the colonnades of oak and poplar on their way to Boislande, and the extraordinary Onassis–Roussel alliance had found a home base.

In the hell-raising phase of her life, Christina had been known to dance on tables and, with the help of chemical stimulants, stay awake for three days and nights on end. However, motherhood had mellowed her in the most delightful way. During the early summer of 1985 she demonstrated her new-found maternal love by spending almost as much time at Athina's side as the girls in crisp white uniforms and the men with guns. Visits to night clubs became a thing of the past as she threw her energies into her new responsibilities. Several times a day she checked the cot while her child slept, to ensure that it wasn't all a dream. There was no mistaking Athina's pedigree. The baby, whom Christina called Tina or *koukla* (little doll in Greek), had her mother's dark hair, 'black as a raven's wing', and the same large, brown eyes, but she had the perfect Roussel nose rather than the huge Onassian beak that had disfigured Christina's face until plastic surgery removed the blemish.

'She's going to be tall like Thierry,' Christina told a friend, holding up the baby for inspection. 'And just look at the size of her feet – she's going to have big feet like me!' Athina had been born with one tooth already in place; as the others turned up and she smiled at her mother, Christina knew a love and a warmth she had never believed were possible. Gradually, the tantrums of early married life when she had tried, and failed, to get pregnant had more or less subsided, and a semblance of bliss descended on Boislande. Sadly, however, it was a bliss born of ignorance.

Christina had married Roussel, heir to a fast-dwindling fortune derived from his family's pharmaceutical business, in two ceremonies – one civil and one Greek Orthodox – in Paris after a whirlwind courtship. Asked to describe himself in a single word, Roussel would probably have said 'businessman', but he was known to many in the Parisian beau monde as a playboy of considerable charm and relentless passion.

Perhaps to restore his side of the family to great riches, the 32-year-old Frenchman had previously involved himself in imaginative business projects that had nothing to do with pharmaceuticals. Beautiful women had always been of great interest to him, and there had been his involvement through one of his companies with his friend Paul Hagnoer in a Paris-based model agency called First. Roussel was all too aware of his playboy reputation. 'It's true that I love life and beautiful women, and it's true that I was born into a rich family,' he said. 'But it annoys me that this is all people remember about me. Success breeds resentment.'

Even at the time of his marriage to Christina, there were those who resented the match to such an extent that they claimed Christina's fortune had played a part in Roussel's decision. She had already given her husband $20 million as a reverse dowry to pay off his debts and place his business interests on a sound foundation, and there were millions more where that came from. Meanwhile, he continued to live a complicated life.

There was nothing new in his attachment to the Swedish model Marianne 'Gaby' Landhage, with whom he had been involved on and off for 15 years. According to a close friend, the bridegroom had telephoned Gaby on his wedding day to assure her that 'nothing had changed' between them. Somehow Christina's extensive network had failed to pick up on a newspaper item, published in Swedish, that reported that, soon after the nuptials in Paris, Thierry Roussel had called Gaby to declare, 'I will start with you again,' to which she had replied, 'And I with you.'

Indeed, the marriage was only a few months old before Roussel turned to Gaby not in the manner of a man resuming a relationship with a former mistress but as a bitterly upset husband who needed a shoulder to cry on. He complained to friends whenever they were apart. 'He was unhappy with Christina,' the close friend told us. 'Initially, he had the upper hand, but he lost it very quickly. Christina started to treat him like a schmuck; it was typical of her to do that if someone were being too nice or too gushy. She could feel if people were only interested in her money.' Christina constantly spied on Thierry at home and checked up on him through friends when he was away on business trips. To test the strength of his commitment to the marriage, she demanded they make love every time he returned to the marital fold. Whenever his ardour seemed to slacken, she reminded him that she was an expert on failed marriages.

Christina's previous husbands were already a source of irritation to Roussel, and he didn't relish comparisons with any of them. Bolker, a twice-married Jew, was old enough to be his father; Andreadis was a hearty eater who collected vintage Rolls-Royces; Kausov had thinning fair hair, a glass eye, gold teeth – and the shadow of the KGB had hovered over his slight figure until Christina had facilitated his escape to the West. But Roussel knew that Andreadis had been dumped after just a few months, while Bolker and Kausov had lasted only marginally longer. Marriage to Christina Onassis was a high-risk enterprise, and he knew she was quite capable of ditching him as well.

Certainly this would have been the outcome had Christina discovered in those fraught early months that he was spending time with Gaby Landhage in between business trips to Paris, Geneva and Marbella. 'He used to see her at a Geneva hotel,' said his close friend. 'She would come down from Sweden to comfort him once in a while.' Whenever he slipped away from his minders and took his Scandinavian paramour in his arms, he told her about the impossibility of living with his demanding Greek wife. Friends later claimed that maintaining this secretive relationship was the only way he could continue in the marriage and still retain his sanity. There was no such problem with Gaby. She had always forgiven her hedonistic, vainglorious lover despite his roving eye and wildly ambitious schemes.

All she had ever hoped was that he would father her children and one day, perhaps, marry her. 'Like a lot of Swedish girls, all Gaby cared about was raising children and having a home,' said a former friend. 'If he gave her that security, Thierry could do as he pleased.'

After each assignation with Gaby, Roussel would return refreshed and level-headed to Boislande. Driving towards the heavy gates that instantly swung open at his approach, he would glance in the rear-view mirror to ensure that the gel he applied liberally to hold down the unruly waves in his long blond hair was doing its stuff. The last thing he wanted was for Christina to suspect that he had been with another woman.

However, Gaby's work required her presence in Sweden and, unnerved by Christina's renewed tantrums after she had failed to test positive for pregnancy, Roussel realized he needed more local support. In May 1984, he decided to introduce a further emotional entanglement into his life by making overtures to Kirsten Gille, a statuesque Danish model with whom he had lived from 1980 until 1983 during a three-year break in his relationship with Gaby. Through an intermediary, Roussel approached Kirsten with a business-like proposition to resume their affair. She was the woman who had smoothed out his rough edges, entertained his more élite friends and fulfilled his sexual needs without ever mentioning marriage or children.

'I had met him in the south of France soon after he had taken up with Gaby,' Kirsten told us during the course of several long interviews. 'When I came to Paris in 1980 I saw him again, and I knew he wanted to start an affair with me. I asked him if he were still with Gaby and he said, "No, she's gone to America – and I've decided I don't want to marry her." So I said OK, and we started our affair quite discreetly. It went on for a few months, and then he went off for Christmas with her. I was in Italy when he broke the news to Gaby that he did not want to marry her. He was only 26, he said, and too young to marry. So his affair with Gaby was finished, and I began three years of living with him.

'When Thierry decided to get married to Christina, Gaby went back to Sweden, where she went to work in the public relations department of a cosmetics firms in Malmö. The day I left him he called her up, but he had already seen her a little before then with the help of his mother, Francine. I didn't know he was still seeing her when he got a relative to contact me three months after his wedding to see if I would speak to him.'

Kirsten was more or less available for such an approach, and she indicated that she was willing to listen to Roussel's proposal. He phoned her, and a meeting was arranged at which he told her he missed her and wanted her back in his life. After some months of soul-searching, Kirsten agreed to resume their relationship. 'I hadn't wanted to see him, and I said, "Look, you're married, and it's finished between us." But he knew I was having some difficulty surviving because I had nothing when I left him. I didn't expect anything, but he knew my dream was to go into showjumping, and he was in a position to help me with that.'

Having agreed to become Thierry's mistress, Kirsten had marvelled at his insistence that she should meet his wife. 'Christina and I have a lot of friends in common like Florence Grinda and her brother Hubert Michard-Pellissier,' she said. 'They're old friends of mine; I've known them since I was 20. I'd seen Christina before, but we weren't friends. I didn't meet her until she and Thierry were married, and I had started to see him again. Then one evening at a dinner party he sort of introduced us, and we spoke together. Christina absolutely wanted to talk to me to find out more about him. She wanted to know everything. She wanted to know how he had been with me compared with how he was with her. She was a hot woman, and I think she had expected more from Thierry than she got.'

The emotional complications of having a wife and two mistresses (one of whom was on speaking terms with his wife, even discussing his sexual prowess) might have been sufficient for even the most daring of men, but Thierry Roussel was not satisfied yet. Kirsten watched in astonishment that summer as her libidinous partner added a fourth young woman to his entourage of 'personal pleasure'. For good measure, he began a new liaison with Teresa Prater, an American girl – blonde like his other two mistresses – after meeting her on the French Riviera. Teresa confirmed that she had had a serious affair with Roussel. 'Well, obviously you know that,' she told us from California. 'So far, Thierry and I have had discretion, and I respect him.'

Thierry had been in the mood for some ego-stroking. Christina had become pregnant in June 1984 and, despite the Onassis name-tag that he reluctantly wore, he knew that nothing could stop the baby from bearing the surname of Roussel. Unlike her three previous husbands, he had succeeded in providing an heir to the Onassis fortune and not even divorce could alter that. Having made Christina pregnant, Roussel felt justified in living his life as he saw fit. He began to spend extended periods apart from his wife, including long stopovers in Paris, where his business interests were located. In November, he also proved the sincerity of his promise to Gaby by impregnating her as well during one of their trysts. The result had been that, not long after Athina had arrived at Boislande for the first time, Gaby had given birth to a son, Erik, in a Malmö hospital in July 1985. By that time, life at Boislande had become so strained that Christina had consulted her lawyers once again to discuss a separation.

'I'm so unhappy,' Christina told a friend. 'My husband doesn't want to be with me. He won't sleep with me.' Roussel had, in fact, left home and was staying at a suite at the Beau Rivage hotel in Geneva whenever he visited Switzerland to see his daughter.

'He left the house because they had continuous arguments,' said a mutual friend. 'Every day Christina would have some terrible crisis. Some Coca-Cola would fall on the floor, and she would make a big drama out of it. She would start screaming like a little Greek woman, and this would go on for one or two hours. This sort of thing was very difficult for him to live with, but Christina wanted him back.' Naturally enough, Thierry kept the news of the birth of his son a secret from his very Greek, very jealous wife as well as from his mistresses Kirsten and Teresa. However, one thing was certain about the future of both his children: they would never want for honorary godmothers.

At Boislande, Christina had completely forgotten about separation as she turned the pages of the huge photographic albums that told her family's story. In terms of human drama, there had been many memorable episodes in the Onassis saga since it had begun with Aristotle's birth at the dawn of the twentieth century. No tycoon in the pantheon of the super-rich had made a bigger impression than her father, and she was proud of him despite his manifest faults. At 5ft 5in tall, he had been diminutive in stature, yet very much larger than life; notorious yet fêted, ruthless yet generous. Although he had hidden many secrets from her, she knew he had fought with utter ferocity to rise from abject poverty to a position of such power that he answered to no one. Like Cartier for jewellery or Bell for telephones or Rockefeller for capitalism, the name Onassis was synonymous with shipping. Even though the name he had chosen for his line was Olympic, Onassis himself had grown immensely bigger than the supertanker fleet he had built up from nothing. Whenever Christina doubted her heritage, she gained strength from looking at her father's face, changing with the passing of time from a brash young boy to a billionaire of international repute to the frail, sorrowing figure whose eyelids she had taped open with strips of Band-Aid to hide his last secret from the world.

Her mother had called him 'Neptune', not only because of his seafaring exploits but also because he believed in mermaids. Onassis preferred to see himself as a modern Odysseus, even if his own conquests had been of a more venal kind. 'The whole world talks of my stratagems,' Odysseus had boasted, 'and my fame has reached the heavens.' This sounded so much like her father, and even if his memory caused her pain, the Onassis legend was part of her own life – and of the legacy she would one day hand down to her daughter.

Among the photographs were a set that she had recently received of Athina's christening on Skórpios on 17 August 1985. The baby's chubby face was surrounded by a lace bonnet, her little arms dangled from vast puffed sleeves, and her tiny body swam in folds of flowing silk. In one picture, Thierry held her like a doll that had suddenly been thrust upon him. His long wavy hair flowed over the collar of his Italian suit, and there was a smile on his handsome face that some might say looked practised. As she studied the photograph, Christina had no idea about the guilty secrets her husband was hiding at the very moment the photographer had captured his likeness on film. Instead, she remembered how her father had sailed around Skórpios with her young lover after they had first met on the Onassis island in 1973. Thierry had told her later: 'He was proud as a peacock with him at the helm and me as crew.' It had always been a great comfort to Christina to know that Aristotle had approved of Thierry Roussel.

But after just 18 months of marriage, the news her husband had to impart upon his arrival at Boislande that night was worse than she could have expected. The strain of living with Christina while secretly seeing Gaby, Kirsten and Teresa had driven him to breaking-point. He was tense, angry and fearful when he faced his wife. But far from admitting that he was leading a bizarre love life worthy of the pages of a Balzac novel, he blamed everything on Christina's possessiveness and the Onassis family. He also announced that this time *he* wanted a divorce.

'I cannot go on,' he told her in words he later repeated to the French press. 'We have not succeeded in coming to an understanding in being able to live together. I have offered you a man's love and given you a child. But I can no longer stand continually being watched over by your bodyguards and permanent closed-circuit television cameras in every room. I don't want to be known as Mr Christina Onassis. It is really too difficult to live with a legend.'

Athina was just seven months old at the time, but her mother knew that her tender age would not deter Roussel from leaving the marriage. Better than anyone else, she identified the true meaning of her husband's outburst. History was repeating itself yet again. Every man she had ever loved had shrunk from the long shadow cast by Aristotle Onassis, the man whose legend was 'too difficult to live with'. For as well as shipping, the name Onassis was synonymous with heartbreak, scandal and tragedy of the most headline-making kind. Thierry Roussel was merely the latest to fall victim to the sinister powers of the curse that had followed Christina all her life.

TWO

RETURN OF THE PRODIGAL

CHRISTINA HAD NAMED her daughter after her own mother, the beautiful Athina 'Tina' Livanos, whose family's wealth had helped Aristotle Onassis to reach the top. Tina had been just 17 years old when he had taken her as his wife at a society wedding in New York in December 1946. 'He wanted to marry me when I was 16,' she said, 'but my parents insisted on us waiting for a year.' In a foreshadowing of the troubled Onassis–Roussel union, the bride had married for love and the groom chiefly for money.

The favourite child of Zeus, sovereign ruler of Olympus, the goddess Athina had sprung from her father's split skull brandishing a javelin. As the carrier of Zeus's thunderbolt, she had protected Odysseus during his perils on the return journey to Ithaca after the siege of Troy. Onassis was a keen student of antiquities, but he had made an even closer study of the Livanos family's balance sheet. Without Tina as his wife, he could never have hit such dizzying, Olympian heights – and his grand-daughter would never have been born. For her part, Tina had chosen to ignore all warnings about 'Flash Ari', secure in the knowledge that her heiress status would give her financial independence from even the most ruthless predator.

Yet nearly 13 years later on a summer's day in July 1959, Mrs Tina Onassis, aged just 30, realized she had lost whatever token power she might have once had in the marriage. Knowing she was still young enough to make a fresh start, she had decided to file for divorce, abandoning the husband who had treated her with callous disregard to whatever fate the gods might have in store for him. In public, Ari sometimes dismissed her as though she were little more than one of the dancing girls from the Crazy Horse Saloon whom he liked to present at black-tie functions in Paris as 'a deb from Debrett's'. From the very start of the marriage, his innate sense of inferiority coupled with a highly active libido had driven him into the arms of other lovers. Only a year after their wedding, he had paid Eva Perón $10,000 for a one-night stand.

However, there was sadness in Tina's heart as she watched him mingle with his latest shipload of guests in his yacht *Christina*. Beside Tina on the deck, eight-year-old Christina gripped the handrail of the yacht that bore her name and wondered about the curious behaviour of adults. The child was sensitive to the hostile atmosphere that had enveloped her parents during the voyage. 'I imagined I was losing something important,' she would later recall, 'but I didn't know what.'

Christina was anchored off the Turkish port of Izmir and, as Onassis prepared to go ashore, his apotheosis into a living Greek god seemed all but complete. He had left Monte Carlo with a full complement of VIPs, including Sir Winston Churchill in broad-brimmed panama hat and three-piece tropical suit, and entered the Bay of the Bosphorus with high hopes for this rendezvous with his past. With *Christina*'s hull gleaming white, its primrose funnel making smoke and its brass fittings highly polished, the shipping billionaire was set to make a heroic return to Izmir, the Aegean coastal city once known to the Turks as 'infidel Smyrna'. Smyrna was traditionally the birthplace of Homer, and it was also the place Aristotle Onassis called home.

For reasons that Tina fully understood, this strange, seemingly unpredictable man was keenly on edge. From the time he had woken up, he had inspected his ship and her company of 60 officers, sailors and staff. 'He is almost like a housewife fussing over it,' said Tina, 'constantly looking to see everything is being done well.' Using a white handkerchief, he searched in remote crevices for even the merest specks of dust. If he had found any, the crew knew from past experience he would shout for so long that he would be rendered speechless for days. He had a voice that could rasp like a chainsaw or flow as smoothly as honey. In English, he rolled his Rs like a Scotsman but retained a heavily Continental accent. Everything was mercifully spick and span, and *Barbas*, or 'uncle' as longer-serving Greeks among the crew called him, allowed a brief smile to crease his sun-bronzed face.

At the controls of *Christina*'s twin-engined Piaggio seaplane, the pilot George Kuris waited for the signal to take off on one of his fetch-and-carry missions: either dropping his master's dirty shirts off at a laundry in Greece and picking up a consignment of fresh oranges from his garden in Glyfada, or fetching the ship's daily bread ration, which had been baked on the Avenue Victor-Hugo and driven by his chauffeur Jacinto Rosa to Orly, where one of his Olympic Airways planes collected it for delivery to an airport near the yacht. It was this gratification of even the tiniest of whims that set Onassis apart from other men of great wealth.

Nor was his indulgence restricted to material possessions such as the El Grecos hanging below in the saloon and his master suite (even if their provenance, like that of their owner, were somewhat suspect). It was typical of Onassis that on this trip he was travelling not only with Tina, Christina and his son, Alexander, but also with his new mistress, Maria Callas. His affair with the most famous opera singer in the world was still a closely guarded secret to all but Tina, which partly explained his nervousness, but the other reason was that he was in considerable physical pain and that rather cramped his style at an inconvenient time.

Showing off for the amusement of his children a few days earlier, he had executed some acrobatic dives into the ship's swimming pool. This was the pool into which he once pushed a fully clothed Stavros Niarchos to show his brother-in-law and chief business rival that nowhere was safe. Misjudging the depth of the pool himself, Onassis had hit the blue-and-white mosaic bottom with a sickening crunch. Carried semi-conscious from the water, he had allowed Dr Theo Garafalides, who was married to his sister Artimus, to examine his head and neck but declined an X-ray in the ship's well-equipped surgery to see if anything was seriously amiss. Nothing appeared to be broken, but he had been badly shaken up, and his back ached. He had started medicating himself with liberal doses of Johnnie Walker Black Label scotch with the result that he had taken his discomfort –

and his hangovers – out on the crew.

When he was finally satisfied everything was in order, Onassis boarded his guests into two of the Chris-Craft launches that were part of the yacht's transportation system and ferried them ashore. They landed at Atatürk Caddesi, the long, palm-lined waterfront where the city's restaurants were quartered. While the locals gawked in amazement, the most famous Greek in the world escorted his unlikely entourage on a guided tour of his youth. The infirm Churchill trundled along in a little electric car that his host had considerately provided for the purpose. For shopping, Onassis took the group past the Moorish clocktower in Konak Square to the network of lanes that formed the bazaar. Here, they delved into little shops packed with jewellery, brassware, clothing and carpets, and Tina, pretending that nothing was amiss, helped Maria Callas to select some shawls. But the real action didn't begin until later that night.

Once Churchill had retired to the Chios suite, one of the yacht's nine staterooms named after a Greek island, and Tina had led the other guests on to the aft deck for coffee and liqueurs, Onassis had gone ashore for a second, less formal, visit. This time, he plunged headlong into one of the grimiest bars in the red-light district of Demiri Yolu, where he proceeded to revel in the surrounding decadence. Perched on a barstool in white cotton pants and open-necked shirt, he ordered drinks for an assortment of old cronies and local riffraff. Egged on by seamen, market traders, hookers and drug dealers, he raised a glass of ouzo and, greying hair tumbling over his forehead, toasted his former compatriots in fluent Turkish. In lurid detail, he recalled his sexual experiences in one of the local whore-houses as a young man. 'January 1921 – that was the year they invented the Thompson machine gun,' he said, 'and the year I discovered my own repeater in Demiri Yolu.'

Onassis liked to play the bad boy. His notoriety in the boardroom and his antics in the bedroom had ensured him a mention on the lips of high-society hostesses from Belgravia to Buenos Aires, if not exactly a place at their table. Superficially, he had developed an armour-plated exterior that was tough enough to withstand the most piercing verbal slings and arrows. 'I'm no Greek god, but I did not waste my life in crying because I wasn't born good looking,' he said with disarming honesty. The secret-service files of every major power bulged with the disputed facts of his life, and the list of his supposed crimes was seemingly endless. The chancelleries of Europe were packed with diplomatic imbibers who eagerly awaited invitations to his receptions on the champagne-and-caviar circuit. Hookers at Madame Claude's salon on Rue Marignan vied for his custom.

To the glittering array of international celebrities, political grandees and unashamed hangers-on who had accompanied him on his sentimental journey, he was a man in his robust prime. Purportedly 53 years of age, he was a figure of towering importance in the worlds of shipping, high finance, Riviera royalty and power politics. However, of those on board only Onassis, Tina and Artimus knew that he was, in reality, just a few months short of his 60th birthday. It was here at Smyrna, once home to a thriving community of Anatolian Greeks whom the Turks had considered 'infidels' that he had chosen to lose those six years.

None of life's mysteries entertained Ari Onassis more than the one he had created around himself. As brazen as any Hollywood press agent, the great deceiver had gilded the legend and then, smiling roguishly, stood back to admire his artistry. This compulsive need to embellish, to exaggerate, to tell downright lies was a key component of his personality. His feats were remarkable for any man born in modern times, but they were not enough for him.

Always a man of extremes, Onassis constantly needed ever greater excess to satisfy the demands of his ego. His tankers had to be the biggest, his women the most glamorous, his yacht the most extravagant, his gifts the most expensive, his exploits the most outrageous. For Onassis, there was no such thing as second place or second best; in his scale of values, moderation equalled mediocrity. 'I would rather take a big risk and lose than drive down the middle of the road,' he explained.

Through sheer willpower and unfailing nerve, he had driven himself until he had proved to the world that he was as good as anybody and better than most. In 1959, his fleet numbered 60 oil tankers and cargo steamers (a total of one and a half million tons deadweight), and he owned two Greek luxury liners, *Agamemnon* and *Achilleus*. He had a 20-year lease on Olympic Airways, Greece's national airline, while the largest cargo vessel in the world, the 65,000 ton *Olympic Challenger*, was being built for him at Kiel. But even the satisfaction of owning and controlling all this didn't bring him a sense of fulfilment.

Long before his accident in the swimming pool, Onassis had

been the victim of mood swings that took him from elation to rage with terrifying suddenness. At one end of the emotional spectrum, there was reckless generosity and, at the other extreme, irrational, violent, even homicidal behaviour. Many of the men who crossed him in business feared for their lives, and the women who loved him bore the marks of physical assault. It was said he never held a grudge for long, but this view tended to come from those who had bettered him and then found to their astonishment that he was magnanimous in defeat. In fact, he courted the friendship of powerful competitors only to neutralize them. 'It is better to make a friend than an enemy,' he would rationalize. But he resented deeply. He flattered the best talent away from his rivals, put them on the payroll and then treated them as curtly as anyone else who took his money. However, he rewarded loyalty, and those who stayed with him were looked after like the subjects of a benevolent despot.

Asked how his enemies saw him, Onassis volunteered: 'They say I'm a Greek shit with too much money.' And he laughed. By his own evaluation, he was nothing less than a one-off. But his need to prove himself over and over again was so strong that nothing mattered more than the next deal, the next conquest, the next surge of adrenalin. 'It's not a question of money,' he said. 'After you reach a certain point, money becomes unimportant. What matters is success. The sensible thing would be for me to stop, but I can't. I have to keep aiming higher and higher – just for the thrill.'

Connoisseurs of scandal recalled the operatic events into which this mania for success had plunged him: high drama at the Baltic Exchange and Lloyd's of London, a feud with Prince Rainier for control of Monte Carlo, a CIA plot to wreck a revolutionary oil deal with the Arabs and an FBI investigation into his commercial and sexual misdeeds. His arrogance showed in the way he referred to his enemies: Rainier was 'a shabby little puppet', and the CIA and FBI agents who pestered him were nothing more than 'hayseeds from Ohio'. But he fawned over celebrities.

'His publicized connections with the great were the keys that opened all doors, that brought him in contact with top bankers, the important businessmen, the millionaires, the moguls,' said the Greek newspaper owner Helen Vlachos. 'From then on, he relied on himself – on his cleverness, charm, persuasiveness – to bring off the most difficult and complicated deals.'

Lord Beaverbrook, former owner of the *Daily Express*, thought even less of Onassis, whom he called Harry, though he continued to receive him as a dinner guest at his Cap d'Antibes villa. 'Oh, he's an amusing dog, an amusing dog,' opined his lordship in the unhurried Canadian drawl he used when firing editors. 'He takes care to get hold of *awl* the important people who come into the bailiwick. Takes the ladies out in his yacht.' As an apparent afterthought, he added: 'I think Niarchos is better at it than the other one.'

However, Beaverbrook envied Churchill's preference for Onassis as host, travelling companion and confidant, and he was secretly as intrigued by the Onassis enigma as anyone else. With his disarming smile, unashamed sensuality and freely spent millions, he attracted the pick of the beau monde to his floating palace like moths to a flame. Richard Burton said of the *Christina*: 'I don't think there is a man or woman on earth who would not be seduced by the sheer, shameless narcissism of this boat.' According to Elizabeth Taylor, Onassis was the only man on earth who could make Burton jealous.

'*Everybody* was jealous of him,' said his first cousin Mrs Stassa Voyvoda, speaking from the Villa Onassis outside Athens. 'He was a wonderful, big-hearted man, the best in the world, and no one has ever written the truth about him. His whole life was to do good. He had the responsibility of the whole family – everybody with the name Onassis – and he was very generous to everyone. He was the nicest person I have ever met in my whole life.'

'Onassis was more than dynamic; he was an incredibly complex creature,' his friend, the international financier Alecko Papamarkou, told us in New York. 'He was so very complex that I don't think anybody fully understood him. He was very close to his sisters, particularly his full sister Artimus, but perhaps they only saw one side of his character. I'm sure that when he died, Stavros Niarchos missed him a great deal. His life wasn't the same without Onassis.'

Despite their great rivalry in the shipping world, Niarchos had not been above joining in the antics that Onassis insisted were an essential part of life. 'Once when sailing in *Christina* we went ashore and the whole company set off to find a bar,' said Greta Garbo, who occupied the Lesbos suite on several voyages. 'Onassis and Niarchos had peashooters with them and started shooting at the lovely plates that had been hung on the bar's walls. They were all smashed to pieces and littered the floor. Onassis just took out his wallet and paid for all the devastation.'

•   •   •

In Izmir, Ari's late-night reunion with old friends had turned into a full-scale pub crawl. Singing loudly and, despite his injury, dancing the *sirtaki*, he smashed more plates and, once again, happily paid for the damage.

Dawn was breaking before he finally called a halt and, noticeably drunk, stumbled back to the quayside. Offshore, his yacht was strung from stem to stern with great bandoliers of light. The illuminations danced upon waters that had once turned deep copper-red from the glow of blazing buildings. This was the scene that still haunted Onassis in every version of his life story he ever told. It was the spectre he had come to exorcize.

Aristotle (or Aristotelis in the Greeks' preferred anglicization of his name) had been born to Socrates and Penelope Onassis in Smyrna on 20 January 1900, when Victoria in her dotage was Queen of the United Kingdom and Ireland, and Empress of India. At his christening in the local Greek Orthodox church, he was also given the middle name of Socrates. 'Since the fall of Constantinople, Greeks living under Turkish domination have given their children classical names in order to remind themselves of their ancient Greek origins and birthright,' he said.

His family lived in the leafy hillside suburb of Karatas, one mile along the coast from the busy port, where Socrates ran a successful import-export agency. Described as 'a very good-looking man like a sultan', Socrates Onassis and two of his five brothers, Homer and Alexander, dealt in cotton, hides, tobacco, opium, raisins, olive oil and carpets. The goods were displayed in bales and casks or piled high outside their premises in the Grand Vizier Hane, a street winding through the maze of the *bedesten*, Smyrna's massive covered oriental market. There was plenty of visible proof of Socrates' position as one of the city's up-and-coming merchants.

However, he was careful not to flaunt his wealth in front of the Turks in his private life, and the Onassis home was an unpretentious stone villa built on one level, with a porch, shuttered windows and a deep cellar. Aristotle and his sister Artimus, who was two years older, played in a garden surrounded by iron railings. Aristo, as he was called, had arrived like a small tornado into this orderly world, and there was conflict between father and son as soon as Aristo was old enough to talk back and run away. Socrates was a disciplinarian who found it impossible to tolerate insurrection in a wilful child. He behaved so badly that Socrates began to beat him, but even lashings with a leather strap failed to curb his incorrigible nature.

When Aristo was six, Penelope died suddenly and unexpectedly from kidney failure, and the boy's slender grip on normality disappeared with her.

'She went into hospital for an operation and never came out,' said Onassis. Socrates' mother, Gethsemane, moved into the house to assume the duties of motherhood. By his own account, the old woman used religion to try to pacify him. 'I even became a choir boy robed in a gold-braided cassock and surplice like a miniature priest,' he said. 'This is where I developed my singing voice – and I've never lost it.'

After an 18-month period of mourning for Penelope, Socrates remarried, and his second wife, Elena, became the target of Aristo's resentment. His open hostility deeply wounded Elena, who had borne Socrates two more daughters, Merope and Callirhoe, and was doing her best to cope with the added responsibilities of rearing two stepchildren. 'I was always arguing with my stepmother,' Onassis recalled. 'I answered back and never did what she told me. My father beat me with the strap, but it had little effect.

'After primary school, I went to the private Aroni School, where I learned to stand up to older bullies – although I was small, I was always fighting – but I didn't do well in class. One of my teachers, Mr Karaplias, would pause when he came to my name, which was always last on the enrolment register because it begins with an omega, the last letter of the Greek alphabet. "Ah, Onassis," he would say, "bottom of the alphabet and bottom of the form."

'I went to Evangeliki Scholi, the Evangelical High School, which had been founded in the 18th century under the British. I spoke Greek and Turkish at home and learned English, German and French at school. My father decided that I should take private French lessons during the summer holidays and, when I arrived, I was determined to behave so badly that the teacher would refuse to see me again. But she turned out to be 25 and beautiful, and my first sight of her excited my imagination on the spot. She was to become my first mistress.'

World War I, which had been raging between the Turks and the Allied forces in the Dardanelles to the north of Smyrna, came closer when Greece abandoned her neutrality and joined the Allied cause.

'My family survived the war very well with my father emerging as one of the three leading merchants in Smyrna,' said Onassis. 'After I finished high school [he failed to graduate], my father took me into his business at his office on the Grand Vizier Hane. He had been dealing in grains and hides as well as tobacco and had provided storage and loans for his customers. I had started to visit the red-light district of Demiri Yolu where I got drunk and went to Fahrie's whorehouse. One of the girls working there told me that, in the end, all women did it for money.'

In 1919, Greek troops supported by Allied warships occupied the city with some loss of Turkish life. The following year, the Turkish government, which had replaced the sultanate, signed the Treaty of Sèvres under which Greece took control of Smyrna and Greek Anatolia in an attempt to recreate Byzantium after 400 years of Turkish domination. Turkish nationalists gathered under the command of Kemal Atatürk, who refused to accept the treaty, and Greek rule gradually collapsed in the face of fierce pressure. Defeated in the field in just 10 days, the retreating Greek army massacred Turkish civilians. When Atatürk's men arrived in Smyrna on the morning of 9 September 1922, they were thirsting for revenge. After the Armenian sections had been 'ethnically cleansed', it was the turn of the Greeks. This was the point at which Onassis found it expedient to lop six years off his age. Only 5ft 5in tall with a slender build despite his muscular shoulders, he passed himself off as a noncombatant of 16.

'Smyrna, with 700,000 inhabitants, was set on fire for weeks,' he said in one of the many interviews he gave about his life, sometimes with self-serving alterations to make him appear more of the villain or the hero according to his mood. 'Executions and pillage took place on a scale I have never seen or heard of since, even in World War II. My own family suffered terribly. My uncle Alexander was hanged for his political beliefs, and my father was taken to a concentration camp outside the city. The rest of the family were interned to await deportation to the Greek mainland. I was permitted to stay at the family home, which had been requisitioned as a billet for a Turkish general. His aide-de-camp was a young lieutenant, and I greeted him politely at the front door and offered to be of service. He asked me several questions about the running of the house, and I showed him how things worked but made it seem very difficult unless you knew what you were doing. The lieutenant agreed to let me stay. You usually find that if you make things comfortable for people they like you.

'The lieutenant grew to like me a lot and took me as his lover. There was no shame attached to it, and it guaranteed my safety; otherwise I would have been conscripted into the Turkish army or imprisoned. Instead, I managed to get a *laissez-passer* from the American vice-consul to enter the heavily armed US Marine zone and found my stepmother and sisters safe in the evacuation centre. With the consul's help, they were put on a boat and taken to Lesbos, although there was no sign of my grandmother. The Turkish lieutenant also gave me a safe conduct pass, so I was allowed to move about Smyrna like an ambassador with two sets of credentials. I visited my father in prison and found him ill and depressed. They were executing between 10 and 20 men each night, and the prisoners didn't know who might be next. One night I slipped down to the port and, in the cellar of my father's burned-out office, opened a secret safe which contained the equivalent of $10,000 in Turkish pounds. I used this money to buy supplies for my father and friends in prison, but my daily visits aroused suspicion, and I was about to be arrested by the prison governor. However, he was distracted for a few moments, and I managed to slip away. The Turks chased me, but I took refuge with the American vice-consul. He put me on an American destroyer, the *Edsall*, which gave me safe passage to Lesbos, where my stepmother and sisters were sheltering in a refugee camp.

'From there, I made my way to Constantinople, where I bribed Turkish officials with most of the money to secure my father's release. Our family was reunited in Athens. Grandmother had made it to Piraeus [the port of Athens] on her own, but a gang of thieves grabbed her purse and she fell from the gangway to the quayside. She had escaped the Turks but died on Greek soil. My father asked me to account for the money I had spent. I felt I had acquitted myself well and went through my expenditure with him. Everything was all right until we reached the final item: the bribe money. He claimed he would have been freed anyway and that I'd wasted the money. I didn't mind my father saying this; it was his money and his life, but I couldn't bear my Uncle Homer's daily reproaches for my extravagance in buying my father's life.

'This is why I decided to go abroad, and had it not been for a few short meetings at the Quai d'Orsay and the Foreign Office, as a result of which Allied policy in the eastern Mediterranean was changed, my family would have sent me to Oxford. I had everything prepared –

clothes and so on – but instead I found myself in steerage, emigrating to the Argentine. I had kept $250 of my father's money and bought my passage out of it. I joined a thousand immigrants on an Italian ship of 8000 tons, the *Tomaso di Savoya*, steaming from Genoa to Buenos Aires, where we had some distant relatives.

'As we passed the lights of Imperia, San Remo, Monte Carlo and Nice, hundreds of emigrants would cry out the names of each place in chorus. For the first time I saw Monte Carlo with its lights blazing. Those really were the gala nights of Monte Carlo. It was shining like a diamond. "See that little piece of paradise?" I said to the guy beside me. "Some day I'll have a house there."'

Before the coast of Argentina showed up mistily to port, the ship entered a shallow, reddish brown sea, through which a winding channel was marked by buoys. This was the great gaping mouth of the Río de la Plata, the River Plate. The shores of the river's estuary formed a natural frontier 30 miles wide with neighbouring Uruguay. Ferries chugged between the capitals of Montevideo and Buenos Aires under the bows of tramp steamers and sailing craft.

Approaching the Argentinian shore, Onassis saw dozens of funnels rising above the hulls of ships docked in lines along the congested wharves. Shipping was the lifeline between Argentina's great ranches and her markets in Europe. Giant cranes swung chains into the holds and cranked up cargoes roped to wooden pallets. Whistles shrieked, foremen bellowed, and stevedores sweated and cursed. The smells were tar, salt and diesel.

All of this frenzied activity was run from a row of shipping offices and freight warehouses that marked the start of the waterfront district, the Boca, in the east end of the sprawling metropolis. Apart from the Kavanagh Building and one or two other early skyscrapers, the city itself was difficult to make out from the deck because Buenos Aires had been built on a low ridge just 30ft above the high water mark on a perfectly flat plain. The only thing Onassis knew for sure was the date of his arrival: 21 September 1923. From his vantage-point, BA was exactly like his future: a vague silhouette on the horizon.

His first jobs were as a hodcarrier to a bricklayer on a construction site and washing dishes at a bar-restaurant on the corner of Corrientes and Talcahuano in the heart of the entertainment district. 'I used to wash glasses used by Carlos Gardel, the great Argentinian tango singer,' Aristo remembered with pride. 'Even when he became famous, he never forgot his roots.'

Onassis came to believe that providence had brought him to *Reina del Plata*, capital of a country that had more millionaires per capita than anywhere else in the world and where men like Gardel could start in the slums and rise to great wealth. 'Make your first million by the time you are 21,' Onassis proclaimed after he had bought Monte Carlo 30 years later, 'otherwise you haven't a chance.' What he had conveniently forgotten was that at 21 he had still been in Smyrna, and even at 23 he was scraping a living out of dirty pots and pans.

THREE

HOW ATHINA'S FORTUNE WAS FOUNDED

UNSHAVEN, UNWASHED AND more or less unloved, Athina's grandfather had appeared in South America like a desperado, young yet with a past, vulnerable yet cocksure. And in his wake trailed the spectre of the Islamic atrocity. Even in a frontier country like Argentina, his Balkan experiences set him apart from other young men of his generation. He had lived through epoch-making times, which most of his new acquaintances had only read about in lurid newspaper headlines. Cruelty and treachery had touched him deeply, but, for all their barbarity, the Turks had taught him two incontrovertible truths: that human life is cheap and that money buys power.

Three months after his arrival, Aristo walked down the great baroque boulevard known as the Avenida de Mayo, wider than the Champs-Elysées and well planted with trees, many of them decorated for the festive season. Although it was Christmas, the southern summer was at its height, and he stopped for a drink at one of the sidewalk cafés. His spirits picked up when he caught a glimpse of high-class Argentinian women in their finery. Beautiful girls with flashing dark eyes flaunted the latest Parisian fashions imported by the boutiques of the Calle Florida. 'They had chaperones or rich boyfriends,' he said, 'and I was just a shabby *émigré* drinking my coffee. You needed real money to buy your way in.'

He jumped into a number of money-making ventures, considering virtually anything that would bring in a few dollars. Aristo wasn't too proud to peddle neckties or trinkets on street corners or to run a game called Surprise, which involved dragging a handcart loaded with sand through the city and charging urchins a few centavos to dip in for hidden prizes. But although he worked hard and, even in his leisure time, played serious poker with his new Greek acquaintances, Calle Florida was beyond his reach.

His luck changed for the better in March 1924 when he was accepted as a trainee electrician with the British-owned United River Plate Telephone Company. Not to be mistaken for a *Turcos*, he gave his birthplace as Salonika on the Greek mainland and, in order to qualify as an apprentice, maintained the fiction about his age. The work entailed converting the old manual telephone system at the Avellaneda Exchange into a modern, automatic switchboard. The pay was little more than adequate, but there was a welcome bonus in the shape of the 200 female telephone operators who worked the day shift.

'I had to work in overalls squatting on the floor behind the switchboard where the girls sat connecting the calls,' said Onassis. 'Whenever I looked up, there was row after row of women's legs.' Nor were the girls averse to looking back at the newcomer, a short, dark, young man with well-developed shoulders, jet-black hair, lascivious eyes beneath thick brows and full red lips. Several accepted his invitation for a drink after work or a night at the pictures, but they lacked the class of the girls on the Calle Florida.

'Aristotle liked the girls a lot and I must admit that he did have the gift of attracting them more than any of the rest of us,' said his distant cousin Paul Kamatropoulos. 'He spoke Spanish with ease and I suppose they must have found his conversation full of charm. But he lost his head over none of them and still less his time.'

One of the movies he saw during this period was a Valentino epic called *Beyond the Rock*. While his date swooned over the Latin hero, Onassis had eyes only for the female star, Gloria Swanson. Here was a woman of class: a genuine Hollywood screen goddess dripping with sexual allure. Somewhere between the fantasies of Sunset Boulevard and the apparitions of Calle Florida, Aristo formulated his idea of the

Desirable Woman. Not only would she be beautiful but she would also possess the right thrust to put his star into orbit.

Aristo volunteered to train as an operator on the men-only night shift at the Retiro Exchange, which had the advantage of being opposite the Buenos Aires branch of Harrods on the Calle Florida. The 'graveyard shift' stretched from 11pm until 7am and, with overtime, paid $25 a week. He had reached the right address, even though he was working unsocial hours, which ensured that he arrived for work just as the night clubs in La Recoleta were hotting up and left in the morning even before the shops had opened.

The job gave him an unexpected chance to share in the stock-market boom of the twenties, albeit as the most minor of players. As an operator, he was able to plug into long-distance calls that came in from London, Paris and New York in the early hours of the morning. His original intention in eavesdropping was to improve his languages, but he suddenly found a lucrative sideline. Many of the calls involved stock-market transactions between wealthy investors and their brokers, and Aristo picked up some useful tips, which he rapidly converted into profit. This was his first encounter with the free-wheeling world of stocks and shares, in which millions were made or lost according to politics, the vagaries of the seasons or even a rich man's hunch. His early sorties returned a profit of $500. 'It was the easiest money I had ever earned,' he said. 'There was very little risk because I was getting expert advice and it cost me nothing.'

He moved to a boarding house on Avenida Esmeralda not far from the Teatro Colón, the city's ornate opera house, where he saw his first opera, a performance of *La Bohème* starring the Italian soprano, Claudia Muzio. He came away fascinated by Claudia's ample charms but professed to be mystified by the music: 'It sounded like a bunch of Italian chefs screaming risotto recipes at each other.' Adding some smartly tailored Italian suits to his wardrobe, he joined l'Aviron, the Oar, an exclusive rowing and yachting club on the Tigre river. Membership of the club allowed him to rub shoulders with young middle-class men and women, many of whom were taken with his friendly manner. The new friends who joined him for drinks at the bar or picnics on the delta's islands would have been astounded had they seen him pursuing his extra-curricular activities. One story, which he told against himself, had him running a string of prostitutes. A second claimed he made bootleg whisky in an illegal still. Yet another had him peddling dope through a tobacco-importing business he was to set up. Thus he was caricatured in gossip as what the Greeks call *mangas*, a cool, tough dude, and this image became part of the myth.

Buenos Aires in the twenties prided itself on being a cross between New York and its chosen spiritual home, the Paris of Haussmann, with bits of Barcelona, Madrid and Milan thrown in. The lusty *porteños*, or men of the port, certainly knew how to spoil themselves. For the élite, there was the well-appointed Jockey Club on Calle Florida. Membership was restricted to the ruling class of Argentinian Creoles, the country's landed aristocracy.

Native-born but European by descent, the Creoles lived in feudal splendour in mansions in the *Barrio Norte*. Socially, they deigned to mix with only the most prominent English, French and German expatriates, who rigidly maintained their national peculiarities in enclaves of mock Tudor, fake Neuilly and neo-Gothic. British investment in railroads, power stations and telecommunications was so enormous that Argentina, to its great annoyance, was often called the fifth dominion of the British Empire. As Aristo contemplated wealthy Europeans disporting themselves in the Parisian-style parks, he remembered Smyrna. 'They watched from the safety of their warships,' he told his Greek friends, 'and did nothing.'

Social distinctions were at their most marked at the opera house and at race meetings at the Palermo, where the class structure was clearly defined. Aristo had never seen such extravagance on display: women swathed in furs and crowned with diamond tiaras, men in morning coats and grey silk toppers; French champagne by the magnum. As social taboos were rigidly enforced, he was consigned to the fringes, but he was getting closer. Excited about the possibilities of Buenos Aires life rather than his position in it, he poured out his hopes in several letters to his father. There was plenty to write home about.

Buenos Aires had transformed itself from a remote outpost of the Spanish empire into the great commercial and industrial capital of a republic that was already the richest, most powerful and aggressive state in Latin America. Rich in beef, hides and just about every kind of cash crop, the one thing Argentina did not produce was tobacco. In his letters home, Aristo reported to Socrates that local cigarettes were made mainly from imported Cuban and Brazilian leaf, whereas only about five per cent contained the milder, more aromatic oriental or Turkish tobacco grown in Greece and throughout the Levant. As his father had reopened his business in Athens and traded in this type of leaf, he saw an opportunity to break into the Argentinian market. He suggested that Socrates send him some samples, which he would try to place with local manufacturers. Socrates chose some of his finest stock and shipped it to his son, but Aristo was turned down flat when he approached the intended buyers. He had no connections, no letters of introduction; therefore he was a nobody. Taking this rejection to heart, he conceived a plan that guaranteed he would at least be noticed.

'I selected Juan Gaona, managing director of one of the biggest companies, because I figured if they could be persuaded to buy a few bales the others would follow,' Onassis said. 'In the morning, I stood outside Señor Gaona's office and, when he arrived for work, I just gave him the eye. The next day, I did the same thing outside his home. This went on for two weeks until he couldn't stand it any longer. He sent his secretary into the street to find out what the hell I wanted. I got to see him and he was so relieved I wasn't a criminal trying to kidnap him that he sent me to the purchasing department. As I had been referred, they inspected the leaf, liked it and ordered $10,000 worth. I charged my father the standard 5 per cent commission and made $500 on the deal. That $500 was the foundation of my fortune.'

The strategy worked out exactly as he had planned – and his ruthless determination to succeed was enacted in all aspects of his life. His first mentor, the urbane and wealthy shipping magnate Alberto Dodero, who lived the high life in Buenos Aires, had introduced him to a young Russian ballerina who was visiting the city with Anna Pavlova's dance troupe. The girl fell deeply in love with Onassis and moved in with him, first into the apartment he was renting and then into a permanent suite at the Plaza. When the time came for the troupe to move on, she defected to stay with him, thus destroying her ballet career. Pavlova herself confronted Aristo over the girl's welfare and when he refused to make a commitment, the Russian ballerina became incensed. 'You are a deeply wicked, wicked young man,' she said. 'You don't know the difference between right and wrong.' There was no right and wrong, Aristo replied coolly, only the art of the possible.

In his new lover's company, he assumed the appearance of a

young lounge lizard in alligator shoes, worldly, arrogant and on the make. In private, her supple limbs and passionate embraces offered him a sexuality that he had never experienced in a woman before. He dressed her from the Calle Florida, wined and dined her in the best restaurants, flaunted her dancing skills at Dodero's parties but refused to consider marriage. For a year, they quarrelled, then made up their differences in bed. When she walked out after one argument too many, Aristo turned to drink.

'I can't understand why she left,' he complained to his new friend Constantine 'Costa' Gratsos, a charming yet tough young man from a Greek shipping family.

'You weren't very kind to her,' replied Gratsos.

'I can't afford to be kind,' Aristo snapped back. 'First, I have to be rich.'

Years later, he gave a censored version of this episode to Dame Margot Fonteyn, one of his guests in *Christina*. 'He said he had greatly admired Anna Pavlova when he was a very young man in Buenos Aires,' she recalled, 'and his eye had been caught by one of the dancers in her company.' There was no mention of his wickedness.

Far to the north in Florida, a B-movie maker called Joe Kennedy was in the process of committing the equally wicked seduction of Aristo's screen idol, Gloria Swanson. Kennedy first bombarded Gloria's suite at the Royal Poinciana Hotel in Palm Beach with flowers. Then he lured her husband away, turned up at the suite in person and jumped on the startled Hollywood star. The affair that resulted from that indelicate coupling in December 1927 would have far-reaching consequences for Joe Kennedy, Gloria Swanson and the as-yet-undiscovered Aristotle Onassis.

By 1928, 'El Greco' was doing so well as a tobacco importer that he had long since quit his job at the telephone exchange. 'Even when you saw him in a bar or simply walking down the street, you knew he was a competitor,' said Costa Gratsos. 'His whole life was to be doing a deal. He was not in shipping when we met, but he was fascinated by ships. They were cheap and people were making money. He got the microbe, the virus.'

The man most responsible for passing on 'the virus' was Alberto Dodero, not simply because he owned ships, but because of the manner in which he had acquired them. The youngest of five sons of an Italian immigrant to Uruguay, Dodero had moved from Montevideo to Buenos Aires to make his fortune. At the end of World War I, he bought 148 US ships with a credit of $10 million, immediately sold them and plunged his vast profits into a shipping company. He now owned the tugboats that hauled big ships into port and the ferries that plied across the River Plate. His mistress was Betty Sunmark, a beautiful American showgirl he had met while she was performing in Paris. 'Alberto Dodero had a fantastic yacht,' said Alecko Papamarkou. 'Before the Wall Street crash, it was the English and North Americans who had the yachts in the South of France, but during the Depression it was the Latin Americans, and Dodero had one of the most splendid.' A luxury yacht became one of the totems of wealth Onassis began to lust after.

For Betty, Dodero later built an estate surrounded by a high, circular wall three miles outside Montevideo. He named it Bet-Alba (for Betty & Alberto) and flew in celebrities from the United States to attend his parties. There was a movie theatre that ran newly released Hollywood films end-to-end, and Aristo was quite likely to find himself enjoying a film next to Tyrone Power or Cesar Romero. Dodero had given him a taste for the good life, and he was a willing apprentice. 'Money was never an end to him,' said Costa Gratsos. 'He never confused accumulation with enjoyment. His money gave him a sense of power, and he used it for his own pleasure, even when he was a young man.'

Nevertheless, he listened attentively whenever the stout, dynamic Dodero outlined his business strategies, especially anything to do with shipping. His expansion, he explained on one occasion, was financed chiefly by credit based on the enormous profits he earned each year from his monopoly on the six ferries that ran between Buenos Aires and Montevideo. Returning from Montevideo on one of these ferries, Aristo noticed a shipwrecked hulk called the *Maria Protopapas* rusting on the riverbank. It seemed that providence had taken a hand yet again.

'I happened to be with him when he conceived the idea of putting the boat back into shape,' said his cousin Paul Kamatropoulos. 'We all tried to dissuade him and convince him that he was going to ruin himself, but we could do nothing. In the company of my mother he set out to look for Greek salvagers who he employed to make the boat as good as new.' The refit took several months, but by the end of it he had a 25-year-old, 7000-ton tramp steamer he could call his own. However, the ship – renamed *Onassis Maria* – played little further part in his life. Aristo claimed she sank at anchor in Montevideo harbour soon afterwards during a cyclone. He told this story to cover up an unpalatable truth. His first ship had gone down off Genoa, probably with its seacocks open, in an insurance swindle.

His tobacco business suddenly faced ruin after the Greek government announced in 1929 that import duty on goods from countries with which Greece had no trade agreement would immediately rise by 1000 per cent. This included Argentina, which threatened to impose a similarly punitive tariff. Equipped with an Argentinian passport and a sheaf of documents, Aristo made his first trip to Greece in six years as a self-appointed envoy with important business to conduct. Single-handed, he persuaded government ministers in Athens that the country's merchant-marine fleet, which relied heavily on shipping cargoes from Europe to Argentina, would suffer irreparable damage in a trade war. The Greeks listened and were impressed. They appointed Aristo to represent Greece in negotiating a trade treaty with Argentina.

The Onassis family welcomed him joyfully, and when he reported on the success of his mission, they fêted him like a hero. Even Socrates acknowledged that his prodigal son had performed a great service to his country. 'Onassis had felt rejected by his father,' said Gratsos. 'He developed this passion for money and power because he wanted to be better than his father.' The reconciliation between them came just in time. Socrates died of a heart attack in 1931 at the age of 58.

'It was hard for him to admit it, and he never did in words,' said Onassis, 'but I know he respected what I'd achieved and the fact that I'd achieved it my way.'

In recognition, Aristo was given a Greek passport and appointed Greece's deputy consul in Buenos Aires, which gave him an official interest in shipping movements in and out of the port. In the offices and warehouses bordering the Boca, he learned a great deal about the spot market, which determined the freight rates that could either make or break a shipping company. He also picked up information about conditions on board ship from disgruntled crews in the waterfront bars. In some ships, a shower with hot and cold running water or a comfortable place to eat were considered luxuries. 'I'll build ships with a swimming pool,' Aristo promised, and although they laughed at him, he wasn't kidding.

The biggest perk of the job was that the Greek government allowed deputy consuls to obtain large sums of western currency at official rates of exchange, which they could sell on the black market at enormous profit. In return, the envoys were expected to act as spies for the Greek secret service. Aristo admitted he was involved in espionage at this time, and his activities were considered serious enough to warrant a mention in US Army Intelligence reports filed from Buenos Aires to one Lieutenant-Colonel J. Edgar Hoover in Washington.

By 1932, Aristo was a dollar millionaire, and he headed for London for the first time to acquaint himself with practices in the maritime capital of the world. He studied the rituals of the Baltic Exchange and made his first contact with Lloyd's of London. Acting on a tip-off, he travelled to the St Lawrence river in Canada, where he bought six laid-up vessels from the Canadian National Steamship Company for the knock-down price of $125,000. He finally had his own fleet – and he had paid cash for it.

In the summer of 1934, Aristo was heading back to Europe again, travelling first class in the Italian liner *Augustus* from Buenos Aires to Genoa, when he met a tall, blonde Norwegian divorcée a few years older than himself. Her name was Ingeborg Dedichen and, as the wealthy socialite daughter of one of Norway's leading shipowners, she filled the role of Desirable Woman to perfection. Aristo taught her to swim in the liner's pool and made her laugh. When *Augustus* docked in Genoa, Ingse accepted his offer to drive to Venice with him, and they became lovers in the Danieli Hotel after he entered her bedroom late at night wearing blue pyjamas with the initials 'ASO' embroidered on the pocket. 'In his arms I took joy in his brown skin that seemed to complement mine,' she said. 'I had never before felt such sensual pleasure. We fell asleep at dawn, alternating confidences with renewed embraces.'

Aristo bought a new beige Cadillac, and they drove to Monte Carlo so that he could examine 'the shining diamond' he had viewed as an *émigré* from the deck of *Tomaso di Savoya*. After a few days at the Hôtel de Paris, they headed through the French countryside for his first taste of Paris. At Maxim's, Aristo was lost in the extensive menu and started craning his neck to see which dishes other diners were enjoying. Then he ordered one hors-d'oeuvre after another, saying to the waiter, 'Bring me a portion of that thing there,' only to cancel the order when something more appetizing came into view. 'He behaved the same way with the next course and with the third,' Ingse sighed. 'He must have changed his mind about 36 times.' She took him home to Norway to meet her widowed mother, and they lived together, although separate bedrooms maintained an appearance of propriety.

Sex, however, was a vital part of the relationship, and Ingse never forgot their lovemaking. 'We would undress and sleep in the nude – lying one next to the other. The scenario was always the same, even if we pretended to go to sleep. Ari would put two fingers on my shoulder and delicately stroke my back. Won over by his magnetism, I felt a tingling all over and pressed myself against him while he continued his caresses. This simple contact gave me the greatest pleasure, and he could make it last for ever. Finally we could no longer resist, our bodies expecting one another, and we let ourselves be carried away in a swirl of love that united us. Often during the course of our amorous rites he would lick me between the toes, carefully, like a cat cleaning itself. He would embrace every part of my body and cover me with kisses before devoting himself to the feet he adored.'

Ingse was more amused than horrified when Aristo dressed in her corsets, skirt and blouse, and minced around her apartment pretending to be 'the Romanian fiancée of the grocer's cousin across the road.' 'I burst out laughing and ran to grab my camera,' she said. 'With good grace, he let me photograph him.'

However, there was nothing feminine about the Onassis who ruthlessly exploited Ingse's shipping connections. He boasted to Costa Gratsos that after a week in Oslo and Sandefjord, 'I've met everyone worth knowing in Norwegian shipping.' In June 1938, *Ariston*, the first Onassis oil tanker and at 15,000 tons the biggest vessel of its kind, was launched at a Swedish shipyard with the help of these contacts. The name was the diminutive of his own name and the Greek word for 'the best'. He paid $800,000 for her, a quarter during construction with the remainder repayable at 4.5 per cent interest over the next 10 years. He astonished the Swedes by including a convertible swimming pool in the blueprint and, for good measure, two huge staterooms. These were put to good use on *Ariston*'s maiden voyage to San Francisco. He and Ingse occupied one, while his cousin Nicos Konialidis and his new bride, Ari's half-sister Merope, took the other for their honeymoon.

While *Ariston* was plying between San Francisco and Japan with her first cargoes of American oil from Jean-Paul Getty's Tidewater Oil Company, Ari ordered two more tankers from the Swedes, *Aristophanes*, also of 15,000 tons, and the even bigger *Buenos Aires*, of 17,500 tons. He was moving with a speed that the established Greek shippers in London found deeply irritating. Beneath the mansard roof of the Ritz on Piccadilly, he boasted about his progress at the salon of the Greek shipowner Panaghis Vergottis. A young Greek called Stavros Niarchos listened to the braggadocio with polite interest. Niarchos came from a merchant family and was, he said stiffly, hoping to become a shipowner himself. Aristo paused to take stock of the newcomer. Niarchos was everything he detested: an Athenian who spoke with an affected English accent, bought his suits in Savile Row and drove a red Bugatti. He barely gave him a second glance.

When England and France declared war on Germany on 3 September 1939, the diverse life Onassis had been leading suddenly became a liability. He was in London, but Ingse had been stranded in Paris. His Cadillac was in Belgium, waiting to be shipped to him at his new address, the Savoy. Two of his three tankers, *Ariston* and *Buenos Aires* (still under construction), were in neutral Sweden, where they were impounded at the insistence of the German Foreign Office. *Aristophanes*, on charter to the Norwegian government, was at sea and in danger of an even more peremptory German sanction.

Ari went to the United States Embassy in Grosvenor Square to enquire about his chances of moving to the United States. The American Ambassador to the Court of St James's since February 1938 had been the former B-movie maker, Joe Kennedy. Staunchly anti-British, a devout isolationist and an admirer of Nazi Germany, Kennedy was an unmitigated disaster. He was, however, concerned about the build-up of Japan's might in the Pacific. When Ari sold two of his Canadian freighters to the Japanese, Ambassador Kennedy reputedly tipped off the US Maritime Commission. This was the opening shot in a private war that continued long after the current hostilities between nations had ceased. As the USA was still a neutral power, there was no reason to prevent Ari from entering the country, but he was given only the bare minimum: a six-month visitor's visa.

Joe Kennedy had become a hugely controversial figure in Europe. His political views enraged male colleagues at the US Embassy, while his unbridled lust alienated women. One of his victims was Barbara Hutton, the Woolworth heiress. Barbara wasn't prepared for what happened during a visit to the Ambassador's office.

'Kennedy shut the door and paced around the room in a very tense state,' she told her friend Lady Diana Cooper. 'He told me that the political situation had changed, and I might have trouble getting back into the States. He offered me a drink, which I declined, but he poured himself a scotch. As he drank, he became more amorous, more direct, more menacing. Within minutes, he was asking me to be his mistress. When I turned him down, he chased me around the desk.' Unlike Gloria Swanson, Barbara was nimble enough to dodge the advancing Ambassador. 'I bolted for the door,' she said, 'and escaped.'

Lady Diana, wife of the British Cabinet Minister Duff Cooper, thought the story 'amusing' and retailed it to her husband and friends, including Sir Winston Churchill, leader of the parliamentary anti-Nazis. Churchill had been in office only five weeks when the Germans swept into Paris, making Ingse a subject of the Third Reich. In just three months, the German war machine had crushed six countries: Denmark, Norway, Belgium, Luxembourg, Holland and France. Ari was making frantic efforts to get his lover out when he received another grievous blow. The Norwegian government had fled to Britain, where one of its first acts in exile was to requisition *Aristophanes*. To all intents and purposes, each of his three tankers had been 'lost in action'. Ari decided it was time to join the thousands of American citizens headed for home in ships from British ports that were being strafed and bombed by the Luftwaffe in the run-up to the Battle of Britain. The news from his family in Athens was equally grim. Italy, which had entered the war on Germany's side, was preparing to attack Greece.

As Hitler boasted he would march into London in two months' time, Ari sailed out of Tilbury in the Cunard liner *Samaria*. The fate of his mistress in Paris and his family in Athens was uncertain, and he still had to reach New York in one piece. One of the last broadcasts he heard before departing was Churchill's famous declaration that he could offer the nation nothing but 'blood, toil, tears and sweat'. It was going to be a tough war for some.

FOUR

ENTER THE GREEK GATSBY

WHILE EUROPE BURNED, Aristotle Onassis became the war's most dedicated recruit of New York's café society. In 1940, the city had 28,593 Greek citizens and 915 night clubs. There was no connection between the two until Ari turned up to make one and, recognizing him as a true party prince, the czars of clubland rolled out the red carpet. He was a refugee once again – but this time a rich one.

No one on board *Samaria* was more relieved than the Greek tycoon when she came out of the Narrows on 10 July 1940, passed the Sandy Hook Light and entered the wide expanse of New York Bay. To port was the Jersey shoreline, to starboard, the Empire State Building and the other towering citadels of Manhattan. On Liners Row, the greatest passenger ship afloat, the 85,000 ton superliner *Queen Elizabeth*, was docked at 50th Street Pier under heavy armed guard, having slipped through the Nazi submarine blockade. But Ari missed this stirring sight. He had been offloaded by immigration officers and taken away for questioning. It was a typical Onassian twist that his last European address had been the Savoy; his first in America the detention centre at Ellis Island.

Owing to what Onassis called 'a little technical irregularity', he spent 24 hours cooped up in this Byzantine prison almost in the shadow of the Statue of Liberty. When he offered proof that he had $500,000 on deposit at Barclay's Bank, he was admitted to the United States on his six-month visitor's visa. 'This island out in the harbour should be called Devil's Island,' he wrote to Ingse. 'It is worse than a third-class prison meant for adventurers and dirty Europeans of the old times.'

Ari found temporary accommodation in a studio apartment on Central Park West, consisting of a living room with a kitchen alcove and stairs leading to an open balcony with a bed and a dresser. After 10 virtually sleepless nights, he didn't make it as far as the bed. He collapsed fully clothed on the floor. 'I can go for three days at a time without sleep at all,' he said. 'At the most I need about three or four hours a night. If I stay up for three days, I can sleep 24 hours without waking up once.' After his Atlantic ordeal, he needed several days of recuperation before he was well enough to face the new city.

When he had recovered, he strolled down Broadway in a slate-blue suit and alligator shoes, just one more Levantine face in this Baghdad-on-the-Subway. Many of the London Greek shipowners were in the process of moving to New York, where they lived at the Plaza, the Pierre, the Sherry-Netherland or the St Regis. Through the Greek Shipowners New York Committee, they had placed their ships at the disposal of the Allies for the duration of the war. Two of the most prominent members of the group would be Stavros Livanos and André Embiricos, who even turned their profits over to the Greek War Relief Association. A lesser member was Stavros Niarchos, who had achieved his ambition to follow Ari into shipping by buying several tramp steamers. However, the man Ari was most pleased to see was Alberto Dodero, by now the owner of the largest private fleet in the world. He flew between Buenos Aires and New York whenever business or pleasure required his presence. Dodero introduced his protégé to his maritime insurance broker, Cecil Stewart, who agreed to handle the risk end of Ari's business.

Although Ari mixed with professionals in the shipping world, he maintained his peasant's habit of hob-nobbing with those lower down the social scale. 'He always had his shoes polished by bootblacks,' said Alecko Papamarkou. 'These guys talked to him non-stop, and Onassis listened with the greatest attention. "You know that universal wisdom exists, but you never know out of whose mouth it's going to come to you," he told me. "Everyone has something important to say if you listen carefully."'

One reason Ari listened a lot was that he was lonely, not for casual friendships but for the company of the Desirable Woman who really understood him. He started to bombard Ingse in Paris with cables and letters, saying he missed her and urging her to come to America to marry him. Taking him at his word, Ingse packed her belongings, closed up her Paris flat and began a hazardous journey south to Marseilles in Vichy France. While she was still in transit to the USA via Spain and Portugal, Ari spent his evenings with Alberto Dodero, who was living with Betty Sunmark at the Pierre on Fifth Avenue.

Betty arranged for him to meet some of her girlfriends from the troupe of Les Girls at Fefe Ferry's Monte Carlo night club on Madison Avenue. Suddenly, he was out nightly with Dodero, Betty and one stunning showgirl after another, and he was no longer lonely. He also found a more suitable address for after-hours entertaining in New York's first residential skyscraper, the Ritz Tower on Park Avenue at East 57th Street. 'We took transit custom in those days,' sniffed the present-day concierge.

As in Argentina, the upper echelons were barred to an *arriviste* like Onassis. Even the established Greeks shunned him. 'My family used to refer to Aristotle as "Parachutist Onassis" because he just dropped in on them from nowhere,' said Milto Goulandris, a member of one of the biggest shipping families. 'He was new money and was looked upon with distaste.' Undaunted, Ari made himself at home elsewhere.

Born in the Jazz Age when old money finally walked out with 'theatrical people', café society had survived the Depression in rude good health. The spirit of the age was summed up by Leo 'the Lip' Durochek: 'Nice guys finish last.' As he was apt to do, Ari purloined this quote for his own purposes. He was in like-minded company when he visited the Monte Carlo, 21, the Stork Club and the El Morocco, known to intimates as 'Elmo's'. In this Argentinian-owned establishment on East 54th Street, revellers sat on zebra-striped banquettes and drank highballs under a sky-blue ceiling. Ari was an instant hit once he got his wallet in the door. He invested in his first tuxedo, an off-the-peg number that made him look like a waiter, and mixed easily with the Runyonesque characters whose exploits were reported in the tabloids in defining capital letters: Broadway

Playboys, Stage Door Johnnies and their Glamour Girl Friends. Among the patrons were the Hollywood mogul Howard Hughes, and the recently returned Ambassador to London, Joe Kennedy. Damon Runyon himself was sometimes there, quietly observing the scene through a haze of cigarette smoke.

Ingse finally arrived in New York to find Ari esconced on the 37th floor of the Ritz Tower in a two-bedroom, serviced apartment with a large living room, kitchen and dining room and a view of the East River. Looking up from Park Avenue, she saw one terraced setback climbing on top of another like layers on a wedding cake. The masonry was decorated with naked nymphs, Grecian urns and classical scrolls, and a Greek mural adorned one wall of the foyer. He wasn't quite on Millionaires Row, but he was close.

While she was adjusting to New York Ingse also had to adjust to a change in her fiancé. For one thing, he no longer considered marriage a priority. 'He had suddenly realized the years were passing,' said Ingse, 'that he was suffocating in his business and neglecting the life that was now within his reach. His friends lived a life he had never known, going out with the most ravishing women. He had begun to deceive me in order to imitate them.' As a consolation prize, he bought her a $15,000 mink from Maximilian. The couple became regulars at 21, the Colony and, in particular, Le Pavillon on East 55th Street run by Henri Soulé, a Parisian whose ample girth confirmed his reputation as a conspicuous gourmet.

One customer who received special attention at Le Pavillon was the FBI boss, J. Edgar Hoover, who ate there with Clyde Tolson, officially his assistant and privately his lover, whenever their search for fifth columnists brought them to New York. The fastidious Hoover was allergic to noisy Greeks in slate-blue suits. Always impatient, Ari had a habit of rapping his knife against a glass and hissing through his teeth to attract a waiter's attention. Ingse also noted with alarm that the cocktail hour was one American custom her lover had embraced with gusto. Hoover learned that the uncouth customer was one Aristotle Onassis, a Greek shipowner from Argentina.

Hoover and Tolson ended their evenings in Manhattan as the guests of Walter Winchell at the Stork Club, where the most flamboyant newspapermen in America held court at Table 50. To Winchell, the Stork was 'the New Yorkiest place in town', and it was here that he dredged up much of the dirt for his *Daily Mirror* column.

Hoover was one of his best sources. The FBI chief leaked damaging material to Winchell to advance a vendetta against any public figure or celebrity who had offended him. Hoover kept note of possible 'troublemakers' and, when he returned to FBI headquarters in Washington, he fed Ari's name into the system. Perhaps it had triggered a flicker of recognition in the back of his mind from past intelligence reports filed from Buenos Aires.

Escaping from New York's summer heat, Ari drove Ingse down to Long Island in a new Cadillac he had bought to replace the one abandoned in Belgium. They spent weekends with Betty Sunmark and Alberto Dodero, who had an estate at Center Island on the north shore where, as at Bet-Alba, they entertained on an epic scale. Other guests that summer included film director Otto Preminger, Greek-born Hollywood studio executive Spyros Skouras, writer-artist Ludwig Bemelmans, Stavros Niarchos and Brooklyn-born actress Constance Keane, who would find fame in Hollywood as Veronica Lake. Onassis also met his screen idol Gloria Swanson at this time, but he did nothing more than exchange pleasantries with her.

Bordering Dodero's estate was one belonging to Cecil Stewart, which included a derelict lodge called Foster House overlooking Oyster Bay. Stewart's wife Dorothy offered it to Ingse as a holiday home for her and Ari. Ingse smartened the place up, furnishing it from junk shops. Soon Ari was throwing parties of his own and inviting people who could be helpful in business. There were French servants to wait on guests and an Italian chauffeur to drive them home. A typical evening *chez* Ari might be a well-primed barbecue followed by an all-night poker session.

'I had no idea Onassis was such a wealthy fellow,' Otto Preminger said. 'He looked as if he slept in his suits.' Indeed he did – often. A contemporary snapshot taken on Long Island showed him in just such attire. Hands sunk deep in the pockets of a creased double-breaster, the brim of his black fedora turned down, his eyes shaded behind dark glasses, only a self-deprecating smile saved him from the image of a B-movie hood. 'He was very short with very broad shoulders, like a barrel with bandy legs,' said Alecko Papamarkou. 'He had a gravelly voice which made him sound like a Mafioso, but a kindly Mafioso, although much more complex than any of those guys.'

Like Long Island's most famous mythical resident, Jay Gatsby, Ari mixed with gangsters in New York night clubs while cultivating a social image on Long Island. This was a feat Gatsby had mastered a generation earlier in Scott Fitzgerald's classic tale of Jazz Age manners, *The Great Gatsby*.

Also like Gatsby, Ari made the mistake of believing the literal truth of the American Dream: that anything was possible for the self-made millionaire, even social acceptance. It was the Hollywood movie producer Darryl Zanuck who first made the comparison between Ari and Gatsby. After sampling Ari's hospitality, he noted that 'his parties were just as compulsive as Gatsby's.' There was, however, a marked difference in style. Gatsby, a non-drinker, always remained sober and detached, a voyeur surrounded by the 'spectro-scopic gaiety' at his West Egg mansion. Onassis, drinking heavily, was the life and soul of the party at Oyster Bay. Hair greased back, his short, dark figure bobbed and weaved through the throng, dispensing a smile here, a joke there. He made contacts and enjoyed conquests but, like Gatsby, never had a chance of penetrating the vast mansions where the old money was. Fitzgerald had been right: the rich *are* different.

Ari took full advantage of his 'amorous holiday', which gave him licence to roam while Ingse was expected to remain faithful. Many of his flings were in Hollywood. When war broke out, Costa Gratsos was in California, where he became Greek maritime consul in San Francisco. As two of Ari's Canadian ships, *Callirhoe* and *Gulf Queen*, were operating out of San Pedro, the port of Los Angeles, he had a legitimate reason to make frequent trips to the West Coast. The ships were under charter to the US government for $250,000 a year each to carry oil from the American oilfields to Vancouver, British Columbia. When one of them was due to dock in San Pedro, Ari would fly from LaGuardia to LA, inspect the ship and take the captain for a debriefing session in one of the port's lowlife bars.

As soon as he had completed his business, he checked into the palatial Beverly Hills Hotel, where Gratsos would join him from San Francisco and the two Greek playboys would go out on the town. 'We sat in LA, screwing the girls, a very pleasant occupation,' said Gratsos. 'There were starlets, semistars, and stars . . . an endless supply.'

Ari gravitated towards Spyros Skouras, whose business skills rather than any artistic merit had taken him to the presidency of

Twentieth Century-Fox. While Ari was taken with the glamour of the star system, Skouras had a more patriotic imperative. As chairman of the Greek War Relief Fund, he raised money, collected supplies, sold war bonds and cajoled the Greek shipowners into giving as much as possible to the Allied war effort. When he tapped Ari for a contribution, he was turned down.

'I've seen what happens to men who get involved in political causes,' he snapped. Skouras was furious, all the more so because Greece had been under Nazi rule since 1941. He shot back: 'You're just a jumped-up shit from Smyrna.' Ari shrugged. 'I've always resisted the temptation to be a nice guy,' he said. 'Nice guys finish last.'

His bitterness towards politics stemmed not only from what happened to his father and uncle in Smyrna but also from wartime strictures imposed by the US government. The Maritime Commission had instructed him to cancel the Panamanian registration on two of his freighters and sail them under the Stars and Stripes, which would have made them liable to US taxes. When Ari tried to sell the ships, the authorities in Washington blocked the sales. This sort of interference made him furious, and he lacked the emotional stability to deal with reverses calmly. His insomnia had become chronic, and he had started to show symptoms of manic depression. Ingse was the first to suffer from these mood swings when he beat her up after a simple domestic argument.

She had insisted on wearing a pair of green and yellow plaid pants, which Ari considered unflattering, to dinner with Stavros Niarchos and his second wife, Melpo. They had argued on the Chris-Craft taking them to the Niarchos house at Lloyd Neck, a point between Cold Spring and Huntington harbours. Ari had drunk heavily during the meal but said little. Once they had returned home, however, he turned on Ingse in a fury, knocking her down with a flurry of punches and kicks. 'He left no marks,' she said. 'He knew how to hit like an expert.' In the morning, Ari remembered nothing of the assault; he had gone into an alcoholic black-out. 'Every Greek, and there are no exceptions, beats his wife,' he told Ingse. 'It's good for them – it keeps them in line.'

Once the attacks had started, they continued at frequent intervals. 'He needed some victim on whom he could release his nervous tension,' said Ingse. 'Oddly, these spasms of pointless violence seemed to satisfy him. He would emerge from them as relaxed and happy as if he had just made love.' In self-defence, she moved into another apartment at the Ritz Tower but did not end the relationship.

During one trip to Los Angeles, Ari renewed his friendship with his old drinking pal Veronica Lake, who had became famous as the languid 'peekaboo girl' in *This Gun for Hire* and *The Glass Key*. She and Ari trundled between Perino's on Wilshire Boulevard and Ciro's or the Mocambo on Sunset Strip. When he wasn't seeing Veronica, who shared her favours with Howard Hughes, he was spotted in the same nightspots with the actress Paulette Goddard or with Simone Simon, the French sex siren. He also looked up Gloria Swanson, who was pleased to receive his call. He had behaved like a gentleman in New York, and she accepted his invitation to dinner. It was through Gloria, the original Norma Desmond in the screen version of *Sunset Boulevard*, that Ari's conflict with Joe Kennedy came out into the open.

Gloria was Hollywood's reigning sex goddess, earning $1 million a year, when she met Joe for the first time in New York in the autumn of 1927. They had an affair that ended in 1929 only after his wife Rose complained to Cardinal Spellman, and the Catholic Church had intervened. When Ari took up with her, Gloria was 45 and still beautiful. She was only 5ft 1in tall, but in a white silk turban she towered over him.

When Joe learned the identity of Gloria's new lover, he was insanely jealous, and the two men were reported to have clashed in a restaurant. Joe had friends at Tammany Hall, where the Democratic political machine ran New York through bribery and corruption. One of the most influential figures at Tammany Hall was the night-clubbing Frank Costello, who often joined Joe for sex with women of negotiable virtue at the Kennedy private apartment in the new Carlyle Hotel. As Mob killings in Little Italy and Hell's Kitchen enlivened the tabloid headlines, there was a chance Ari might wind up in the East River.

Joe simply wouldn't go away. Once, he flew to Los Angeles to collect Gloria and take her back to New York. For some unexplained reason, she went with him. There was an embarrassing scene when they arrived at LaGuardia at 1.30 in the morning. Rose's father, 'Honey Fitz', jumped out of a limousine that had driven on to the tarmac apron and berated his son-in-law: 'How dare you, you sonovabitch, cavorting with that floozie while my daughter is at home.'

Joe knew J. Edgar Hoover well and, after 1943, acted as an unpaid, 'special service' informer for the FBI. He played an indirect part in the problems Ari suddenly faced with the bureau. Until America came into the war in December 1941, he had been able to fly between New York, Buenos Aires and Los Angeles without attracting too much attention. But after Pearl Harbor, the authorities took a close look at every frequent traveller on the South American route. Onassis, the authorities noted from the files, had sold two of his former Canadian freighters to the Japanese early in 1940, not a crime but the vessels were now actively engaged in the war against the USA. Further enquiries revealed that he kept questionable company in Argentina, and several of his close friends were outright Fascists.

One of them was Fritz Mandl, a Jewish arms and munitions maker who had smuggled his fortune out of Austria in 1938. He supported the Nazis from Buenos Aires and maintained contacts with the Hermann Göring steelworks. US intelligence had added his name to the Anglo-American blacklist, which barred him from entering the United States. Ari had met Mandl and his wife Hedy, later the actress Hedy Lamarr, at one of Dodero's parties at Bet-Alba.

When Ari returned to Buenos Aires in the summer of 1942, agents working out of the US Embassy checked up on him in person. Ari was far from being a Fascist, but his apparent Nazi sympathies were reported to Hoover. 'Before Onassis left Argentina, somebody put in a report in Buenos Aires saying he was anti-American,' said his friend, the writer Doris Lilly. 'He didn't know it at the time, but this report went to the FBI and was considered important enough for Hoover to personally write a letter to Rear Admiral Emory S. Land, then the head of the War Shipping Administration.' The letter, dated 16 July 1942, was marked 'Personal and Confidential by Special Messenger' and read:

> My Dear Admiral
> Information has been received from a confidential source that Mr Aristotle Onassis, who is reportedly part owner of the tankers *Calliroy* [sic] and *Antiope* was scheduled to depart for the United States on Thursday, June 18, 1942, by Pan American clipper from Buenos Aires, Argentina. According to the informant, the purpose of Onassis' visit is to continue the negotiations for the sale of these two tankers to the War

Shipping Administration.

The informant advised there is no information available indicating Mr Onassis has any other motive for making a trip to the United States, but it was reported he has expressed sentiments inimical to the United States war effort, and that his activities and movements while in the United States should be carefully scrutinized.

Sincerely yours,
John Edgar Hoover

Ari was followed from the moment he stepped off the clipper, and the heat intensified after Hoover received another despatch from Buenos Aires, which claimed that he 'possessed Fascist ideas and was considered shrewd and unscrupulous.' Hoover immediately alerted the Los Angeles field division of the FBI, and the earlier surveillance was upgraded into an espionage investigation. 'We could see that we were being followed,' said Costa Gratsos, 'and that our phones were tapped.'

Ari learned what was going on from an acquaintance with intelligence contacts who let him read copies of FBI reports bearing his name. 'They claimed that I was a shyster and a Fascist,' Ari said. 'The Fascist shit was mostly innuendo, making a lot out of my friendships with Mandl and some people in Buenos Aires. They covered a lot of ground. They were certainly thorough. There was even stuff in there about insurance claims that went back years and which they said weren't on the up and up.'

Costa Gratsos promised to make enquiries among his maritime contacts in Washington, who confirmed that Ari was indeed under official scrutiny because of his regular trips between Argentina and America. 'They think you're a Nazi – but you're only one name on a very long list,' Gratsos told him. To find out who was behind this 'persecution', he consulted Howard Hughes's top political fixer, Johnny Meyer. The head of the Hughes Tool Company had recently hired Meyer from Warner Bros studios to help him secure war contracts from the US government. His job was to procure beautiful women as bedmates for top military brass to give Hughes leverage in his negotiations. 'He [Meyer] was lavish with hotel suites, fancy dinners, champagne and caviar, not to mention $100-a-night beauties,' said the top Hughes aide, Noah Dietrich. Onassis told Meyer that somebody was trying to destroy him, and the procurer came up with two strong possibilities.

One was Spyros Skouras, who had reported Ari's hostile attitude towards the war-relief effort to the Maritime Commission. Meyer discovered that these comments had been duly passed to the FBI. Using Hughes's friendship with the FBI chief, Meyer went straight to Hoover and was told that somebody in the Greek Embassy had also sent an adverse report on Onassis to the bureau. Onassis suspected a man who was working as assistant to the naval attaché at the embassy after seeing action in the Atlantic convoys: Stavros Niarchos. Whatever the truth, Onassis believed Niarchos was guilty, and the great feud that would characterize their relationship for the next 30 years had begun.

In the meantime, Onassis decided to do something about the Kennedy vendetta against him. He approached a Kennedy foe, Joseph E. Casey, to act as his American lawyer. Casey, a Congressman of liberal persuasion, had returned to the law after his political career had been ruined by Joe Kennedy. A mutual mistrust of the Kennedys provided a bond between lawyer and client, but the real business they discussed was shipping. This was the start of a dialogue that would ultimately bring Ari into confrontation with Joe's younger son, Bobby. In 1943, however, Ari's immediate concern was to find a lawyer who could act as lobbyist in Washington as part of his strategy to join the major league of Greek shipowners. Ari did not explain that his desire to assert himself had become a matter of urgency as he had recently met the girl he intended to marry.

Athina Livanos was the younger daughter of Stavros Livanos, a strait-laced man whose idea of a good night was a game of bridge in his suite at the Plaza. Ari was engaged in one of these contests with Livanos, Niarchos and some of the other New York Greeks when Arietta Livanos entered the room with her two daughters, 14-year-old Tina and 16-year-old Eugenie. Tina had injured her leg in a riding accident and hobbled into the room on crutches. Balancing on one leg, she shook hands with Ari and the other guests.

The sisters departed to another room with their mother, and the men returned to their cards, although Ari admitted he found it hard to concentrate. He had been so struck by the young girl, then a brunette but later a blonde, that he noted the exact time and date in his little black book: 7pm, Saturday, 17 April 1943. Tina already had a young admirer and wasn't remotely interested in middle-aged, bridge-playing playboys. All she remembered of Ari (then 43, but admitting to 37) was that he was better looking than most of her father's friends and that she had felt 'somewhat intimidated' by him. 'My leg bothered me and I did not pay much attention,' she said. 'But Ari told me later it was the moment he fell in love with me.'

Tina had been born in Kensington, West London, on 19 March 1929 and had been educated in England. She spoke with an upper-class English accent and was everything Onassis was not. His normal routine of wining and dining girls at 21 before whisking them on to the dance floor at El Morocco was clearly not an option in this case. For once in his life, Ari employed stealth, bided his time and slowly inveigled his way into Tina's affections.

As invitations to the well-regulated Livanos household were few and far between, Ari dropped in uninvited with gifts of flowers and little luxuries for Arietta and the girls. He spent as much time as he could with Tina without arousing suspicion. She told him about her strict upbringing in London, where a chauffeur-driven limousine had taken her from the Livanos home in Holland Park to services at the Greek Orthodox church every Sunday. At the age of 10, she had been sent to Heathfield, a boarding school for young ladies at Ascot, where her ambition had been to be a laboratory assistant. The family had taken its holidays on the island of Chios, a Greek possession just off the Turkish coast in the Aegean.

Ari knew that the Livanos dynasty had originated in Chios, where Tina's forebears had progressed from a single, island-hopping caique to a fleet of ocean-going steamships. He also knew that Chios was the setting for one of the bloodiest massacres in history when its Greek citizens had rebelled against Turkish rule in 1822. The Sultan, furious at subversion on his favourite island, ordered his admiral Kara Ali to end the revolt. In a few days, 30,000 Greeks were slaughtered and 45,000 taken into slavery, an atrocity that had moved Delacroix to paint his stirring canvas, *Massacre at Chios*.

Exactly 100 years later, Onassis told Tina, the Turks repeated the carnage at Smyrna. He told her about the martyrdom of his uncle Alexander, his father's imprisonment, his own adventures in securing his release and the family's flight to Athens. Tina was moved. She began to look upon Ari with a new interest that wasn't entirely platonic.

Placing his dreams in the hands of a woman little older than a child might have seemed foolhardy. However, the age of Ari's intended bride was not an insurmountable problem because Livanos was proud that he had married Arietta when she was only 15. A bigger obstacle was Ari's position in society, or rather his lack of it. To the Greek shipping community at large, he was an unsuitable candidate for matrimony, a womanizer with a shady past who had somehow conjured up an annoyingly visible present. In their eyes, he was a chancer, an opportunist and, by birth, practically a Turk.

When he drove out to Long Island in his Cadillac on a summer's day in 1945, he had more secrets than Jay Gatsby under the brim of his black fedora. His enemies had muttered darkly into Livanos's ear that he was not only a Nazi but was also involved with the Mob. It was true that Ari, like anyone else using the American waterfront, had dealings with gangster-controlled labour unions. He could also count known hoodlums among the fraternities of the night to which he belonged. But there was absolutely no evidence linking him to extortion, prostitution or drug-dealing in the United States. As Hoover found it convenient to reject the concept of 'organized crime' because of his own kickbacks from Murder Inc., it was impossible to accuse anyone of actually belonging to an organization that the FBI chief insisted didn't exist. Still, the rumours persisted, and Ari knew the time had come to make a move. His plan was to take Tina's virginity, then marry her to avoid a scandal.

In outline, Long Island looked like a huge white fish hooked to Manhattan by the Brooklyn Bridge. Slouched behind the wheel on the hour-long run from Midtown to Oyster Bay, Ari pointed the Cadillac east along the 25A and crossed the line into Nassau County. The ribbon of road threaded past shingled farmhouses and over wooded hills, where he caught a glimpse of silver inlets winding down to the sea. Villages were knotted like bows in the ribbon, and here and there was a town with a Main Street, shops, a movie theatre and a soda parlour. Occasionally, a great house showed up in wooded grounds, perhaps a Tudor-style mansion or Norman manorhouse.

As far as espionage was concerned, the FBI had drawn a complete blank, despite a two-year probe into Ari's affairs. The files contained only details of his past misdeeds, namely insurance frauds over tobacco imports into Buenos Aires and currency swindles he had perpetrated as deputy consul. FBI agents assigned to the case had decided that his alleged anti-American utterances arose from the sabotaging of his Panamanian tax-avoidance scheme. These outbursts, the report speculated, 'may have been occasioned by annoyance over disruption of this undoubtedly profitable plan'. The final report, dated 1 April 1944, concluded: 'Investigation to date has not reflected any activity of a subversive nature on the part of the subject. No further investigation is deemed warranted and the case is hereby closed.'

Accelerating up Sagamore Hill in Oyster Bay, the Cadillac swept past colonial saltboxes and lunged down to the beach near the Livanos mansion. Parking the car, he changed into swimming trunks, picked up a large furled banner and headed down to the Chris-Craft moored at his boathouse. When he took his boat out into the bay, the banner trailed behind spelling out the letters T.I.L.Y. Back on shore, he told Tina they stood for 'Tina, I Love You.' To mark the moment of their first meeting, he gave her a gold coin bearing the profile of Alexander the Great and the inscription: *Saturday 7pm 17th April 1943. T.I.L.Y.*

Tina accepted his invitation to go for a ride in the launch. Ari was at his most romantic and persuasive. The war was ending with America in great economic shape; the dollar was king, and he had millions. (One source estimated his personal fortune at this time at $10 million.) He told her he planned to build the biggest tankers the world had ever seen and yearned to name one of them after her if she would become his wife. For all his self-aggrandizement, he fascinated Tina as no other man could. They became lovers that day. 'He took my virginity in a Chris-Craft in Long Island Sound when I was sixteen,' she said. Ari knew he was taking a huge risk. If Livanos found out, he could have him charged with statutory rape, but he also knew that taking the young girl's maidenhead had seriously damaged her chances of marrying anyone else.

Early in 1946, the long-suffering Ingse was given a Parisian apartment and sent to live in it – permanently. Then Ari approached the patrician Livanos for Tina's hand but was turned down. The age-gap wasn't the problem, Livanos explained, remembering his own nuptials, but there was a matter of protocol to consider. Tina could not marry until her elder sister, Eugenie, had walked down the aisle ahead of her. 'He treats his daughters like ships,' Ari grumbled to a friend. 'He wants to dispose of the first of the line first.'

Help arrived from an unexpected quarter when Stavros Niarchos stepped forward and made the same proposal. Livanos was outraged. Niarchos's marriage to Melpo – his second – had only recently ended in divorce while Ari had at least remained single. At this point, Tina asserted her New World equality and demanded the right to break with the Greek tradition of arranged marriages. She told her father she loved Ari and wanted to marry him. Arietta, who knew about her daughter's lost virginity, sided with Tina, and Livanos reluctantly gave his consent.

Ari and Tina were married on 28 December 1946, at the Greek Orthodox Cathedral in New York City. She was 17, he was 46 – although he kept up the pretence of being six years younger. 'Greek marriages are not infrequently arranged,' said Tina. 'It would have been the usual thing in my case, too. But my marriage to Ari was arranged only by Eros, the god of love.' Ari was described in the social columns of the *New York Times* as 'Aristo S. Onassis of this city and Oyster Bay'. At a reception in the Terrace Room of the Plaza, he gazed at the assembly of wealthy Greek shipowners reflected in the arched mirrors and told Costa Gratsos: 'I'm looking to beat the shit out of these sons of beetches.'

It was at the Plaza that Gatsby had been exposed as a phony who had made his wealth from crooked dealings, but Onassis suffered no similar come-uppance. The reception passed without incident, and Ari took Tina up to the bridal suite. The newly-weds were guests of the Doderos at Bet-Alba during their two-month honeymoon. They returned to the lodge at Oyster Bay while waiting for renovations on their new four-storey town house at 16 Sutton Square down by the East River to be completed.

They had barely taken possession before they had a new neighbour. This was Ari's rival, Niarchos, who married Tina's older sister, Eugenie, in November 1947 despite Ari's strong and outspoken opposition, and they had bought a somewhat larger house just around the corner at 25 Sutton Place.

Ari had hoped that the kudos of the Livanos name would give him an edge over Niarchos in business, but his rival had become his brother-in-law with exactly the same advantage. Their rivalry spurred Ari into taking the biggest gamble of his career. Using the First National City Bank as an intermediary, he secretly signed long-term contracts with John D. Rockefeller's Standard Oil Company, which he then took to the Metropolitan Life Insurance Company. Met Life agreed to advance him the huge sum of $40 million to build the world's first supertankers, accepting the contracts as collateral. 'I am the first Greek shipowner Wall Street ever lent money to on ships,' said Onassis. This deal was to become the real source of his multi-million dollar fortune.

Ari's heir, Alexander Socrates Onassis, named after the uncle hanged by the Turks, and his own father, was born in New York City on 30 April 1948. As the empire his son would one day inherit now stretched from Buenos Aires, Montevideo and New York to London, Paris and Athens, Ari decided it was time to return to Europe. He bought a seaside villa near Athens and an apartment on the top floor of 88 Avenue Foch in Paris. He took Tina to Maxim's, showed her the wonders of Versailles and drove south through the Loire Valley to the Riviera. There, he rented the Château de la Croë at the tip of Cap d'Antibes. Returning to New York, he closed the house at Sutton Square and moved Tina and Alexander to their new French home. Once the residence of the Duke and Duchess of Windsor, the white château was a worthy neighbour of the most sumptuous retreat on the Riviera, the Hôtel du Cap.

Shortly after they moved in, Tina returned to New York to give birth to their second child, Christina, on 11 December 1950. Ari managed to be in New York for the birth, but he spent most of his time conducting business from the Monte Carlo. The joke in there was that as he liked the place so much he ought to buy it. Instead, he bought the real thing.

FIVE

ONASSIS VERSUS AMERICA

THE MONTE CARLO takeover started over a quiet lunch, but the ink was barely dry before all hell broke loose. On Monaco's rugged cliffs, Onassis found he had risen not so much to the pinnacle of fame as to the twin peaks of intrigue and notoriety.

This episode in a career that had already attracted its fair share of odium began over dinner at the Café de l'Opéra in Paris during the early months of 1953. Ari mentioned to the French banker Charles Audibert that he had been thinking of moving his headquarters to Monaco. He was living nearby at the Château de la Croë, and his yacht, *Olympic Winner*, was berthed in the Port of Monaco. 'My ships sail under flags of convenience,' he said over an aperitif, 'so why not a headquarters of convenience?' The move made good economic sense. The principality was strategically placed between the great ports of Marseilles and Genoa, Ari explained, and there were considerable tax advantages. However, a problem had arisen. He had tried to rent the old Winter Sporting Club, which was rundown and unoccupied, but his offer had been flatly rejected by the owners, La Société des Bains de Mer et Cercle des Etrangers (the Seabathing Society and Foreigners' Club, SBM for short). The board of this curious entity had made it plain to Ari's agents that they did not consider him a suitable person to operate within their midst. This was a mistake, said Ari, because snubs like that always provoked a reaction. 'They know I have money, but they don't think I've got class,' he said. 'If you have enough money, you can buy other people's class.'

Audibert checked the price of SBM shares, which were openly quoted on the Bourse despite the pervasive air of secrecy surrounding the tiny sovereign state. They were surprisingly cheap. Scribbling on his napkin, he worked out that Ari could acquire control of SBM for 800 million francs ($3 million). Over the *digestif*, Ari instructed the banker to start buying on his behalf, spreading the orders through a number of his Panamanian holding companies to avoid forcing the price up.

As the share raiders moved stealthily into action, Ari returned to his château and, like any other Riviera resident, took to strolling through the streets of Monaco. Sometimes Tina and the children accompanied him; sometimes he ventured there alone. Surreptitiously, he checked out the real estate that the SBM either owned or controlled. The list was formidable. There was the Monte Carlo Casino, the Hôtel de Paris, the Hermitage Hotel, the Monte Carlo Beach Hotel, the Café de Paris, the Country Club, numerous villas, and the golfcourse and the magnificent gardens on Mont Agel. The total holdings occupied more than one third of the principality's 375 acres. Suddenly, the hillsides heaved with possibilities.

There was, of course, a very sound reason for the modest SBM share price. Entertaining guests aboard *Olympic Winner*, Ari politely questioned them about Monaco's finances. They were, he was told, in a parlous state. Gambling, which the SBM had controlled since 1862 in exchange for a levy of 10 per cent of the takings, had slumped to a mere fraction of its previous worth. Paid annually into the treasury, the bounty now amounted to a paltry 5 per cent of the principality's revenue. The Casino and the *belle époque* hotels on the hill that gave Monte Carlo its name had become relics attesting to the principality's slow and inexorable decline under the playboy rule of Prince Rainier III. One of his guests asked if Ari were perhaps thinking of playing a little roulette. He shook his head. 'My whaling fleet is out and might earn or lose me $5 million within three or four months,' he said. 'That's what I call gambling.'

Ari's representatives swooped at the SBM's annual meeting in the summer of 1953. When the startled SMB executives checked the share register, they found much of the stock had been bought by 49 Panamanian companies registered at the same address. It was also the address Onassis had used to secure a single block of shares in his own name. In just 48 minutes, his nominee Charles Simon was voted in as chief executive, and Ari swept the winnings off the table. He moved his family from the Château de la Croë to the Hôtel de Paris across the road from the Casino. Olympic Maritime set up shop in the old Winter Sporting Club at 17 Avenue d'Ostende, halfway down the hill separating the Casino from the harbour. He ordered the builders in to turn the top floor into an apartment. When they had finished, he would have realized his dream of actually *living* in a night club. Just inside the breakwater and in full view of his penthouse (and Prince Rainier's Pink Palace), he would moor *Christina*, a Canadian frigate that was being converted into the most luxurious yacht in the world at a cost of $5 million. 'She's worth more than all of Monte Carlo put together,' he said.

Initially, Rainier welcomed Onassis, thinking not so much about the man but more about the wealth his presence would attract. However, the FBI had no doubts about who was really in charge. A memo from J. Edgar Hoover to Assistant Attorney General Warren Burger of the US Justice Department commented: 'Onassis's agent, one Charles Simon, was elected General Manager of the SBM on 29 June 1953, and Onassis, therefore, except for the prince of Monaco, whom the French regard as an inconsequential person whose only real interest is in a reliable source of funds for his pleasures, may be regarded as the real ruler of Monaco.'

The FBI had reactivated the Onassis file as part of an investigation that had been secretly mounted to bring criminal charges against him. The probe by the Justice Department related to a scheme Ari had discussed with Joseph E. Casey about the purchase of surplus American ships after World War II. Ari had tried unsuccessfully to buy 20 T-2 tankers from the US Maritime Commission in 1946. The commission had informed him that the 16,000-ton tankers were available only to American citizens or US corporations. As the asking price was a mere $1.5 million each, it was a bargain that Ari was not prepared to let pass. He consulted his American lawyers about ways of skirting around the law without breaking it. Casey set him on the trail of eminent American citizens who might be prepared to lend their names to such an adventure in exchange for a slice of the profits. Ari recruited several Americans better known for their social prominence than any knowledge of shipping, and made them majority shareholders in a new company called United States Petroleum Carriers. In two years the company had bought 10 T-2s, seven Victory ships and two Liberties. Millions of tax-free dollars had been made out of these American ships after they had passed into Ari's grasp through a labyrinthine maze of subsidiaries. 'Onassis was only one of a dozen Greek shipowners who had bought surplus ships through American corporations set up for the purpose,' said Doris Lilly. 'But he was the biggest fish because, since his conquest of Monte Carlo, he was the best known to the public.'

Niarchos, who had also acquired ships in the same secretive manner, was the first to feel a blast of the hot wind blowing off the Potomac. Ari was back at the Café de l'Opéra celebrating the Monaco coup with his French bankers when news reached him that a grand jury in Washington had handed down an indictment against his brother-in-law. Niarchos was accused of circumventing the Ship Sales Act of 1946 to get control of tankers whose sale to foreign operators was strictly forbidden. If convicted, he faced a prison sentence and a huge fine. 'Onassis couldn't give a sou about Niarchos's troubles, but he was worried about the terms of the indictment,' said one of the bankers at the lunch. 'It was not to be unsealed until Niarchos returned to the States. He was convinced it was a trick to put pressure on Niarchos to co-operate in other investigations.'

'I don't like to think of Stavros's goose stewing in the States,' Ari mused. Then he went back to his pâté de foie gras.

In New York, Joe Kennedy wasn't particularly concerned about the fate of Niarchos, but he had a personal interest in Ari Onassis and Joe Casey. His younger son Bobby, who had graduated from Harvard Law School, was involved in the investigation against them. Ironically, Casey himself had been responsible for the débâcle. He had given evidence before the Senate Permanent Committee on Investigations, which was probing corruption in the administration of President Harry S. Truman. Questioned about a $75,000 fee he had received from a Brooklyn steelworks for working on its behalf as a political lobbyist to secure government funding, Casey had dismissed the amount as trifling. It was, he said, inconsequential

compared with the $250,000 he had raked in on an investment of
$20,000 in surplus tankers. 'Since when is it a crime to make money?'
he demanded and, in passing, mentioned that 'several million dollars'
had been made from sales of surplus shipping. Casey stopped short
of informing the senators that the Greeks, Onassis and Niarchos
among them, had received the lion's share of the market, but the
damage had been done. The senators had been given a glimpse of the
clandestine world of shipping, and they were anxious to know a great
deal more. By the time the committee had reconvened in March
1952, the question of the ownership of surplus ships had turned into
a big political issue.

America had been on Red alert ever since the North Korean
forces of Kim Il Sung had crossed the 38th parallel and swept south
on the night of 25 June 1950. Ten Communist divisions had made
four major thrusts against the South Koreans, and by 28 June Seoul
had fallen. American troops committed to the field against the North
Koreans and their Red Chinese allies found themselves being shot at
with bullets made in their own munitions works. When Dwight D.
Eisenhower replaced Truman in the White House in January 1953,
no subject was more emotionally charged in the public mind than
trading with the enemy.

As the legal skirmish developed into a full-blooded purge,
Onassis found himself clashing head-on with Bobby Kennedy.
Working as counsel to the Senate Permanent Investigating
Subcommittee, which included Joe McCarthy, the Red-baiting
demagogue from Wisconsin, Bobby was making his mark in
Washington dredging along one of the tributaries that flowed off the
poisonous mainstream of McCarthyism. His task was to investigate
the shipment of American goods to Red China and other Iron
Curtain nations with which trade was prohibited.

By law, the captain of every ship departing US shores was
required to sign a document swearing that none of the American
goods he had picked up was destined for Communist countries.
'What would happen was that some Greeks would swear to it and
would abide by the letter of the law,' said Roy Cohn, chief counsel for
McCarthy. 'They'd simply take the goods to Portugal, and then
another ship would pick the stuff up and take it to China. Bobby held
some hearings – ironically one of the people he cross-examined was
Aristotle Onassis – and he did a good job.'

Even though he was one of Joe Kennedy's greatest friends,

McCarthy had hired 25-year-old Cohn as chief counsel in preference to Bobby. The son of a judge, Cohn had strong links to the Mob and boasted that he was able to fix political appointments through Frank Costello at Tammany Hall. But he had used simple guile to get the job that Bobby had coveted. Knowing that Hoover and McCarthy were close friends, he had phoned the FBI chief to ask for access to FBI reports on people he was investigating. Hoover had readily agreed to hand over the files and rated Cohn so highly that he attended a party to celebrate his appointment in January 1953.

However, the guest of honour at Cohn's 1953 celebration had been the new Vice President, Richard Milhous Nixon. He had also been a member of the subcommittee involved in the Onassis investigation and saw an opportunity to make political capital out of the Red phobia gripping America. With Onassis's unwilling help, he might even make President after Eisenhower had stepped down from office. Nixon recalled to mind the name of a young American he had met during a recent trip to Mexico City. The man had slipped his calling card into Nixon's pocket at a reception at the US Embassy. *'My wife and I want to thank you for the magnificent job you're doing for our country,'* said the handwriting on the back of the card. The other side announced in printed letters: *E. Howard Hunt, Jr, Attaché.* Hunt would later achieve notoriety as one of the convicted Watergate burglars, but his first job for Nixon was to make life tough for Aristotle Onassis.

Just four days after Ari had taken over Monaco, Joe Kennedy had celebrated the engagement of John F. Kennedy to Jacqueline Lee Bouvier. Marriage into 'the old guard' of American society to which Jackie belonged represented a significant step up for the Kennedys, and, for Jack, it was a vital milestone on the road to the White House. At 36, he had dallied long enough. Since returning from the war against the Japanese as the hero of PT 109, he had indulged his sexual appetite with some of Hollywood's most beautiful women, including Zsa Zsa Gabor, Hedy Lamarr and Gene Tierney. FBI files also linked his name with Joan Crawford and Susan Hayward, and he was spotted with Lana Turner. When he attempted to seduce Joan Fontaine, she told him that his father had already tried – and failed. Jack wasn't abashed. 'I only hope I'm the same as him when I reach his age,' he chuckled. However, the most important of all his movie star contacts was Marilyn Monroe, who was still struggling to make her name as an actress. He probably met Marilyn as early as 1951 at the Hollywood home of her agent, Charles Feldman. Feldman was a friend of JFK and always invited him to his parties whenever he was in Los Angeles. Marilyn was one of the regulars, and she and Kennedy were remembered at the same parties.

While Jackie prepared to become a Washington housewife, Onassis managed to elevate himself from international irritant to America's Public Enemy No. 1. He embarked on a scheme that, if it came to pass, would snatch a huge section of the world's oil supply away from the mighty American petroleum industry. Infinitely bigger than the stakes he was playing for in Monaco or with his whaling fleet on the high seas, this gamble had its origins in a conversation between Ari and a middleman called Spyridon Catapodis at the Carlton Hotel, Cannes, in August 1953.

The concept was that Onassis would provide the King of Saudi Arabia with a fleet of tankers that would carry Saudi oil to Western refineries under the Arabs' national flag. This was a privilege that the Arabian American Oil Company (Aramco), the consortium dominated by four major American companies, Standard Oil Company of California (or Socal), Mobil, Exxon and Texaco, had enjoyed since 1933. The American oil giants had signed a treaty with the Saudis that gave them the right to extract, refine and export Saudi oil until the year 2000. Only one man, Jean-Paul Getty, had managed to break this monopoly, and he was, at least, an American. If the King accepted Ari's offer, the Greek would become richer and more powerful than even Getty; indeed he would achieve the status of some nations. 'I was about to stick my finger into the American pie,' he said.

The plan was still a secret when Jackie and JFK took their wedding vows at St Mary's Catholic Church on Rhode Island a month later. Joe's mission to make his son the first Catholic President was evident in the arrangements he had forced upon Jackie's mother, Janet Auchincloss. The Kennedy family retainer Archbishop Cushing had celebrated nuptial mass with no fewer than four Catholic assistants, including Monsignor Francis Rossiter of the Boston Archdiocese. Joe had hired Luigi Vena, a tenor soloist from Boston, to sing an 'Ave Maria' and had arranged for Pope Pius XII to bless the bride and groom in Rome.

Jack had invited the entire US Senate, but he was disappointed that his idol, Joe McCarthy, had failed to appear. McCarthy had been delayed en route but had sent a message to say he still hoped to attend 'if official Senate investigation duties permit'. McCarthy loathed social occasions at which his drinking had to be curtailed for the sake of decorum. Even Hoover had chided him about his fondness for bourbon.

The most notable absentee, however, was the bride's father, Black Jack Bouvier. He had become indisposed through drink at the Viking Hotel, where he was staying. When relatives went to fetch him, they found he could hardly stand. 'Uncle Hughdie', as Jackie called her stepfather, was deputed to walk down the aisle with the bride. Although she looked radiant in a wedding gown of ivory tissue-silk taffeta, the smile behind her rosepoint lace veil was as fixed as the Sphinx's, and white-knuckled hands gripped the bouquet of pink and white orchids. Standing amid the parasol-topped tables set up on the rolling lawns of Hammersmith Farm, Joe Kennedy raised his glass in yet another toast to the bride and groom.

'Jack will make a great President,' he said to his son's best friend in the Senate, George Smathers. Joe and George had met before the war when they had gone racing at Hialeah in Florida several times.

'Yessir, he sure will – and Jackie will make a great First Lady,' the Senator said, raising his glass.

'You've helped him a great deal, and I'm grateful,' Joe Kennedy continued. 'We'll have the same arrangement as before: whenever you're out with Jack, you pick up the tab and send me the bill. He's just hopeless with money.'

'It'll be my pleasure,' said Smathers. 'But you know as well as I do that Jack isn't sold on politics. He still says his greatest ambition is to be a writer.'

Bobby Kennedy, Jack's best man, joined them as the strains of the Meyer Davis society orchestra tootled over Narragansett Bay.

'How's the father of the bride?' Bobby enquired.

'Roaring drunk,' said Joe Kennedy. 'I told the *New York Times* he's got flu so he owes me a favour.' In fact, as they were speaking, Joe's old enemy was being trundled into the back of an ambulance for the ride to his home in New York City.

Bobby knew that what impressed his father most was the taking of political scalps and working for McCarthy had given him the perfect hunting ground. 'He's a great kid,' Joe Kennedy said. 'He hates the same way I do.' Top of Bobby's hate list was Roy Cohn, but

Onassis wasn't much further down. As the Greek shipowners he was investigating included Stavros Livanos, Bobby summoned the old man to Washington and told him he knew his ships had been trading with Red China, and there was 'other dirt' against him. If Livanos signed a secret pact agreeing to cease trading with the enemy, the committee would drop its case against him in the matter of the surplus ships. However, Onassis would not be exempt from prosecution even though none of his ships had traded with the Communist bloc. Livanos had little alternative other than to sign, leaving his son-in-law at Bobby's mercy.

A secret indictment against Onassis and two of his associates in the surplus ships sales was returned by a Federal grand jury in the District of Columbia on 13 October. The following week, Hoover informed his New York bureau that warrants had been issued for the arrest of Onassis and two associates, Nicolas Cokkinis, his managing director in New York, and Robert L. Berenson. Although Ari didn't know it at the time, there were five civil charges in the indictment and just one criminal charge, a big one: conspiracy to defraud the United States of America.

Ari spent most of the winter months in Monaco, which was on the same parallel as New York but enjoyed a more temperate climate. When he did venture abroad, it was to Saudi Arabia, where a draft agreement was drawn up between himself and the new monarch of the desert kingdom, King Saud. Known simply as the Jedda Agreement, it called for Onassis to supply 500,000 tons of tanker shipping towards the establishment of the Saudi Arabian Maritime Company, or Samco, to transport oil from Saudi wells. The fleet would have its headquarters in Jedda and fly the Saudi flag. Samco would get priority rights on the shipment of Arabian oil with a guaranteed 10 per cent (or a minimum of four million tons) of the country's annual output, while Aramco ships would gradually be phased out. Within a decade, Ari would have a monopoly on the transport of more than 45 million tons of Saudi oil a year.

In January 1954, Ari and Tina arrived in Saudi Arabia aboard *Tina Onassis* to a respectful welcome. There were picnics by the Red Sea and banquets attended by senior members of the royal family. As a sign of goodwill, the King presented Ari with Arab ponies for Christina and Alexander and a pair of gold-sheathed scimitars for him and his wife. The agreement was signed at the villa of the Finance Minister on 20 January and needed only the royal assent to make it law. Armed with this secret weapon, Ari decided it was time to go to the United States to confront the authorities about the unfinished business of the surplus ships.

Although the deal had been kept secret from Aramco, garbled versions of the Jedda Agreement had started leaking to the American oil companies and the western press. Aramco was outraged by what they saw as rank treachery and lodged a strong protest with the Saudi government.

Flying into freezing New York on 1 February, Ari braced himself for a tap on the shoulder of his black overcoat, but he passed through immigration and customs unimpeded. He visited his office at 655 Madison Avenue and met with his lawyers, then toured his old haunts. Nothing untoward happened, although FBI files show that Hoover knew exactly where he was. After three days of official inactivity, the suspense was killing him, so Ari sent a telegram to Attorney General Herbert Brownell Jr at the Justice Department, which read: 'I wish to inform you that having arrived from Europe on Monday night I place myself at your disposal during my visit for any information you or your department might care to have.'

Working for a New York law firm, Brownell the lawyer had actually scrutinized the sales contracts for Ari and Joe Casey. However, Brownell the lawman immediately sent a Federal marshal to New York with an arrest warrant for Ari and orders to bring him to Washington in handcuffs. The scene was rich in irony, and Ari voiced his feelings about Brownell's duplicity in playing both sides of the street.

He was lunching at the Colony when the marshal arrived to take him into custody. However, he was allowed to make one phone call, which he used to contact his chief lawyer, Edward J. Ross. Ross persuaded the marshal to allow his client to surrender voluntarily in Washington, and the officer departed empty-handed. A few days later, scores of reporters were present when Ari arrived at the district court building in the capital to face the conspiracy charge against him. In dark-blue suit, blue shirt and black tie, he was photographed from several angles, fingerprinted and locked up with a group of Puerto Ricans who had tried to bomb Congress the previous day. Reminded of his father's captivity, Ari later admitted that the 40 minutes he spent in the holding cells seemed like an eternity. When he appeared before a judge, he pleaded not guilty and was released on $10,000 bail.

By the time he got to see Assistant Attorney General Warren Burger, the case had proved so costly that he sensed the government was anxious to settle out of court. 'I'm not going to back down, Mr Burger,' Ari told the man who would rise to the eminence of Chief Justice of the United States. 'I'll litigate for the rest of my life if I have to because I know I'm going to win.'

He also knew that the Justice Department had recently brought charges against the American members of the so-called Seven Sisters oil cartel, including his four Aramco enemies, under America's anti-trust laws. A grand jury had investigated the Sisters' monopoly of the international oil market and handed down subpoenas against them. Ari knew that, in this instance, the Attorney General had dropped criminal charges in favour of a civil action. 'Mr Burger, what is the ransom?' he demanded.

Burger laughed and airily suggested a fine in the region of $20 million, the profit Ari had made from his control of the American ships. Even if Burger were joking, he had opened up a dialogue and, in that moment, Ari knew he had a chance of settling the case without going to prison. Instantly, he reverted to type; he was prepared to buy his way out of trouble but not without arguing about the price. In his own words, 'the horse trading had begun.' He was haggling for his freedom just as he had done with the Turks on the far side of the Bosphorus to secure his father's liberty. Cleverly, he reworked a quote from American oilman Robert Wilson about the plight of the US oil giants. Wilson had said: 'In England they knight their leading businessmen, over here they indict them.' Ari's version was: 'Mr Burger, if I had done all this in England or some other country, I would have been knighted. Here, I am indicted.'

It was a cheeky move, but it worked. Burger recognized the quote. He reconsidered. Perhaps the fine should be linked to the current market value of the ships, which was around $12 million, rather than the profit figure. Ari agreed this would be more appropriate. He knew the market price was too high and was bound to drop. With a deal agreed in principle, Ari and his cohorts celebrated over dinner at Harvey's restaurant. He chose this venue because he knew it was the favourite eating place of J. Edgar Hoover and Clyde Tolson. Sure enough, the FBI chief and his lover were *in situ*, eating prime ribs and drinking whisky from miniatures hidden under a napkin. Ari had to be restrained from giving them a piece of his mind.

By the time the paperwork had been sorted out, the ships had indeed lost $5 million in value. 'It was all dressed up to look like a government victory,' said Edward J. Ross, 'but even they knew we had won.' Ari was even allowed to pay the $7 million fine over several years.

The Jedda Agreement was an entirely different matter. 'Never before in the history of business was so much power combined to fight and destroy an individual,' Ari remarked. As well as Aramco, he found himself up against the State Department, the CIA and his old enemy Stavros Niarchos. Having settled his differences with the administration with a cheque for $5 million, Niarchos was as anxious as Aramco to scuttle the Jedda Agreement because it threatened his own position in the Arab world. Through his New York office, he contacted Robert Maheu, one of the smoothest private investigators in the United States, and instructed him to take whatever steps were necessary to sabotage the deal. Maheu was an inspired choice. A former FBI agent, he had quit the bureau in 1947 to form Robert A. Maheu Associates and had since been involved in various CIA escapades.

Maheu and his CIA friends bugged Ari's offices in Madison Avenue and the penthouse in Avenue Foch for a week, but the results were disappointing. He rarely did important business across his desk, in his home or over the phone. In Monaco, he made calls from a communications system specially set up in the Salle Empire of the Hôtel de Paris. For really private conversations, he could always raise anchor and sail away, knowing that *Christina* was almost impossible to bug at sea. Moreover, Ari always spoke to his closest associates in rapid-fire Greek.

Although Maheu was on the Niarchos payroll, he kept the CIA informed about his moves and consulted Richard Nixon. The Vice President, whose political battlecry was 'Find out who hates who,' detested Onassis, but made one stipulation: 'If you have to shoot the sonovabitch, don't do it on American soil.' Maheu submitted a breakdown of the Jedda Agreement to the President's National Security Council, which proved that its terms were prejudicial to US interests in the region. The State Department instructed its Saudi ambassador to contact Aramco's director in Saudi Arabia to express the government's concern. When news of this official intervention reached King Saud, he paused to consider his position. He wanted the prestige (and the profits) of carrying Saudi oil in Saudi ships provided by Onassis, but the risk of alienating the US government was unacceptably high. The Jedda Agreement started to founder on the rock of power politics.

Alerted to the stalemate, Onassis flew to Jedda and made some minor concessions to Aramco, which enabled King Saud to proceed. In its revised form, the deal was given the royal seal on 18 May 1954. Aramco refused to recognize the validity of the contract on the grounds that it violated their own concession. Ari was told that when his ships arrived at an Aramco terminal to take on their first loads of Saudi oil, they would be turned away.

Ari's response was a masterpiece of seat-of-the-pants diplomacy. He told the King that the latest 46,000-ton tanker being built for him in Hamburg, originally to be called *Alexander Onassis*, would now be named in his honour. Not even Aramco would dare to reject a ship carrying the monarch's own name. Maheu and the CIA were in serious trouble if the plan went ahead. The only option open to them was to prevent the launching of the ship through industrial sabotage. They fomented a strike among the German workforce, but even this failed to stop Onassis. 'He got the ship built somehow,' said Maheu. One hundred thousand people saw the *Al Malik Saud Al-Awal*, annointed with holy water from the fountain of Zem Zem near Mecca, slide down the German slipway.

From the outset, the weak link in Ari's camp had been the middleman, Spyridon Catapodis, who felt he had been cheated. He claimed that Onassis had promised to pay him $1 million on the signing of the deal; Onassis maintained it was up to the Saudis to look after him. There had been an ugly encounter between the two men in the departure lounge at Nice airport. After a heated argument, Catapodis had wrestled Onassis to his knees and shouted: 'You are not even a Greek but a goddam Turk.'

On 24 September 1954, in the presence of the British consul in Nice, Catapodis signed an affidavit in which he accused Onassis of bribing Saudi ministers and palace officials to advise the King in his favour. This might have been deemed corruption in the West, but in Saudi Arabia it was nothing more than a business courtesy. Unfortunately for Catapodis, he was unable to produce the contract between Onassis and himself, which, he said, proved these charges. Onassis had signed the contract in disappearing ink, he claimed, and he had returned it for a new signature. It had never been seen again.

It was left to Robert Maheu to fly into Jedda to tell the King that some of his closest courtiers had accepted Ari's baksheesh. Maheu undertook the mission with some trepidation. The Saudis issued exit visas to visitors only after their business had been concluded satisfactorily, a problematical definition in this case. However, King Saud received the allegations of bribery with hardly a raised eyebrow, thanked Maheu politely through an adviser and allowed him to leave the country with his person intact. Maheu had, in fact, provided the King with a reasonable excuse for backing gracefully out of the deal. Ari's Saudi fleet was dead in the water, but he was philosophical in defeat. 'My mistake was that I woke up too early and disturbed those who were still asleep,' he said, 'and as a result I got into the biggest mess of my life.' Then he returned to Monaco to devote his attentions to Prince Rainier.

SIX

THE FEUD WITH RAINIER AND GRACE

MONTE CARLO WAS the jewel in Onassis's crown, but it lacked the required lustre. When Ari decided to stage *The Prince and the Showgirl* Riviera-style, Prince Rainier learned that the tycoon's interference in the principality and its affairs extended even to his own lovelife.

The curtain opened with Onassis sitting at his gold-inlaid Louis Quinze desk in his office on the Avenue d'Ostende. He was studying an article on Marilyn Monroe in a copy of the American magazine, *Look*. Considering the complexity of the empire he controlled from here, the desk was sparsely appointed. Onassis preferred to pile work on to his subordinates at Olympic Maritime and keep his own desk uncluttered. Most of his secrets were contained in a little black notebook that he carried with him everywhere.

He picked up the telephone and spoke to George Schlee, who was acting as his ambassador-at-large in the United States. Ari had consulted Schlee, a friend and mentor of Greta Garbo, about the best way to breathe some life into the deserted Casino. In particular, he wanted to attract the dollars that were flowing into the new money-traps of Las Vegas. Schlee confessed he hadn't made much progress in drumming up new business.

Onassis had discussed the problem with Mike Cowles, the publisher of *Look*, who had pointed out the pulling power that royalty had among his readers. Monaco had a royal family, and a royal wedding there would create enormous international interest in the principality.

'Why don't you and Onassis marry Rainier off to an American celebrity?' Cowles had suggested.

'Who did you have in mind?' asked Schlee.

'Well, what about a movie star?' Cowles said. 'Why not start at the top – Marilyn Monroe.'

Schlee had put the idea to Onassis, who held Monroe in high regard. At the time of her wedding to Joe DiMaggio, he had sent a cable to Spyros Skouras, saying: 'Would like to be in DiMaggio's bed tonight.' His time in Hollywood had given him an enduring faith in the star system. 'Celebrities are important to Ari,' said Tina. 'All his fantasies are connected with them.' He gave Schlee the go-ahead to approach the star of *How to Marry a Millionaire*. Behind him on the mantel was a large-scale model of his flagship whaler, the first *Olympic Challenger*. There was a map of the world with magnetized markers showing the disposition of his fleet. A wooden harpoon stained with whale blood was mounted on one wall like a trophy. However, there was nothing to show that he had earned the unofficial title of His Monte Carlo Majesty.

'I love this country, but it is a legend which is in decline,' he had told the citizens of Monaco soon after he swept in. 'I will do my business and I will do yours, too. I'll build, I'll embellish, I'll renovate. The new administration of the SBM will give Monte Carlo a new grandeur.'

These stirring words had quickly lost their meaning. There had been very little grandeur of any sort, and his dream of turning Monte Carlo into the richest playground in the world was as remote as ever. In truth, he had been too preoccupied with other problems to do much about it. A worldwide boycott of his tanker fleet in the aftermath of the Saudi Arabian fiasco had cost him $20 million. His whaling fleet had sailed into serious trouble for killing out of season and harpooning protected species. The Peruvian air force had even fired a machinegun burst across the bows of *Olympic Challenger* to stop the slaughter. Onassis had provided exciting fodder for newspapers, but the publicity had done nothing to pull Monaco out of its slump. Europeans and Americans alike had been disgusted to learn that the barstools in *Christina* were covered with the foreskins of sperm whales. On a trip to London to defend his whaling activities, he realized he had become a celebrity for all the wrong reasons. Monroe must have been on his mind because he snapped at a bunch of photographers who followed him everywhere: 'I'm not Marilyn Monroe, you know.'

In New York, Marilyn responded to George Schlee's call in characteristic style. 'Did you say Prince Reindeer?'

'No, Rainier.'

The actress was between DiMaggio and her third husband, the playwright Arthur Miller, and was legally free to marry. She agreed to meet Schlee at Cowles's farm in Connecticut the following Saturday. There, they discussed the idea in more detail as they walked around the pool.

'Is he rich?' asked Marilyn.

'Sure he is, he belongs to one of the oldest monarchies in Europe,' said Schlee.

'Is he handsome?'

'Yes, very regal.'

'Where did you say Monaco was again? Africa?'

'No, that's Morocco – Monaco is on the Riviera.'

'OK, I'd like to meet him.'

Cowles sounded a note of caution. 'Do you think the Prince will want to marry *you*?' he asked.

'Give me two days alone with him,' she replied, 'and of course he'll want to marry me.'

But Marilyn never got the chance to prove her point. The prospect of becoming a princess excited her greatly, and she told her friends, including Jack Kennedy. Word passed along the Catholic grapevine to Rainier's personal chaplain, the Very Reverend Francis Tucker, formerly of Baltimore. A robust, portly figure with a fondness for motorcycles, Father Tucker had known Onassis was up to some mischief ever since Marilyn's name had cropped up in conversation during a visit he had made to *Christina*. The priest had thought Ari was joking: Marilyn was twice-divorced and notorious. However, he suddenly started to take the threat seriously and was relieved to discover that Rainier had secretly been corresponding with another actress, the wholesome Grace Kelly, whom he had met at the Pink Palace earlier that year. Grace was an Irish Catholic and winner of an

Academy award for her role in *The Country Girl*. At 26, she had beauty, style, class – and, above all, she was the right religion.

The priest urged the 32-year-old Prince to act as a matter of urgency. After some preliminary contacts, Rainier visited the Kelly family home in Henry Avenue, Philadelphia, on Christmas Day 1955, with Father Tucker and his personal physician, Dr Robert Donat. Rainier held Grace's hand and stayed the night. When he drove her to New York three days later, they were already engaged. 'We happened to meet each other at a time when each of us was ready for marriage,' Grace said.

However, Grace had to submit to the formality of a medical examination to establish she was fertile. She knew this would reveal that, despite her girl-next-door image, she was not a virgin, an important consideration for a would-be princess in 1955. She managed to convince the doctor that her hymen had been broken while horse-riding as a teenager. When she had been declared physically fit to bear Rainier's children, the Prince announced their engagement in January 1956. One of the first to telephone Grace was Marilyn Monroe. 'I'm so glad you've got out of this business,' she said.

When Ari was asked to comment, the bitterness he felt over yet another failure clouded his judgment. 'It must be very lonely for him to be stuck up in that place surrounded by all those old courtiers,' he told reporters. Rainier had been fully appraised of Ari's plot and was deeply offended. Asked his opinion of Onassis, Rainier replied: 'That man! I won't have anything to do with him. He'd like to turn Monte Carlo into Monte Greco. Last time Onassis came to the palace I told him, "Mr Onassis, your money has brought you everything except an education. You were badly brought up."'

The reporters scurried back to Onassis to repeat this insult. 'Did that kid have the nerve to say something nasty about me?' he asked. 'I thought that when we got him that boat he wouldn't talk so much.' This was an equally unfair crack. Ari had been instrumental in helping Rainier obtain the 135-ft yacht *Deo Juvante II*. Rainier had paid the $200,000 asking price in full himself, but Ari had made it sound like a gift.

Ari stopped short of giving his views on the Prince's choice of a bride on British television, although a film crew were given permission to shoot scene-setting footage in *Christina*. He had been sorely tempted to take this opportunity to show who really ran the principality, but he held back. Assailed on all sides over whaling, he needed to step out of the limelight. He heeded the advice of one of his aides that the forthcoming marriage could be used to tempt British MPs to Monte Carlo 'to counteract prevalent rumours that your normal parties consist of nothing but film stars and playboys'. Ari listened when the aide told him: 'The main danger at the moment is the headline UNCROWNED KING OF MONTE CARLO, which will become acute at the time of the wedding.' In fact, Ari had already started his counter offensive. Just 11 days after the engagement was announced, he had contrived a meeting with Sir Winston Churchill through his son Randolph. If Rainier were bringing Hollywood spice to Monte Carlo, he would retaliate with the sage of Westminster.

At this sensitive time, Rainier was more worried than ever about the state of his inheritance. He and his government had invested 55 per cent of the national reserves in Monagasque concerns, which had subsequently plunged into bankruptcy. Moreover, members of his family were in secret revolt against him. His sister Antoinette was planning a *coup d'état* with the help of her lover Jean-Charles Rey, a senior member of the principality's National Council. Her idea was to oust Rainier as ruler and have herself declared regent. He found out about the conspiracy and was on the brink of banishing his sister from Monaco when Ari stepped in with an ultimatum: 'Settle the family squabbles or I won't invest a single franc in Monaco's future.' Rainier pulled back and, instead of deporting Antoinette in disgrace, issued a statement saying the allegations against her were completely unfounded.

It was on the *Deo Juvante II* that Rainier brought his bride into Monaco's harbour. Monagasque and American flags waved from every building, cannons on the ramparts of the Pink Palace fired a 21-gun salute, yachts sounded their sirens, fireboats spouted streams of water and a band played 'Love and Marriage'. To crown the arrival, Ari had ordered his seaplane to shower the harbour with thousands of red and white carnations. He watched from the deck of *Christina* with his daughter as Rainier and Grace stepped ashore. 'A prince and a movie star,' he sighed. 'It's pure fantasy.'

But Onassis didn't really believe in the fairytale. He had already checked up on Grace, which wasn't difficult considering his contacts in New York, where she had lived, and Hollywood, where she had worked. She had frequented the Stork Club, and her love of champagne had been duly noted. Ari's spies had dug into the

Hollywood hills and surfaced with pure dirt. Far from being a lily-white virgin, Grace had enjoyed secret affairs with several of her leading men, including Clark Gable, Ray Milland, William Holden and even the crooner Bing Crosby.

As hundreds of reporters, columnists, feature writers, photographers and moviemakers swarmed in for the wedding of the decade, they were showered with hospitality – Onassis hospitality. Rainier tried to control the media through a Monegasque director of communications, who was based in a converted schoolhouse. Taking protocol to the extreme, he briefed the world's press, many of them British and American, over a loudspeaker in diplomatic French. Police were involved in violent clashes with the media when cameramen tried to snatch photographs of Rainier, Grace and their families. While Rainier blustered and dithered, Onassis was the personification of charm and common sense. Along with canapés and Dom Perignon, the most important newsmen were discreetly fed his view of Monaco and its future. His wedding gift to the couple, he let drop, was a painting by his friend Ludwig Bemelmans who had painted the murals in *Christina*'s children's room.

Ari was satisfied with the way things were progressing when he entered the cathedral to watch Rainier and Grace take their vows on 19 April 1956, to the accompaniment of whirring MGM cameras, which were recording the ceremony for the world's cinemas. The congregation consisted of a diverse social mixture, from ex-King Farouk of Egypt, the Aga Khan and the Duchess of Westminster to David Niven, Cary Grant, Ava Gardner and Grace's mother, who had greeted Rainier's family with the rousing egalitarian cry, 'Hi, I'm Ma Kelly.'

'The impression gained by the press visiting Monte Carlo at the time of the wedding could not be better, particularly the British Press who were inclined to think of Monte Carlo as the residence of the handsome and innocent young Prince and the wicked Mr Onassis,' an aide reported to him in a memorandum. 'Thanks to your energy and personal handling of them, they have largely reversed their opinion. They were all extremely disappointed with the public relations and press arrangements organized by the Prince.'

Onassis could afford to wait patiently for the couple to return from their honeymoon cruise to Corsica. He had great power over the new Princess, and he intended to use it. 'Onassis had a lot to say about Grace and her sex life,' confirmed his bodyguard-cum-private spy Frank Monte, who later worked for him in Rome. 'He knew about her love affairs from information he had received. He had used other people in this type of work before me.' His main 'dirty tricks' operative was the American, Johnny Meyer, whom he had coaxed away from Howard Hughes.

One of the events the newly-weds attended after their return was a dinner in the Salle Empire at the Hôtel de Paris. A vast canvas painted by Paul Gervais in 1909 covered the north wall with scenes of nubile young women playing with peacocks and cheetahs under the gaze of a catlike Sphinx. Onassis was in his element. Waiters bore silver trays of champagne through a forest of black and white marbled pillars and, overhead, the brightest crystal chandeliers dangled from a gilt ceiling. Reflected in the mirrored west wall, the distinguished throng seemed to double in size until it presented an occasion worthy of Versailles itself. With a party hat askew on his head and a lopsided grin on his face, Ari told Grace about his escapades in Hollywood. 'He was out to do the best by himself, and he moralized and whitewashed a lot of the decisions he made for business reasons,' said Monte. 'When he got it against somebody, he was really out to get them – and he was out to get Rainier and Grace.'

Ever since the engagement, the new Princess had been plagued by guilt over her previous liaisons. If she had any doubts that Ari knew about her past, he completely removed them during that dinner. 'Onassis boasted to me that he could have taken Grace as his lover any time he had chosen,' said Monte. But Ari had no wish to ruin the Princess's marriage, which had undoubtedly been good for business. In the months following the wedding, hotel bookings had boomed, and the volume of money going through the Casino showed a healthy increase. His objective was to win his battle against Rainier through a combination of insults and threats followed by unexpected overtures of peace. Ari refused to use the Prince's deferential titles of 'Altesse' or 'Monseigneur', addressing him to his face as 'Rainier' and to his staff as plain 'Mr Grimaldi'.

'He told me he thought Rainier was a terribly weak man who had inherited a block of land which he didn't know what to do with until he came along,' said Monte. 'He said he had secretly flown in a Savile Row tailor to make some new uniforms for the Prince because "he looked like a shabby little puppet". Onassis said he paid for that; it was a story he recounted many times. I remember he said, "We can't make him taller, but we can pad his trousers to make him look better." He swore they put padding in Rainier's pants.'

The dispute between the two men came down to a fundamental difference of opinion over the manner in which Monaco should be developed. Ari despised games of chance, even though the odds were stacked in favour of the house – *his* house. When Rainier suggested installing slot machines, Ari explained that it was anathema to him to profit from the lost earnings of ordinary people. 'He was not setting himself up as a sort of moral authority,' said Rainier, 'but he believed that less rich people were corrupted by gambling. He knew the odds against winning, and he thought they shouldn't be allowed to take those sort of risks. It probably had to do with his poor origins. For all his wealth and generosity, he was always very careful with his money.'

The only building projects Ari would consider paying for were a new wing with a rooftop restaurant, Le Grill, at the Hôtel de Paris and an indoor swimming pool. Anything else, he maintained, would ruin the intrinsic character of the place. In this, he appeared to show an enlightened spirit of conservation, but the suspicion lingered that his real plan was to build luxury apartments on any available site and sell them to very rich clients. His aim was to restore 'the gala nights of Monte Carlo' as he had perceived them from the deck of *Tomaso di Savoya* in 1923: refinement acted out against a backdrop of enormous wealth; plutocrats at play in their very own resort. 'Monaco will always be prosperous,' he said, 'so long as there are 3000 rich men in the world.'

Rainier's plan was more or less the complete opposite. He wanted to modernize Monte Carlo by attracting package tours, building medium-class hotels, including a Holiday Inn, and establishing a convention centre. The result, Ari wailed, would be Las Vegas-sur-mer. To prove his point about the magic 3000, he drew up lists of famous people to visit him, and they accepted his invitations in droves. There were free rooms at the Hôtel de Paris, cocktail parties on board *Christina* and nights in the Casino. The guaranteed presence of Her Serene Highness Princess Grace added the necessary touch of class. Everyone from Cary Grant, Gregory Peck and Greta Garbo to Winston Churchill and the Windsors turned up. The celebrities weren't expected to lose vast amounts at the tables. In fact, Ari frequently gave them chips on the house or made good their losses. The idea was that they would attract the high rollers of the new Jet Age, and they did just that. Greek shipowners, oil-rich

Arabian princes, American movie producers and deposed royalty, embodied in the bulky form of Farouk, showed up in increasing numbers. The Casino profits soared.

However, the truce that Onassis had imposed on the two Grimaldi factions proved to be illusory. Antoinette was openly insulting towards Grace, until Rainier, at his wife's insistence, kicked his sister out of her rooms at the palace. On 29 January 1959, Rainier declared in a radio broadcast to his subjects: 'I cannot tolerate any pressure whatsoever which might undermine my complete rights.' He suspended the Constitution, dissolved the National Council and abrogated the rights of political assembly or demonstration. One way or another, he was going to curb the power of his uncrowned rival.

Ari's other problem was the distress of his wife, which culminated in Tina suffering a nervous breakdown in *Christina* in 1959 as her marriage crumbled in front of her eyes. Her married life hadn't just been difficult, it had been impossible. Ari's long absences, psychotic rages and multiple infidelities had turned her into a social butterfly flitting from one distraction to another. She hated his nomadic lifestyle, claiming all she wanted was for him to be at home with her and the children. Ironically, she had become just as much of a nomad as her husband.

'It would be ridiculous for me to generalize on marrying very young, but it is true that both of us have managed to work it out well,' she said in a guarded interview in June 1959. 'I am totally unambitious. Everything happened to me so soon and so young. I feel a woman's place in life is to be a wife and mother, and there is certainly plenty to do running the house whether it be in New York or in Paris or entertaining in *Christina*. Maybe this sounds pompous, but I have never been bored or blasé at all. For the past 10 years, we have always been on the move. It's the greatest luxury to be able to travel; it's a divine life. My dream is to travel around the world in the yacht and see places like India, Nepal, Siam, Japan and the South Pacific.'

Tina had realized soon after the royal wedding that no matter how much she admired Princess Grace, Monte Carlo wasn't big enough for both of them. As she had no wish to usurp Grace's pre-eminence, she distanced herself from the Monaco court. Anyway, she preferred the Paris or Rome collections to the boutiques of the Avenue des Beaux-Arts and the Broadway theatres to performances at the Salle Garnier. 'I buy all my town clothes in Paris at Chanel, Desses or Dior,' she said. 'In the spring and then in the late summer I get usually six dresses, say two evening frocks, two cocktail dresses and two for the afternoon. I simply adore summer clothes. I get them all from Italy, usually at Emilio Pucci.' Personally, Tina knew she was superior to the smug Monegasque matrons who felt duty-bound to snub her because she was married to Onassis. She came from a dynasty that measured class in terms of wealth and manners rather than titles. The place she felt most comfortable was St Moritz in the Swiss Alps, where she was definitely among equals and felt free to roam as she pleased without the scrutiny of her husband. Ari detested the slopes. 'When I went skiing,' he said, 'it was mainly on my backside.' Stavros Niarchos was an excellent skier and, although married to her sister, he began to exhibit an interest in Tina.

Tina and Ari had been leading separate lives amicably enough until 1957, when she had caught him in bed with Jeanne Rhinelander, an attractive American school friend of hers. Tina had bumped into Jeanne at the pool near the Eden Roc restaurant at the Hôtel du Cap and invited her to visit the Château de la Croë. Until then, Ari's affairs had been brief flings suited to his lifestyle, but he was captivated by Jeanne's film-star looks. After catching them in her own home, Tina began to flirt more openly with other men. She had always had plenty of offers; now she took them up. Ari ordered his aides to have her followed, and the investigators prepared a dossier on a weekend she had spent in Rio de Janiero with one lover. Ari reacted in character. A guest at the château, the English writer Alan Brien, watched in horror one night when he saw Ari beating Tina. Ari screamed, 'You whore, you whore,' as Tina sobbed uncontrollably. Just as Brien was about to intervene, they fell into each other's arms and retired to bed. Her most serious affair was with Reinaldo Herrera, the dashing 18-year-old heir to a Venezuelan oil fortune. Despite an age difference of eight years, he proposed marriage to Tina, and she accepted.

When she asked Ari for a divorce, he was nonplussed. He begged her to reconsider for the sake of the children and, in the meantime, gave Tina permission to bring her lover on to *Christina* whenever she felt like his company. Although he complained about Tina's insensitivity towards his feelings, he was an active participant in this arrangement and even allowed it to proceed in front of his children. 'He had his friends, and I started to find mine,' Tina said, although her infatuation with Herrera soon petered out. But she was finished with the Château de la Croë, and Alexander seemed to sense her dislike of the place; one morning he shattered every ground-floor window with a stick. When the property came on the market, Tina forced Ari to let it go, and it was promptly bought by Stavros Niarchos.

Alerted to his brother-in-law's apparent interest in his wife in the *après-ski* conviviality of St Moritz, Ari insisted that Tina spend more time in Monaco, though not necessarily with him. Apart from attending business dinners and social functions with him, she could do what she liked. The principality was divided into three sections like a block of Neapolitan ice cream: the old town of Monaco, dominated by the Pink Palace, the Condamine or port area, where *Christina* was anchored, and Monte Carlo itself, the hill with the Casino and hotels. If Ari were in one place, she was liable to be in another. To Tina, Monte Carlo was 'the dead zone', a baroque prison, a last resort. When she simply couldn't avoid being there, she alternated between the apartment Ari had built above the old Winter Sporting Club and her bedroom in *Christina*. Although she always looked ravishing, she was wilting inside. 'This life is killing me,' she told a friend.

Ari assumed Tina was still happy with the prospect of the next party, or a new wardrobe or a diamond bracelet. He had seriously misread his own wife. She told friends it was precisely this kind of ostentation that had destroyed her husband. And it was all so vulgar. 'All that Monte Carlo stuff! Buying up the place! I can't tell you how much I dislike Monte Carlo.' She took no pleasure in the liberty-style Casino with its rounded feminine forms, nor the Hermitage's art-nouveau façade. To Tina, the place was as hollow as the sea caves permeating the honeycomb rockface; the people as shallow as a roulette wheel in the Edwardian plush of a *salle privée*. This disenchantment emanated largely from her belief that her husband had never appreciated her true worth. 'Ari never gave me my due in his life,' she told a titled English friend. 'He never recognized my contribution.'

Certainly, she received no credit when Ari gave interviews about the secret of his success. Goronwy Rees visited Monte Carlo in 1959 for the *Sunday Times* and found him full of *bonhomie*. 'He is vivacious, amusing and amused by himself, but perhaps what is most impressive about him is an extraordinary combination of modesty and frankness which has its own particular dignity,' he wrote. 'He is a man of wide general education and culture, and only someone with his own prodigious capacity for work and concentration could have achieved this in the course of building up and operating his great shipping business. He regards himself and his own achievements with a kind of amused wonder and is completely without any form of affectation or pomposity.'

In other words, Aristotle Onassis was an entirely self-made man. The only time Tina's name was mentioned was in the context of one of his ships: 'the *Tina Onassis* of 45,000 tons'. In the eyes of the world, she had been reduced to a possession, a mere chattel. It was almost the final insult.

SEVEN

CHURCHILL AND THE GREAT BRITISH CONSPIRACY

STAVROS NIARCHOS WAS outspoken in his view that Onassis's primary purpose in buying Monte Carlo had been 'to bribe and subvert' politicians and businessmen. The unpublished Onassis Papers, a large number of documents to which we were given access during our enquiries, lend a considerable amount of weight to his allegation. They disclose for the first time the extremes to which Ari was prepared to go to win over members of the British Establishment.

The Onassis Papers show that the shipowner spent lavishly to gain influence over oil-industry executives, Fleet Street journalists, royal aides – anyone, in fact, with the power to promote the Onassis name and enrich his companies. Onassis money bought Pimm's for VIPs at the Henley Regatta and champagne dinners at the Royal International Horse Show. For groups of friendly journalists, there were free trips to Athens, Rhodes and, of course, his Monte Carlo showpiece.

While Ari would never admit to such base motives, he once privately referred to Sir Winston Churchill as 'the biggest fish I've netted yet'. And Churchill, once he had taken the bait, became the sprat to catch some even bigger mackerel. The first time the Greek tycoon had met Britain's wartime leader, they argued. The meeting took place at La Pausa, the Riviera villa of Churchill's foreign-rights agent Emery Reves, just 10 months after Churchill had resigned as Prime Minister in April 1955. Although Churchill had retired to bed that night grumbling about 'that bloody Greek fool', the following day he had reconsidered and described his opponent as 'a man of mark'.

Within a matter of weeks, Churchill had moved six miles west from La Pausa to Monte Carlo and was enjoying views of the Corniche and the Mediterranean from the penthouse of the Hôtel de Paris, where he stayed as Ari's guest. By the autumn, he was sailing along the coast in *Christina*, the first of eight cruises he enjoyed around the Mediterranean, across the Atlantic and down to the Caribbean.

The magnetism that drew the two men together was mutually intense, but the extraordinary friendship that developed from that rowdy first encounter would throw a long shadow over the final years of Churchill's life. When he had called Onassis 'a man of mark', he hadn't realized that *he* was the 'mark' in Ari's game.

For his part, Churchill had been only too willing to be netted. The Greek maverick's rise to prominence in the shipping world had intrigued him for many years. As Prime Minister, he knew only too well of Britain's dependence on the Suez Canal for its oil supplies, and he regarded men such as Onassis, the industry's fetchers and carriers, as essential links in a chain stretching from the Persian Gulf fields to British refineries. At 10 Downing Street he had worked behind the scenes to bring Onassis (and his ships) into the British fold. But Ari's misadventures in America and Saudi Arabia had fuelled the xenophobia that invariably applied, as Onassis put it, to 'crooked little dagoes' in the British mind. The more that British oil companies shunned him, the more determined Churchill became to befriend him.

While still Prime Minister, he had discussed the problem with Sir Lionel Heald, the Member for Chertsey who was Ari's legal representative in London (and later Attorney General), and Churchill's adviser Brendan Bracken, founder of the *Financial Times*. In 1955, Churchill decided to plant a go-between in the Onassis camp with the help of Sir John Rogers, a director of J. Walter Thompson. The man chosen for this delicate mission was Nigel Neilson, a former

Never Happier: Christina Onassis proudly presents her three-year-old daughter Athina to the world in spring 1988. Her smile reflects the happiness that her daughter had brought into her often troubled life. After Christina's death in Argentina six months later, the little girl became sole heiress to the fortune made by her grandfather, Aristotle Onassis.

(Rex Features)

Daddy Dearest (*above*): Aristotle Onassis displays his devotion to his daughter, Christina, in this intimate portrait taken on the yacht that bore her name. Onassis had subjected his daughter to a life of opulent neglect and emotional cruelty throughout her childhood, but he came to love her deeply.
(Rex Features)

Upwardly Mobile (*above*): The young Aristotle Onassis poses with his first automobile in Argentina when he was an up-and-coming businessman in the tobacco trade. Although he claimed to be 24 when the picture was taken in 1930, he was actually 30 years of age. He often covered up his early life.
(Central Press)

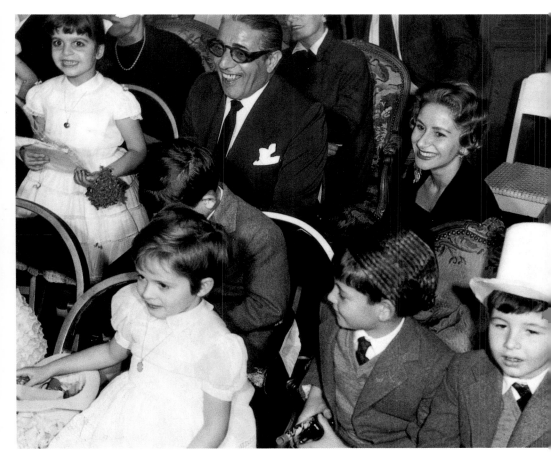

Petite Princesse *(above)*: Christina *(left)* smiles happily at her 1955 fifth birthday party given by her parents in their penthouse apartment at 88 Avenue Foch, Paris. Aristotle joins in the fun with his first wife, Tina, the former Athina Livanos.
(Studio de France)

Flying Family *(right)*: Two years earlier, Christina posed with her parents and older brother, the tragic Alexander, after touchdown from one of the flights the children made with their roving father. In 1973, Alexander died in an Athens plane crash.
(Associated Press)

Sting in the Tale *(below):* Aristotle Onassis bought the scorpion- shaped isle of Skórpios in the Ionian Sea for $100,000 in 1963. But the happy times that the modern Odysseus had envisioned there were marred by tragedy.

Ari's Envoys *(right):* Jackie Onassis and Aristotle's public relations chief Nigel Neilson (*left* in the picture) are surrounded by security guards during a visit to a Belfast shipyard in 1969. Jackie later withdrew from her Greek millionaire

husband's life, but Neilson remained a loyal aide to the Onassis family for 30 years. He was kept busy.

Opera Bluff *(right):* Aristotle welcomes Maria Callas and her husband Battista Meneghini to a reception in her honour at the Dorchester Hotel in June 1959. The gala evening was part of his bold scheme to seduce the famous diva. He succeeded.
(Desmond O'Neill)

Gracing Manhattan
(right): Film star Grace Kelly and His Serene Highness Prince Rainier celebrate their engagement at the Waldorf-Astoria in January 1956. In Monte Carlo, Rainier fought a running battle with Aristotle Onassis over the principality's development as a tourist playground. Onassis lost.

(Range/Bettmann/UPI)

Jumping Jack (*left*):
President John F.
Kennedy, pictured here
on his 46th birthday
just six months before
his assassination in
Dallas, Texas, in
November 1963. JFK
had just banned
Aristotle Onassis from
the United States, but
five years later the
Greek go-getter
married his widow.
(Range/Bettmann/UPI)

Greek Gladiator (*left*):
Aristotle's most famous
foe was his former
brother-in-law, Stavros
Niarchos, pictured here
in 1959 at his desk in
the suite he kept at
Claridge's in London.
Niarchos, who first met
Onassis just before
World War II, became
his rival in shipping and
in love. After failing to
win the hand of Tina
Livanos, Niarchos
married her sister,
Eugenie, and after
Eugenie died of a drug
and alcohol overdose
and Tina had divorced
Onassis, he married his
sister-in-law in Paris in
1971. Onassis was
devastated.
(Popperfoto)

Darling Clementine
(*above*): Aristotle
listens respectfully to
Lady Clementine
Churchill, but it was
her husband, Sir
Winston, who really
held his attention.
(Associated Press)

Taking Off (*left*):
Homburg and cigar
firmly in place, Sir
Winston Churchill
boards an Olympic
Airways aircraft for a
flight with its owner,
Aristotle Onassis.
(John Chillingworth)

Black Widow: Jackie Kennedy Onassis guides a distraught Christina across the tarmac after she arrived in Greece in the aircraft carrying Aristotle Onassis's body from Paris in March 1975. While Jackie smiled for the cameras, Christina was dazed with grief. 'How can you?' she asked her stepmother. Jackie replied: 'Take it easy. It'll soon be over.'

(Associated Press)

actor and war hero who worked for the powerful American-owned advertising agency in London.

'Sir John came to me and asked if I could recommend someone to represent a man whom Churchill considered to be very important to Britain. It turned out to be Onassis,' said Neilson. 'Churchill was worried because he had moved into the big league of shipping as an oil carrier, and the British oil companies were refusing to deal with him. Churchill felt this was a mistake which could leave the country vulnerable in time of trouble. I didn't know anyone suitable for the job and said so. Sir John told me to do it myself. Lord Bracken and Sir Lionel Heald had made it plain to me that Churchill was adamant: Britain had to befriend Onassis.'

This was the background to that first meeting at La Pausa, which had taken place at the behest of Ari's carousing friend Randolph Churchill on Monday evening, 16 January 1956. Playing the *arriviste*, Ari presented himself at La Pausa clutching a bunch of roses as though calling on a sweetheart. Swiftly downing a couple of drinks while waiting for Churchill to come downstairs, he appeared nervous and discomposed. In fact, his behaviour was so totally out of character as to rate as one of the best performances of his life. ('Onassis used to walk up and down the deck of *Christina* rehearsing conversations with himself,' said a former crew member.)

No one ever described Ari's conversational style better than Randolph Churchill: 'He is a born orator with a poetic sense and can build up a list of adjectives in an ascending order of emphasis and weight which are as perfect as a phrase of music. Just as his listener is caught by the spell, he will suddenly bring the whole edifice tumbling down by a deliberate piece of comic bathos. He will burst into laughter at the very moment when almost any other man would be exploding into passion.'

Tonight, the spellbinding touch was noticeably absent. After trying to kiss Churchill's hand, he had muddled up his words of greeting, and the born orator's adjectival edifice collapsed before it had even started. He seemed to know he was making a bad impression and that only precipitated greater gaucheries. Fortified by more drink, he laughed at everything anyone said whether it was funny or not. 'We talked about oil and politics,' Churchill said. 'I told him that 30 or 40 years ago I had got Anglo-Persian for the Admiralty. He said he knew all about it.' An argument arose when Churchill challenged Onassis to explain his country's 'monstrous conduct' over Cyprus, where terrorists were murdering British troops in the fight for enosis, or union with Greece. Although Churchill roundly cursed Ari, the outburst had snapped him out of his depression. Surprisingly, Churchill, who had been in a melancholic mood for some weeks, started to lighten up.

The Onassis Papers indicate that Churchill had indeed found Ari's company stimulating. At a cocktail party at the Dorchester hotel in London a few months later, Churchill's private secretary, Anthony Montague Browne, ventured as much to an Onassis aide. 'He assures me that as far as the Government is concerned, they have absolutely nothing against you,' the aide reported to Ari in July 1956. 'He told me that although Sir Winston cannot agree with some of your theories, he likes you very much.'

Although Ari claimed he had no wish to make his friendship with the former British Prime Minister known to the world, he had tipped off photographers about Churchill's first visit to *Christina*. The pictures had been published everywhere, much to Winston Churchill's embarrassment and Ari's secret delight. After the American freeze-out, he had been desperate to find customers among other nations involved in shipping oil. Britain was the strongest economic and military power in Europe at that time and a leader in the energy field. Ari wanted to do business with British Petroleum (BP), where Churchill's friendship could only help. What is described in the Onassis Papers as 'the British Petroleum Company Campaign' became his main objective.

Churchill had been one of the earliest advocates of oil as a replacement fuel for coal, and as First Lord of the Admiralty he had converted the British Navy to its use in 1911. Three years later, he had persuaded the government to buy 51 per cent of the Anglo-Persian Oil Company, which was exploiting huge fields in Iran. The company later became British Petroleum, and control of it had cost the Treasury just £2 million. Ari knew that, for these historic reasons as well as his wartime Prime Ministership, Churchill's name carried a fair amount of weight with the BP board.

As one of the world's most mysterious figures, interest in Onassis ran high among oilmen. But he soon discovered that Tina, Alexander and Christina had important roles to play. The Onassis Papers report that 'at a cocktail party, Mrs Neville Gass, wife of the managing director of British Petroleum, and various other "oil" wives asked a series of questions about Mrs Onassis and the family.'

This natural curiosity to meet and observe the Onassis family in their Monte Carlo habitat played right into Ari's hands. The newly appointed BP chairman, Basil Jackson, was 'rather wary' of receiving him formally at his office in London, but Jackson was amenable to meeting him in the more social climes of the Riviera, provided secrecy could be guaranteed. As Jackson and his wife were spending Easter in Cannes, it was arranged for them to drive to Monaco for a visit to *Christina*. Mrs Jackson was particularly anxious to see the *Christina*, while her husband's only reservation was that a picture of him and Onassis might appear in print with the caption: NEW CHAIRMAN OF BP CONFERS WITH ONASSIS. This time, there were no photographers. The secret meeting went ahead as planned and was, according to the Onassis Papers, 'a great success'. Basil Jackson 'thoroughly enjoyed himself' and was interested in everything Onassis had to say. 'The main thing is that the myth about you being unapproachable, as conveyed to Basil Jackson, has now been exploded,' a summary of the occasion concluded.

The next step was to convince sceptics on the BP board that Ari was a proper person to carry their oil. Over dinner on 1 June 1956, Jackson told an Onassis aide it was rumoured that Ari was 'apt to make negotiations behind the backs of oil companies'.

'He said that obviously the whole difficulty could be traced to the Saudi-Arabian deal, but he felt that the prolongation of this might be due to "a rather narrow-minded Scotsman in a position of authority,"' the documents reveal. The Scotsman in question was named Robert Gillespie, and Jackson offered to talk to him and other doubters on his board. He volunteered to report back to the Onassis camp on the outcome. There were urgent political and economic reasons behind Jackson's willingness to find a way of ending the hostility towards Onassis. In a few days' time, British troops were due to withdraw from the Suez Canal under the terms of the Anglo-Egyptian agreement of 1954, leaving the fate of Britain's vital oil route in the hands of the Egyptian President, Colonel Gamal Abdul Nasser. As Churchill had foreseen, Britain might need Onassis sooner rather than later.

Jackson was as good as his word. In the chairman's office on 26 June, he disclosed a memo by Bob Gillespie outlining the case against chartering Olympic tankers. First Gillespie pointed out that it was against BP policy to use ships sailing under flags of convenience. He also claimed Onassis 'had done something unpleasant to the Jersey

Oil Company' (the Standard Oil Company of New Jersey, known as Exxon or Esso, and one of the Seven Sisters whom Onassis had opposed in Saudi Arabia). Finally, he alleged Onassis 'had negotiated for "pirate" oil in Persia', which had always been BP's fiefdom.

Jackson didn't believe any of these objections amounted to much and invited Onassis to lunch with him and his colleagues in London at the Savoy on 13 July. In the interval, Ari was briefed on the opposition. As well as Gillespie, another antagonist on the BP board was known to be Neville Gass, who 'may be the hardest nut to crack'. According to the Onassis Papers, 'he is extremely charming, but always against any new move that might have repercussions.' Ari was well prepared when he bowled through the revolving door of the Savoy. At lunch in a private room, 'we were having a liqueur when Ari suddenly took them on,' said one who was present.

'I'm told you've got several nasty things to say about me,' Ari told the oilmen. 'If there is anything, please do tell me.'

'There was a lot of coughing and spluttering into the vintage port,' said the witness. 'They were clearly embarrassed. But one finally repeated a story which had been planted by a large American oil company. In his marvellous way, Ari put him right. He went on to answer every question they put to him.'

With the Suez Crisis looming, Ari was pushing at an open door. Asked about the opposition of Gass and Gillespie, Jackson said: 'They *will* change their minds, but nothing can happen overnight.' Then he went on holiday. On 26 July, Nasser nationalized the Suez Canal or, more accurately, he took over the Anglo-French Suez Canal Company, inviting the imperialist powers to 'choke to death on their fury' if they didn't like it. The British Prime Minister, Sir Anthony Eden, warned Nasser that Britain would not allow him 'to have his thumb on our windpipe'. While emergency plans were drawn up for armed intervention in Suez, the charter arm of BP started to negotiate with Onassis, but it wasn't until the invasion of Egypt by British, French and Israeli forces in October that the first contract was signed. The breakthrough was leaked to reporters on the *Sunday Express* and the *News Chronicle*, although 'the official story is that they found things out for themselves.' This was just one of many examples of the manner in which Onassis manipulated Fleet Street for his own ends.

Nasser retaliated by blocking the 103-mile-long waterway with the hulks of scuppered ships. Randolph Churchill had already warned Ari this was likely to happen, and he was ready to take advantage. As most of his tankers had been idle owing to the American boycott, he was ideally placed to provide the extra tonnage required to carry oil from the Gulf around the Cape of Good Hope to Europe. Suddenly, he was the darling of the US oil companies, and he screwed every last cent out of them. In just six months, he said he made between $60 million and $70 million on the spot market. He also shipped a great deal of oil for his new British client, validating Churchill's faith in his 'man of mark'.

Asked to confirm that there had been an initial prejudice against Onassis, Sir Eric Drake, who was managing director of BP in 1958 and later chairman of the company, said: 'We were a bit worried to start with because he was very brash in those days. He used to go in for all sorts of adventures, but he never did anything crooked as far as we were concerned. We chartered a few of his ships at that time, but the majority were after Suez.' As for Churchill's claim that he had bought Anglo-Persian for the Admiralty, Sir Eric said: 'Churchill objected quite a lot, but he did give £2 million to keep us going because he believed in oil for the British Navy. He was very gaga by the time he was going on board *Christina*.'

Many found the rapport that had sprung up between the statesman and the tycoon difficult to fathom. Churchill's doctor, Lord Moran, said: 'Ari, as Winston calls him, hardly takes his eyes off his guest; one moment he will fetch him a glass of whisky and the next, when Winston finds it cool on deck, will tuck him in a blanket. Once, noticing hairs on the collar of his coat, he hurried away to find a clothes brush.' One night in the Caribbean, 'Ari held a teaspoon of caviar to Winston's lips, as one feeds a baby. Three times he repeated this little ritual.'

Apart from his yacht and all its luxuries, Onassis's most important gift was that he could snap Churchill out of his gloomy moods. Using the tactic of waving the name of one of his enemies in front of him like a red flag, he asked provocative questions, such as: 'Was Stalin as bad as they say?' The resulting verbal conflagration had the effect of jolting Churchill back to life. Publicly, Ari demonstrated some of the statesman-like skills he had picked up from the master. 'We are all deeply indebted to him for the system of life we enjoy,' he said. 'He has given that system an extension of life: let us hope that the extension will last long.'

• • •

In his old age, Churchill had become prone to forming ill-advised infatuations for beautiful women. He had a crush on Emery Reves's fiancée, the American model Wendy Russell, which Noel Coward recorded in his diary in June 1956: 'There was this great man absolutely obsessed with a senile passion for Wendy Russell. He followed her about the room with brimming eyes and wobbled after her across the terrace, staggering like a vast baby who is just learning to walk.'

However, there was never the slightest suggestion of loose behaviour whenever Churchill was accompanied by his wife Clementine. She tolerated Ari for the sake of her husband and joined him on several cruises in *Christina*. 'She thought he was keeping bad company,' her grandson, Winston Churchill II, told the *Sunday Times*. 'She disapproved of rather a lot of his friends.'

Onassis also provided the devoted couple with free seats on Olympic Airways. In February 1959, an entire aircraft, a DC6, was placed at their disposal for a special flight from London to Marrakesh. Churchill wanted to spend a holiday at the Mamounia Hotel, where he could paint the snow-capped Atlas mountains. According to the Onassis Papers, Ari met Lord Monckton on this flight and noted that he 'could prove to be a great ally in the future ... Apart from his ministerial duties in the past and among other important positions, he is chairman of the Midland Bank and also chairman of the Iraq Petroleum Company.'

The bill of fare on the flight to Morocco gave some idea of Ari's hospitality to the Churchills:

MENU

Les Canapés Moscovite

La Tortue Verte au Xères

Le Filet de Sole Joinville

Le Tournedos Poelé aux Champignons
Pommes Duchesse
Haricots Vert au Beurre

Le Savarin aux Fruits

Le Plâteau de Fromages Assortis

La Corbeille de Fruits

Café

The wine list offered Champagne: Pol Roger 1949 (Churchill's favourite); White Burgundy: Chassagne Montrachet 1955; Claret: Château Ausone (château bottled) 1949; Brandy: Hennessy 1900; Liqueurs: Bénédictine, Crème de Menthe (Cusenier), Cointreau, Kummel Wolfschmidt; Whisky: Johnnie Walker Black Label.

After this gourmet lunch had been devoured, a poker game started up among Onassis, Churchill and two other passengers. Churchill lost so badly that the pilot's request for the players to fasten their seat belts for landing seemed like a timely intervention. Down on the tarmac, the reception committee was lined up, the band was waiting to play, and 500 Frenchmen were poised to shout: 'Vive Churchill!' However, the guest of honour insisted on continuing with the poker game.

'Lawd!' he said. 'This is the first decent hand I've had on the whole journey. Tell the pilot to go round again.'

The pilot circled the airfield – and Churchill scooped up the pot. But the old man was growing uncomfortable about the extent of Ari's largesse, and he insisted on a bill for his suite at the Hôtel de Paris at the going rate the next time he stayed in Monte Carlo. It was only a token payment, but it saved his dignity.

The Churchills were very fond of Tina Onassis and were sadly aware that her marriage to Ari was breaking down. They tried to speak to their host about it, but Ari politely told them he knew what he was doing. When the dénouement came later that year, the Churchills found themselves the occupants of front-row seats at an unedifying performance that a librettist might have entitled The Tycoon, His Wife, An Opera Singer and Her Husband.

EIGHT

THE NIGHT ONASSIS AND CALLAS GOT MARRIED

AS IN EVERY other arena, Aristotle Onassis liked to make the rules in matters of the heart. He also liked to say, 'The only rule is there are no rules.' Even for the richest playboy in the world, this sounded too glib – and so it proved. When he launched himself at Maria Callas, he was fully prepared to ride roughshod over his wife, his family and his friends to get the woman of his dreams. But instead of happiness, he set himself on the path to destruction.

The matchmaker in the romance between Ari and Callas was the suitably wicked American society hostess Elsa Maxwell, who loved orchestrating the ritual dance between changing partners. Although proud of her own virginity, the roly-poly Maxwell could sense the sexual tension of lesser mortals across a crowded room. She perceived just such an arousal in Ari in the first time he saw La Callas, who was guest of honour at her ball in Venice during autumn 1957. On that glittering night he had been attracted to Callas's Greekness, which she wore like a neon sign. However, he did nothing about it for more than a year. It wasn't until he saw her perform in Paris on 19 December 1958 that his political antennae registered even more pleasing signals than his senses. After that, she had his undivided attention.

Callas had given a gala concert at the Opéra for the Légion d'honneur, which was shown on television throughout Europe. It wasn't so much her singing that appealed to Ari, but the manner in which she commanded the adulation of the famous audience. The President of the French Republic, René Coty, topped a celebrity list that included ambassadors, politicians, the Duke and Duchess of Windsor, the Ali Khan, the Rothschilds, Charlie Chaplin, Juliette Greco, Brigitte Bardot and Sasha Distel. More star-struck than ever, Onassis decided he had to have this Desirable Woman and her fame.

'I believe the Greek shipowner was very impressed by what he saw,' said Callas's husband, Battista Meneghini. 'He, with all his money, would never have aroused so much interest. It was this consideration that put into his head the idea for his diabolical project.'

Ari's first move was to phone Callas soon after her Paris triumph to offer his congratulations. By the time they met in person, they were at least on speaking terms. This was at another ball organized by the Countess Castelbarco in her Venetian palace. Ari and Tina had arrived in *Christina*, which was berthed at the entrance to the Grand Canal. Tina looked sensational in a gown by Jean Desses with her long blonde hair entwined in an exotic headdress.

But Tina was left talking to friends while Onassis wheeled the somewhat taller diva around the dance floor. Again, he invited Callas and her husband for a cruise, boasting about his ship and reeling off a list of the important people who came to see him. Callas was polite but lukewarm. A short time later, he got Tina to phone from Monte Carlo to extend the same invitation. Callas was doing *Médée* at Covent Garden, and Onassis, taking over the phone, said, 'I'll come to London for your answer, and we'll have a party.'

With indecent haste, he flew to London, snapped up 30 tickets for the performance and dispatched last-minute invitations, which announced, 'Mr and Mrs Onassis have the pleasure to invite you to a party in honour of Maria Callas, which will be held at the Dorchester at 23.15, Thursday, 17 June, 1959.' He had, in effect, hijacked the occasion. Arriving early at the theatre, he waited at the foyer bar for his guests to arrive. As Callas was at the height of her fame, he had had no difficulty in finding some high-ranking takers. They included Tina's friends the Duchess of Kent, her daughter Princess Alexandra, the Queen's cousin Lord Harewood and the actors Douglas Fairbanks Jr and Gary Cooper.

After the performance, a fleet of limousines carried the distinguished guests to the Dorchester, where everyone waited in eager anticipation for Callas to appear. It was well after midnight before the diva, wrapped in a huge fur, walked into the lobby with the balding Battista Meneghini frowning nervously at her side. When the couple had celebrated their tenth wedding anniversary at Maxim's a few months earlier on 21 April, she had called him 'my Battista' and remarked, 'I am the voice; he is the soul.'

But from the moment he walked into the Dorchester that night, Battista Meneghini was very much a lost soul. Onassis pounced. Ignoring Meneghini and Tina, he led Callas into the party and monopolized her until 3am as camera flashbulbs lit up the salon like exploding fireworks, and the gossip columnists composed glowing tributes to the two most famous Greeks in the world. Towards the end of the evening, Onassis sidled over to Elsa Maxwell with a questioning look on his face. How was he doing? Maxwell patted him reassuringly on the arm and indicated that the diva was his for the taking.

For the next 24 hours, Onassis swamped Callas's suite with phone calls, flowers and affectionate messages. He had rarely worked faster to bring a relationship to the boil. By the time she had agreed to join *Christina* in Monte Carlo for the long-awaited cruise, they were already lovers. The setting for their first tryst was a mews house in London's Grosvenor Hill, a short walk from the Dorchester. When *Christina* sailed at midnight on 22 July, Callas, Battista Meneghini, the entire Onassis family, Winston Churchill, Clementine, Lord Moran and other Greek, American and English guests were on board. Prince Rainier, a genuine opera lover, waved goodbye from the quayside.

The first port of call was Portofino, followed by the Isle of Capri, where Callas and Tina went shopping together. From the Mediterranean, *Christina* headed into Onassis waters through the Aegean to the Gulf of Corinth. From the start, Meneghini was the odd man out, and the choppy seas soon had him reeling with seasickness. He could not even find solace in his cabin, which was hot and stuffy, because Callas refused to allow the airconditioning to be switched on in case it affected her voice. When he did join the others for dinner, he lived up to his reputation as old opera roué and provincial Casanova. Women tried hard to avoid sitting next to him because he had the habit of engaging their legs with his own under the table. Tina dubbed him 'Meningitis.'

Christina entered the Bay of the Bosphorus on 29 July and anchored off Smyrna. 'The Greek wanted me to go to dinner with him and meet his old boyhood friends,' said Meneghini. 'Near the port we went to various local dives which Onassis knew intimately, and we made merry all night in the company of dealers, prostitutes and assorted sinister characters. At five in the morning I persuaded him to return to the yacht. He was so drunk he couldn't stand up.'

But his wife was drawn ever closer to Onassis no matter how badly he behaved. Meneghini watched in astonishment a few days later as the Patriarch of Constantinople honoured 'the greatest singer in the world' and 'the greatest sailor of modern times, the new Odysseus'. 'He blessed them as if he were performing a marriage rite,' said Meneghini. 'She was no longer the same woman. And how could I have defended myself against the new Odysseus?' Soon afterwards, Tina saw her husband having sex with Callas in the saloon late one night and told Meneghini. When he challenged Callas, she laughed in his face.

As soon as the cruise ended, Callas walked out on the millionaire industrialist who had made her a star, declaring: 'I had a feeling of having long been held captive in a cage so that on meeting Aristo I became a different woman.' At Harry's Bar in Venice, Ari responded: 'How could I not have been flattered by a woman of Maria Callas's class falling in love with me? Who would have reacted differently?' Meneghini replied unsportingly: 'I created Callas. When I met her, she was fat and clumsily dressed, as poor as a gypsy. She had nothing.' Even less sportingly, he said he had put a curse on the couple, revealing a hitherto unsuspected knowledge of the black arts.

The only one who kept a dignified silence was Tina. Gathering up Christina and Alexander, she flew to New York and filed for divorce. She said nothing until 25 November when she read a prepared statement to the press at her home in Sutton Square: 'It is almost 13 years since Mr Onassis and I were married in New York City. Since then he has become one of the world's richest men, but his great wealth has not brought me happiness with him nor, as the world knows, has it brought him happiness with me. After we parted this summer in Venice, I had hoped that Mr Onassis loved our children enough and respected our privacy sufficiently to meet with me – or, through lawyers, with my lawyer – to straighten out our problems. But that was not to be. Mr Onassis knows positively that I want none of his wealth and that I am solely concerned for the welfare of our children.' The marriage was eventually dissolved in June 1960 on the grounds of mental cruelty. Christina cried herself to sleep every night for a year.

Onassis quickly discovered that although he might have liberated Callas from her cage, he had imprisoned himself. In Monte Carlo, the break-up of his marriage strained his relationship with Prince Rainier and Princess Grace even further. Defying everyone, he began to live with Callas in *Christina*. They spent many of their evenings in a new night club called Maona, short for Maria and Onassis, where the singer announced her intention to merge her name with Onassis's even more directly through holy matrimony. As Catholics, their Serene Highnesses viewed the prospect of a marriage between the two divorcees with alarm – as did Onassis. 'He sort of shrivelled up,' said Rainier, 'and perhaps because it was here that all his trouble started, he may even have taken an unconscious dislike to Monte Carlo.' However, the Grimaldis continued to mix socially with Ari and even attended one of the shows Callas put on for guests in *Christina*. The Grimaldi family accompanied them on a cruise in 1961, and Ari gave Rainier the full run of his yacht to entertain his friends and business associates. This wasn't as generous as it seemed. All the cabins were bugged as part of Ari's spy network. By monitoring private conversations, he found out exactly what Rainier was saying about him.

In the middle of this farcical situation were the Grimaldi children, Caroline, Stephanie and Albert. They loved sneaking up on Uncle Ari whenever he took a siesta on the deck. 'They would tease him, tweak his ears and pull him into the pool,' Rainier said. 'He wasn't young then, and we used to get rather worried. But he loved it and although he did not appear to be the typical playmate for the children, they adored him.'

Onassis had far greater difficulty getting any sort of a laugh out of his own children. He had given almost no thought to how the changing circumstances of his life would affect them. Alexander was 11 and Christina 9 when their parents' divorce became final, but they were old enough to blame Maria Callas. If she hadn't blundered into their father's life, they reasoned, the split would never have taken place. They avoided her whenever they could or ignored her if they were forced to spend any amount of time in her presence, usually in *Christina*. Her presents were left unopened, and they never responded to anything she said. The war of nerves took on a more openly hostile note when Onassis gave his son a Chris-Craft as an outright bribe. The boy waited until Callas was taking a nap in her stateroom or practising at the Steinway before revving up the powerful engines and circling *Christina* with a deafening roar. Callas's equilibrium was shattered even further when her lover refused to stop him.

Nearly 40, her voice faltered and her career suffered, but she received very little support from Aristo. Everything about her started to infuriate him. He forbade her from wearing spectacles and sent her to a Paris *coiffeur* to have her long, dark hair shortened. Whenever she complained, he turned on her: 'What are you? Nothing! All you have in your throat is a whistle which no longer functions.' In truth, he was furious with himself for having driven Tina out of his life, but he was too proud to admit to Callas he had made a monumental mistake.

Behind the scenes, the power struggle between Ari and Rainier had reached a new intensity. As the largest single shareholder, Onassis could appoint his own men to the SBM board. But Rainier had the power of veto over these appointments, and he used it unsparingly. There were frequent changes in the executive line-up, and very little business was actually getting done. To end this futile impasse, Ari suggested that the company acquire a special negotiator to act as an intermediary between himself and the prince. But the man became a mere pawn in the Riviera's biggest chess game. Scampering from Ari's office to the palace, he told Rainier that Onassis had finally agreed to finance an artificial beach, a heliport and a new luxury hotel.

'And in return?' asked Rainier.

'You must give up your power of veto and allow the SBM to run without outside interference,' replied the messenger.

Rainier raged against this typical Onassian duplicity and sent the man back with his answer: a resounding no. So Ari resorted to the tactics that had brought him to Monaco in the first place. He bought up more shares until he controlled 500,000, making him the majority shareholder, regardless of Rainier's holding. 'I am the boss here now,' he remarked to Louis Vuidet, the *maître de* of the Hôtel de Paris.

Rainier appeared to be in trouble on all fronts. When the

National Council opposed an extravagant scheme to build an aquarium and an underwater laboratory, in which his friend Professor Jacques Cousteau could study marine life, Rainier promptly dismissed the assembly. He set up the Monaco Development Corporation to attract foreign capital and business. Hundreds of businessmen from America, Germany and the United Kingdom clamoured to take advantage of the climate and the liberal tax concessions. Real-estate prices shot up, and Monaco office buildings proliferated with shiny new brass nameplates. President Charles de Gaulle became alarmed when it was revealed that many of the investors were French, a large number of them former colonialists who had been forced out of Algeria, Morocco and Indo-China.

In 1962 the gangling Gallic giant gave the Prince six months' notice of his intention to overrule the convention that governed relations between the two countries unless he banned French tax dodgers. Temporary customs barriers were set up at Monaco's frontier, and Rainier was warned that gas and electricity supplies would be cut off if no agreement were reached. The Prince had no alternative but to surrender. A concordat was signed, which effectively excluded French citizens from using Monaco as a tax haven. Two-thirds of the estimated 16 billion francs held by Frenchmen in Monte Carlo was transferred overnight from Monaco's financial institutions. But instead of returning to France, these deposits simply crossed the Alps into Switzerland, taking Monaco's prosperity with them.

With Monaco and its Casino headed for bankruptcy, Rainier abolished the antiquated concept of 'rule by divine right' in favour of a constitutional monarchy with regular elections and a supreme court. He focused public attention on the foreign ownership of the SBM and demanded that Onassis present a plan for land reclamation. Explaining his objection to the landfill scheme, Ari said: 'We cannot really turn the place into a second Brighton.' He was prepared to build one hotel – no more. In return, Rainier had to give up his veto power over the SBM and take over the running of such cultural activities as the Monte Carlo National Orchestra. He threatened to halt the regattas, operas and rallies that the SBM had traditionally organized.

Rainier turned to de Gaulle, who loathed Onassis and everything he stood for. As a sign of goodwill to the Prince, the French President ordered the Quai d'Orsay to take a tough line against Onassis. A whispering campaign was orchestrated, which did considerable damage. *Sotto voce*, French diplomats took to referring to Ari as 'an undesirable presence' in Monaco; not so softly, Rainier dubbed him a speculator 'devoid of any real concern for his adopted country.' 'Monsieur Onassis often repeated to us that gambling was immoral,' he said. 'That is one point of view. But we do not know whether financial speculations are less immoral than gambling, which is regulated strictly according to the law. The only solution appears to be a test of force. My government and myself are resolved upon it.'

On Rainier's orders, Jean-Charles Rey, now his brother-in-law, concocted a scheme under which the state would create 600,000 new shares in SBM, thus acquiring a clear majority. It would also purchase any other shares that the existing shareholders wished to dispose of at a price fixed halfway between the high and low points during 1966, plus a small bonus. Ari exclaimed that Rainier must be joking, but the decree was drawn up and passed just the same. Onassis's appeal against the legislation as unconstitutional was rejected by the newly formed supreme court. He received a check for 39,912,000 francs ($10 million) for his 500,489 shares, and his reign was over.

'We were gypped!' he complained before *Christina* weighed anchor and sailed out of the harbour. The Pink Palace on the Rock was to starboard and the spot-lit Casino to port. Heading east, the serrated shoreline swept past new Legoland apartment blocks to the even newer Sporting Club at the point of a wooded headland. As the place that had been his home since 1953 slipped from view, Ari remained below deck. The 'gala nights' had returned to Monte Carlo, but he was no longer in charge of the illuminations.

'He told me that as far as he was concerned, Monaco had been a pleasant little retirement village, and he had put it on the map,' said Frank Monte. 'He felt he had lost out on his investment. He hated not being there, and he hated Rainier and Grace for kicking him out.'

The terrifying thing for Onassis was that Callas had recently become free to carry out her intention to marry him. 'The fact is that I have always been afraid of spending my old age in poverty,' she said. On 18 March 1966, Callas, who had been born in New York, renounced her American citizenship and handed in her American passport at the US Embassy in Paris. In April of that year, she became a Greek citizen, which nullified her marriage to Meneghini everywhere except in Italy. According to a Greek law passed in 1946, a marriage between Greek citizens was legal only if the ceremony had been performed by the Greek Orthodox Church. As the lovers were both single at last, there was no longer any real impediment standing in the path to the altar. Ari's last excuse had disappeared. Rumours that Ari and Callas did, in fact, become man and wife persisted for years.

They started early in November 1967 when the couple left Régine's in Paris at two o'clock in the morning looking happier and more relaxed than usual. A reporter asked them: 'Is it true you are about to get married?' 'You're too late,' said Onassis. 'We are already married. We married 15 days ago. It was a wonderful thing.' Enquiries at the time failed to establish whether he had been telling the truth. The matter might have ended there if Ari hadn't repeated the same story in private. 'Ari told a friend of mine that he and Maria were married,' said his friend, the writer Doris Lilly. 'He didn't usually lie for the fun of it, and it seemed a strange thing to say if it wasn't true. When Maria overheard him, she wagged her finger at him and told him, "No, no, you mustn't do that."'

The *Sunday Times* followed the trail to Las Vegas, where it is believed the marriage might have taken place. Our enquiries there brought us in contact with a local property millionaire. 'They weren't married here, they were married on a ship,' he claimed. 'A chef from one of the Vegas hotels – the Stardust – went to work on *Christina*, but left after about a year because he couldn't stand it. He said he was woken up in the middle of the night to make Greek dishes for Onassis and Callas. They even had to have a certain kind of orange flown in for their juice. I remembered the story because I love hearing about other people's tastes in food. The chef who worked on the yacht was an Italian, but he died a few years ago. He came back to Vegas and told me about the wedding ceremony. He said it took place at sea on the Onassis yacht. Onassis kept people quiet, and it didn't take a lot of money because they feared him – he was a very tough guy.'

The vision of Ari summoning the captain during a night of revelry to officiate at an impromptu wedding ceremony to placate his irate diva sounded very much in character. Doris Lilly had spotted Callas in Las Vegas in the summer of 1968, a few months before Onassis married Jackie Kennedy. 'What was Maria doing there?' asked Lilly. 'She was certainly out of her social element there, and she wasn't singing. Don't people usually go in that direction when they get a divorce?' In fact, Callas was in the company of three friends on a recuperative sightseeing trip that took them from Santa Fe to San Francisco with a stopover in Las Vegas.

'The qualifying time for a divorce in Vegas was then six weeks,' said the millionaire, 'but the date of arrival could be backdated, so you could be divorced in a matter of days. There would be no record to show you had even been here.' An interesting point of authenticity in this story was that one of the lesser known facts about life on board *Christina* was that Onassis had oranges from his garden in Glyfada flown to him by Olympic Airways once a week – just as the chef had claimed.

Nadia Stancioff, who became Callas's private secretary in 1969, denied that the couple had married in 1967 or that Callas had gone to Las Vegas for a divorce. 'There wasn't any deep, dark meaning behind the trip,' she said. 'She was footloose, and she was being protected by some of her friends. She needed moral support, and she found it in America.'

In Washington in 1963, the marriage between Jackie and JFK was proving far from settled, and the image later woven around the romance of Camelot was a clever journalistic fiction. Fate had decreed that this was the moment Aristotle Onassis would make his entrance in their lives, with shattering consequences for all concerned.

NINE

JACKIE'S SECRET LOVER

THE CRUISE THAT would ultimately make Jackie Kennedy a fully fledged member of the Onassis dynasty hit serious turbulence before it had even begun. By the time it had ended, many strands of the Kennedy–Onassis saga had been woven into a thread that would bind not only the lives of Jackie and Ari but those of their children and grandchildren as well.

In the summer of 1963, Jackie lost her third child, Patrick Bouvier Kennedy. The baby had been born five weeks prematurely and survived less than three days. The grieving mother wanted the comfort of her sister, Princess Lee Radziwill, who was spending much of her time with Ari, either in *Christina* or on flying trips to London and New York. She told Ari over dinner in Athens that Jackie was deeply depressed and unhappy over the loss of her child. Ari suggested a convalescent cruise in *Christina*.

When Lee telephoned her sister with the suggestion, she immediately accepted. 'It's the dream of my life,' she told Lee. However, JFK was opposed to the trip. The prospect of Onassis acting as his wife's host was shot through with danger. The Kennedys were the world's first Catholic family, and Ari, a divorced man, was involved in two liaisons with married women – a public affair with Maria Callas and a secret one with his own sister-in-law. A presidential election was due in 1964, and Ari's gallivanting, jet-set lifestyle stamped him as the sort of person the voters of middle America heartily detested. This was a man who had been indicted by the Justice Department, accused of shipping oil to Red China and Cuba (falsely, as it turned out), and was friendly with America's sworn enemies, Nasser of Egypt, Perón of Argentina and Duvalier of Haiti. But an even more pressing consideration seemed to override these patently political objections.

'Bobby Kennedy got all upset when Lee Radziwill started playing around with Aristotle Onassis and was supposedly going to divorce her husband to marry him,' said a Kennedy aide. 'That really sent Bobby up the wall, and he told Jackie to put a stop to it.'

The situation played perfectly into Ari's hands. He had drawn on his well-honed playboy instincts after he met Jackie when she visited *Christina* with JFK in the summer of 1956: 'There is something damned wilful about that lady; something very provocative indeed. She has got a carnal soul.' In his most self-deprecating manner, he volunteered to stay behind, knowing full well that if Jackie wanted to talk to him about Lee, he would have to be there in person. He had guessed correctly. Jackie dug her heels in, maintaining: 'I can't possibly accept this man's hospitality and then not let him come along. It would be too cruel.' To save face, the President ordered a member of his administration, Franklin D. Roosevelt Jr, to accompany his wife as chaperon. 'I didn't really want to babysit for Jackie,' Roosevelt complained. 'I was Undersecretary of Commerce at the time, and I didn't think the trip would add much lustre to my political image.'

However, the reluctant Roosevelt joined Onassis, his sister Artimus, Jackie, Lee and her husband Stas and the rest of the party on *Christina* in the Greek port of Piraeus on 4 October 1963. There was no sign of Maria Callas, the one woman who could have made things difficult for Ari. The scene was set for his bold plan to switch from one sister to the other. He held a dinner in Jackie's honour that night, followed by dancing on the raised mosaic floor of the swimming pool. In the morning, ships' victuallers filled the yacht's vast refrigerated holds with buckets of red mullet, canned hams, crates of grapes, black figs, pears, peaches and pomegranates and eight varieties of caviar. Before setting sail, Ari told reporters: 'We'll go wherever Mrs Kennedy wants to go. She's in charge here. She's the captain.'

Before a single tub of caviar had been emptied, the cruise had turned into a hot political issue in Washington. Questions were raised in Congress about the propriety of the President's wife being the guest of a foreigner who had been under indictment and was now 'turning over to the disposal of a Presidential and Department of Commerce party a luxury ship, with 60-man crew, including two *coiffeurs* and dance bands at a personal cost of many tens of thousands of dollars'.

Ari initially kept a discreet distance from his guests, declining to accompany them ashore when the ship stopped at Lesbos for a sight-seeing tour. After she returned to the ship, Jackie sent Roosevelt to enquire why he was 'hiding away' and let it be known that she would appreciate his presence as a guide and companion. When the yacht reached Crete, Ari resumed his customary role as host, enchanting the company with recitations of Greek myths interwoven with fragments from his own past. Jackie, he noticed, smoked heavily and bit her nails, but she hung on his every word. When the ship was in port, he and Jackie began slipping away to tavernas, where they talked privately over dinner, and Ari demonstrated his skill at bouzouki dancing.

Ari knew that Jackie's hauteur masked an inner conflict that she would only express to someone she trusted – and she came to trust Onassis. As well as being a gifted raconteur, he was also an astute listener, and he remained silent as Jackie poured out her troubles. Her husband's philandering had reached epic proportions, and although she could live with his meaningless flings with female staffers in the White House, the affair with Marilyn Monroe had humiliated her in public. Even though Monroe had died the previous summer, Jackie had been badly shaken by subsequent whispers about the star's involvement with her husband. Certain members of the Kennedy family knew exactly what had transpired between them because much of it had taken place at the Santa Monica beach house that JFK's sister Patricia shared with her husband, the actor Peter Lawford.

'Everybody knew that Jack was moving around a little bit and that Jackie spent a lot of money,' ex-Senator George Smathers told us, 'but I don't think he was for one minute unhappy about his marriage.' Jackie, however, saw it differently. While she didn't believe that her husband would divorce her and marry someone like Marilyn, she had reached the point where she was no longer prepared to turn a blind eye. She didn't want revenge against her husband; she wanted protection from him. When *Christina* reached Skórpios, she summoned the nerve to tell Ari she never wanted the cruise to end.

One of the guests was Alexis Miotis, director of the Greek National Theatre, who had directed two of Callas's operas, *Norma* and *Médée*. As he watched Ari dote on Jackie, he realized that Callas was no longer in the running. 'Ari wanted to be Emperor of the Seas,' he said, 'and he wanted a Cleopatra to sit by his side.' Sailing back to Piraeus on the last leg of the cruise, Ari knew it was time to test his instincts. When he went to Jackie in the Chios suite late at night, she overlooked his lack of decorum and invited him to stay.

Jackie encouraged his advances for two reasons. Not only would this end the troublesome affair between him and her sister but it would also make an ally of one of the world's richest and most powerful men. By common consent, Onassis was wicked, but to Jackie he was a necessary evil. No one was more suitable than this deceptive man, charming yet ruthless, in dealing with the pain her husband had inflicted upon her. Ari was a father figure who made her feel like a little girl again; she could tell him of her innermost problems. Also, like Black Jack, he was often irrepressibly high-spirited with an enviable capacity for enjoyment, laughter and self-mockery. As Jackie judged every man she met by her father's memory, Ari left the Chios suite certain in the knowledge that he had not been found wanting in this or in any other respect. Jackie began to call him 'Telis', a contraction of the Greek word for Aristotle.

Asked if the affair had started before the events in Dallas unfolded a few weeks later, JFK's secretary Evelyn Lincoln replied: 'I think so. Yes, I would say so.'

The not-so-subtle shift in Onassis's affections became apparent to Lee Radziwill at the end of the cruise. As was customary, Onassis presented gifts to his guests at a dinner party. Jackie got a $50,000 diamond and ruby necklace that uncoupled to form two bracelets. 'Oh, God,' gasped Lee, 'it's so stunning I can't believe it.' She wrote to JFK that she had received only 'three dinky little bracelets that Caroline wouldn't wear to her own birthday party'. Intentionally or not, she had alerted the President to Ari's interest in his wife. When Jackie returned to the White House on 17 October, a member of the staff said: 'Jackie had stars in her eyes – Greek stars.'

She was far from coy about her feelings, describing Ari as 'an alive and vital person who had come from nowhere . . . Onassis is no more conscious of his wealth than Rock Hudson is of his good looks,' she explained to friends. 'It just comes natural to them – even though Rock was born with his blessings while Onassis had to work like a galley slave to get his.'

Jackie confided to her friend, the British writer Robin Douglas-Home, about the cruise, and he remarked on her new composure. 'Gone was much of the bewilderment, the repressed frustration, the acidity – and, yes – even the bitchiness,' he said. Ari lapped up the gossip from inside Camelot. There also seemed little doubt that JFK guessed what had transpired on the yacht, or perhaps Jackie told him in the manner of a warning. The President informed Onassis through one of his aides that he would not be welcome in the United States until after the 1964 election. Ari was furious. 'Who do they think they're kidding? The Kennedys are just a bunch of Irish politicians,' he said. 'The only one with any class is Jackie.'

In Washington, JFK asked Jackie to accompany him on a trip he was making to mend some political fences in Texas. Jackie agreed to go, and on 21 November 1963, she and her husband set off for the Lone Star state. A member of the entourage recalled that Jackie was so edgy she chainsmoked a full packet of Salems during the flight.

In fact, she was furious with JFK and, according to visitors to the White House, they had had what looked like a physical fight the previous evening. Jackie had returned home to learn that her husband had taken full advantage of her absence to pursue his extra-marital activities. When the Kennedys arrived in Dallas for a motorcade through the streets on 22 November, Jackie was more grateful to Aristotelis Onassis for his friendship than JFK would have liked to hear.

The real reason Jackie Kennedy married Aristotle Onassis was a mutual antipathy towards members of the Kennedy family. Money and personal security were important, but secondary, considerations in Jackie's choice of a husband to replace JFK. Had she simply wanted to marry a very rich man, there were numerous millionaires in America who would have been prepared to offer the same terms as Onassis: $3 million down and $30,000 a month. Instead, she chose a man whose very nationality, appearance and reputation were anathema to her Irish in-laws. As well as freedom from Kennedy control, there was an element of pay back.

However, Jackie and Ari didn't hate the same members of America's First Family. Jackie despised only the women, particularly her mother-in-law, Rose, who had never missed an opportunity to denigrate Jackie in the eyes of her daughters and daughters-in-law. Jackie also harboured a deep grudge against JFK's sisters Kathleen and Pat, and Bobby's wife, Ethel, for the way they had treated her during her marriage to JFK. They had scoffed at her pretensions to a French aristocratic background and even parodied her name: 'Jackleen – it rhymes with Queen' was a favourite dig at the young, insecure Jacqueline Lee Bouvier even before she had joined the family. 'The Kennedy women had always flaunted their money and power,' said George Smathers. 'This was Jackie's opportunity to say to them, "OK, what are you going to say now that I can buy and sell you?"'

For his part, Onassis nurtured a long-standing hatred of Joe and Bobby Kennedy, while he dismissed Teddy, even before Mary Jo Kopechne's death at Chappaquiddick, as 'a weakling'. He had had little contact with the Kennedy women but was only too willing to exploit Jackie's desire to show off in front of them. Nor had he been in awe of the President, knowing as he did that JFK's telegenic smile and slick haircut hid many guilty secrets.

Towards the end of 1963, his feelings towards the President had bordered on the homicidal. JFK had been responsible for his blacklisting in America, which had opened up old and painful wounds at a time when he was trying to renovate his image. He had huge holdings in the United States, yet the President's personal proscription denied him the right even to visit his American lawyers. He had been treated like a dangerous criminal when his only breach of the law in the United States had been the disputed purchase of some surplus ships many years earlier. Yet Onassis knew that the pretexts JFK had given were mere window-dressing. The real reason behind the blacklisting was his pursuit of the President's wife.

For Onassis, it was a timely and convenient death. In the aftermath of the events that took place in Dallas at 1.30pm on Friday, 22 November 1963, a thorough investigation would have uncovered the fact that the tycoon had coveted the victim's wife. Had the Dallas

Police Department treated JFK's assassination as a routine homicide, Onassis would have emerged as a prime suspect. In police jargon, he had the motive, the passion and the capacity to have plotted the removal of his rival. In the words of one who had suffered at his hands, he was 'an extremely dangerous person who would stop at nothing to get his own way'.

However, no one in authority – from the Attorney-General Robert Kennedy to the head of the FBI J. Edgar Hoover to the US Chief Justice Earl Warren – wanted to believe that the political crime of the century was anything other than the work of a single assassin, Lee Harvey Oswald, acting entirely alone. This view was endorsed by Jackie, who repeatedly said that proving a conspiracy wouldn't bring her husband back. But as subsequent enquiries have shown, it was anything but a simple slaying.

Onassis was launching a tanker in Hamburg when he heard the news and immediately flew to Washington after first checking that he would be allowed in. He was assured that he was no longer on the Immigration blacklist at any of the country's ports of entry; the First Lady herself had ordered the lifting of the ban. As further proof of his relationship with the President's widow, Ari stayed in the White House as her official guest, one of the few non-family members to be afforded that privilege. He comforted Jackie behind closed doors and offered whatever help he could provide through his vast network. On the morning of 25 November, three days after the assassination, he accompanied Queen Frederika of Greece to the funeral ceremony at St Matthew's Cathedral, where he sat with the Kennedy family, and he followed the cortège to Arlington Cemetery for the interment. As all eyes were on Jackie and her children, Caroline and John, Ari's presence was hardly noticed.

After dinner in the White House later that evening, Bobby Kennedy left the family circle and joined Ari for a drink. The two men talked about money or, more specifically, about the origins of Ari's fortune in Argentine. Bobby suddenly dashed off and returned with a formal document, which he handed to Onassis. Privately, Bobby called Onassis 'a complete rogue on a grand scale' because his ships sailed under flags of convenience to avoid tax and other legal responsibilities. The paper was an oath stipulating that Onassis would give half his wealth to the poor of Latin America. Onassis joined in the spirit of the occasion and signed – in flowing Greek. He told Doris Lilly he had given his personal IOU to Bobby for $250 million 'but it was all in fun – just a joke. Of course, if he had ever wanted to cash it he could have.'

Shortly after the funeral, Onassis flew to Paris to help Maria Callas celebrate her 40th birthday, but the woman on his mind was Jackie Kennedy. Although Ari stood to gain from the President's death, he seemed to take the manner of his passing to heart. It was, he decided, a professional hit and not simply the work of a lone madman. He spoke with conviction when he later told Costa Gratsos that JFK was the victim of a conspiracy. 'I'm sure he was,' were the exact words he had used. The reason Ari was 'sure' was not that he had foreknowledge of the plot, but that he had used his contacts to find out after the event. 'Onassis owned the finest intelligence network money could buy,' claimed one of the bankers. At times, he shared information with Howard Hughes, who was not only a close friend of Hoover but also a crony of senior mobsters.

Suffering from hereditary deafness, an addiction to codeine and a phobia about bacteria, Hughes had dropped out of sight in 1958. An anonymous document circulated to influential citizens in Los Angeles accused Onassis of kidnapping him. In fact, he had smuggled himself into Las Vegas, arriving at midnight in the back of an ambulance and taking over all the high-roller suites on the ninth floor of the Desert Inn for himself and his Mormon entourage. Bankrolled with $500 million in cash from the sale of his 77 per cent stake in TWA (which Ari had tried to buy to merge with Olympic Airways), he embarked on a reckless spending spree, starting with the Desert Inn, for which he paid $13.2 million. He bought seven hotels and gaming establishments including the Sands, Castaways and the Silver Slipper as well as a great deal of land at vastly inflated prices. Robert Maheu, the private eye-cum-CIA operative, had been brought in to run the casino/hotel side of the Hughes organization.

It was an open secret to men like Maheu and Johnny Meyer that JFK had gangland links via the Kennedy political machine long before he became President. In office, he used Sam Giancana, the Mafia boss in Chicago, and Santo Trafficante, the Mafia boss in Florida, in plots to kill Fidel Castro. Official investigations revealed that the go-between orchestrating the plot between the CIA and the Mafia to assassinate Castro was none other than Robert Maheu. Bobby Kennedy told Hoover in a memo dated 10 May 1962, that 'he had been advised by CIA that CIA had hired Maheu to approach Giancana with a proposition of paying $150,000 to hire some gunmen to go to Cuba to kill Castro.'

As unofficial inquests into the Bay of Pigs fiasco later proved, the Mob were actively involved in attempts to reclaim Cuba as a Mafia fiefdom. One popular theory was that pro-Castro gunmen had shot Kennedy in retaliation for the plots against the bearded leader's life. The involvement of Oswald, a pro-Castro activist, had pointed the finger of suspicion straight at Havana. This, however, was one of the few points Oswald had been able to clarify after his arrest. 'I'm just a patsy,' he had insisted to reporters at the police station before the strip-club owner Jack Ruby had shot him dead on orders from the Mob. Our enquiries showed that the true motive for the assassination of JFK was much closer to home than Cuba.

Bobby Kennedy had sworn to destroy the power of organized crime in America, and three of the Mob chieftains he had targetted were Giancana, Trafficante and Carlos Marcello, head of the New Orleans branch of the outfit. The former Florida senator George Smathers said: 'I don't believe the Cubans had a damn thing to do with Jack's assassination.' Smathers maintained powerful contacts in Washington and had his own sources of information on the assassination. 'I don't have any doubt that it was the Mob – gangsters from Detroit, New York and Chicago – who were behind the whole thing,' he told us in Miami. 'The reason was that Bobby was killing 'em. As Attorney-General, he had got J. Edgar Hoover off his ass and turned the FBI loose on them. They were really closing on those gangsters; closing down the rackets. So those guys – Giancana, Trafficante and so on – had to get rid of Bobby somehow. He was too tough for them.'

Smathers knew quite a lot about the racketeers from visits they had made to Florida in the fifties. 'They used to come down here to stay at the Key Biscayne hotel,' he said. 'As I had been a district attorney, the Secret Service would tell me when these guys were in town. They were bad guys; I never did get friendly with any of them, but I knew who they were.' The former senator was adamant that Bobby Kennedy was the original target of the conspiracy. 'The FBI got on to that, and Bobby was so well protected he became infinitely difficult to get into an assassination position. Nobody thought that Jack was in any great danger, but they finally decided to knock him off. Lyndon Johnson was Vice-President, and he didn't like Bobby, and Bobby didn't like him. When Johnson became President, they [the Mob] figured he would get rid of Bobby.'

Bobby's biggest enemy was Jimmy Hoffa, the Teamsters Union leader who was indicted for extortion on 18 May 1962. 'Jimmy Hoffa was very close to those Mob guys,' said Smathers, 'and they were the ones who masterminded the assassination. In my mind, I don't have any doubt about it. That's exactly the way it happened; they arranged things. They found a kook and used him – and that was Oswald. They were out to stop Bobby, and they finally decided it was easier to get rid of Jack because he was more exposed and easier to target.'

Leaving Washington for good, Jackie moved into a duplex at 1040 Fifth Avenue with Caroline and John, and began to visit her favourite restaurant, the Côte Basque. She was spotted out on the town with a vast array of men: the composers Leonard Bernstein and Alan J. Lerner, politicians Averell Harriman, Robert S. McNamara, Roswell Gilpatric and Franklin D. Roosevelt Jr, writers Truman Capote and Randolph Churchill, the diplomat Lord Harlech, the banker André Meyer and the actor Anthony Quinn. The one escort no one noticed was Onassis, even though he frequently visited her apartment.

When Alecko Papamarkou asked Doris Lilly why women found Ari attractive, she said: 'He's got charm, and he's obviously very rich, but it's more than that. I get the feeling – and my girlfriends agree with me – that Ari's best quality is that he keeps himself in reserve. He doesn't plunge into affairs. He stands back and keeps himself for something special. Everything is done brain first.'

By the start of 1967, Onassis felt he had stood back long enough. He was determined to make Jackie his wife, but he discovered that he had to contend with an unexpected rival for her favours. 'A former Kennedy mistress told me that Jackie was in love with Bobby Kennedy,' Doris Lilly revealed over lunch at 21 in New York. 'Everybody knew it. If you could have seen the way she clung to him, put her head on his shoulder and looked up into his eyes . . . She was hooked.' Jackie and Bobby had been spotted one evening at the Carlyle hotel and, the following morning, were seen leaving the same suite after apparently having spent the night together. Jackie made no secret of her feelings for Bobby. 'I'd jump out of a window for him,' she said.

Putting his brain first, Ari invited Jackie to spend a few days with him in Paris during the spring of 1967. It was a clever move; for a Francophile such as Jackie, there were few better places to receive the spirit of the City of Light than from the balcony of his penthouse apartment. No. 88 Avenue Foch was a mansion block of polished white sandstone built along classical lines during the Second Empire of Louis Napoleon. Apart from its eminent position among the Parisian *haute bourgeoisie*, the feature that appealed most to Ari was the building's western façade. Facing the setting sun, it was shaped like the prow of a great ocean-going liner, which seemed poised to sail through the Bois de Boulogne to join the Seine. No. 88 was also conveniently close to the George V hotel and one of his favourite nightspots, the Crazy Horse Saloon.

Ari had made careful plans to protect the identity of his guest from everyone, including his servants. The meal had been prepared before Jackie's arrival, and he ordered his maid Eleni Syros and his major-domo Jorge to stay in their rooms for the rest of the evening. He would serve his guest himself, he said. The rest of the staff were banished from the apartment for the whole night. There was, however, one witness whom Onassis could not order to turn a blind eye, the concierge Madame Maggie. 'I knew Maria Callas when she lived here with Mr Onassis, but after 1967 I didn't see her again,' she told us. 'Then I saw Jacqueline Kennedy coming in through the street door. It was such a surprise I could hardly believe it.'

Jackie had slipped through the gate in the 7ft-high spiked railings and walked down a path lined with pink geraniums to enter the building through a wrought-iron doorway. Seven years had passed since Jackie had become the darling of Paris during a visit with JFK. Her reception in the French capital had been so spontaneous and overwhelming that Kennedy had been moved to introduce himself as 'the man who accompanied Jacqueline Kennedy to Paris'. President de Gaulle had taken careful note of Jackie's allure and remarked to one of his ministers: 'I can see her in about 10 years from now on the yacht of a Greek oil millionaire.'

Over a dinner of the finest French cuisine in the intimate surroundings of his own home, Ari resumed the dialogue they had started on *Christina*. No one knows for sure what was said that night, but it was certainly a prelude to a proposal of marriage.

After dinner, Ari led his guest out on to the balustraded balcony, which ran like an upper deck around the rim of the building. Straight ahead was the Bois de Boulogne and Longchamp and, to the south, the flood-lit spire of the Eiffel Tower reared up beyond the Palais de Chaillot and the Trocadéro gardens. Eastwards, the broad, tree-lined sweep of the Avenue Foch ran uphill to join the twelve-pointed star at the Arc de Triomphe. The Paris Jackie had dreamed about ever since she had been a student at the Sorbonne was suddenly within her grasp.

A few days later, Ari whisked Jackie off to Greece and, between the Greek salad and the brandy at his favourite night club, Zampetas in Glyfada, he asked her to marry him, although he had already proposed to Maria Callas. The first the Kennedys knew about the seriousness of the relationship was when Jackie called Bobby from Greece to tell him that 'Telis' had proposed. Bobby was flabbergasted – and very angry. Onassis, whom he always referred to as 'the Greek', was one of the last people he wanted to find out the truth about his relationship with Jackie. He was also immediately aware of the political damage to his plan to run for the presidency in 1968. When he found his tongue, he decided to turn this ludicrous proposition into a bad joke. 'For God's sake, Jackie,' he quipped, 'this could cost me five states.' Jackie replied: 'He's been wonderful to me, Bobby, and so good to the children.'

When he returned to Paris, Ari attended a cocktail party at the George V, where he gave an impromptu press conference about Jackie. 'She is a totally misunderstood woman,' he said, knowing full well that Jackie would read his comments. 'Perhaps she even misunderstands herself. She's being held up as a model of propriety, constancy and of so many of those boring American female virtues. She's now utterly devoid of mystery. She needs a small scandal to bring her alive. A peccadillo, an indiscretion. Something should happen to her to win our fresh compassion. The world loves to pity fallen grandeur.' In his own way, he was preparing the ground for the emotional tremors that the announcement of his engagement to Jackie would inevitably create.

Both Bobby and Teddy Kennedy knew that Onassis posed a serious threat to the family's political ambitions. Their wives, Ethel and Joan, interceded with Jackie to point out to her that Onassis was 'too foreign' to be accepted by the American people and too involved with the right-wing Colonels who had seized power in Greece. Jackie listened while the Kennedy women poured out the family's concerns, but it was only after Cardinal Cushing urged her to reconsider that she agreed to wait until after the presidential election. 'I know this is what the Ambassador would want me to do,' she said, referring to Joe Kennedy. In December 1961 after realizing a lifelong ambition to put a Kennedy in the White House, he had suffered a massive stroke from which he never recovered. Semi-paralysed and speechless, he had struggled out of bed on the day of JFK's funeral with the intention of burying his son but had been gently led back to his room.

On Easter Sunday 1968, Ari and Jackie were spotted dining in a private room at Mykonos, a Greek restaurant in New York, with Margot Fonteyn, Rudolf Nureyev and Christina. According to Doris Lilly, Ari arrived like a nervous lover an hour early to check the arrangements. They had barbecued baby lamb and moussaka washed down with red wine. During that spring Jackie and Ari were often together at the Colony, where they sat at his usual corner table and ordered his favourite spaghetti. They visited Jackie's friends in Palm Beach, swam together at Bailey's Beach Club in Newport, where they were guests of Janet Auchincloss, and Jackie flew to Nassau in the Bahamas for a weekend aboard *Christina*.

The image Onassis projected was that of a man who had risen above politics and wished nothing more than to be of service to America's most tragic widow. He tried to distance Jackie from the political turbulence in Greece, where the young King Constantine had been driven into exile, and a military junta was in power, but he wasn't always successful. 'I was berthed next to *Christina* in Miami, and we arranged a soccer match between the two crews,' said publishing executive John B. Evans. 'The game had to be stopped after an almighty fist-fight broke out on the other side. The rival political factions in Onassis's crew were fighting the Greek civil war on the pitch.'

When Bobby Kennedy was shot at the Ambassador Hotel in Los Angeles on 5 June 1968, no one was more pleased than Hoover, Jimmy Hoffa or the Mob, but neither did Onassis try to hide his satisfaction. 'She's free of the Kennedys,' he told Costa Gratsos, 'the last link just broke.' Until Bobby's death, the relationship had been finely balanced, but after that Jackie's feelings changed dramatically.

'I hate this country,' she told a Kennedy aide. 'I despise America, and I don't want my children to live here any more. If they're killing Kennedys, my kids are No. 1 targets. I want to get out of this country.' Ari and Jackie visited the Kennedy compound at Hyannis Port on Cape Cod, its centrepiece the big white house with a circular drive at the foot of Scudder Avenue. When JFK was in office, the presidential standard had flown from a flagpole in the front yard during his visits. Before she had departed, Jackie had left the Kennedys in no doubt that she was incensed over the manner in which she and her children had been exploited for political ends. She intended to live the rest of her life as a modern woman, she said, not as a holy icon in widow's weeds.

During his stay on Cape Cod, Onassis invited Teddy Kennedy to escort Jackie for a week's cruise in *Christina* in August. 'As I did not expect a dowry, there was nothing to worry about,' Ari said.

The high point of the trip was a bouzouki party held aboard the yacht while she was moored at Skórpios. A Greek reporter, Nicos Mastorakis, tricked his way into the group using the bogus title of 'social director'. He described the scene: 'Jackie is standing at the door. She is resplendent, wearing a flame-red blouse with a check scarf around her neck and a long, checked, gypsy-style skirt. The Greek sun has bronzed her. She is a sweet woman who watches the world with interest and smiles at everybody with the same warmth and without pretence. Onassis introduces her. She squeezes our hands warmly and to each says something kind.

'Teddy comes in. He holds a blonde goddess by the shoulders. He is wearing a light pink shirt and matching scarf. The indications are that the party will be explosive. The musical evening begins with pepper tips, ripe red tomatoes, spinach purée, black caviar and liquor. Teddy drinks ouzo, permanently. Jackie prefers vodka at first. A crooner sings, and Jackie is rapt with fascination. From time to time Onassis translates with whispers in her ear, and she stares with those big eyes. The bouzouki music reaches its peak, and Teddy gets up and tries to dance . . . Teddy returns to his ouzo.' Mastorakis's cover was blown when he tried to sneak a photograph of the dishevelled Senator. Onassis had the journalist arrested on his return to Athens, and his film was seized.

Sources close to the discussions that took place between Ari and Teddy the following day said Teddy had opened with the words: 'We love Jackie, and we only want what's best for her.'

'So do I,' murmured Onassis. 'I want her to have a secure and happy future.' Teddy told Ari that Jackie would lose the $150,000 annual income she received from the Kennedy trust. As Ari's fortune was estimated at $500 million in 1968, he said this would not be a problem. Under the *nomimos mira* rules of Greek law, a husband had to leave at least 12.5 per cent of his wealth to his wife and 37.5 per cent to his children. This law was strictly enforced, making it impossible for a Greek to disinherit his family. However, Onassis told Teddy that he required Jackie to waive her rights under *nomimos mira* in a pre-marital contract. In return, Jackie would receive $3 million for herself and $1 million apiece in a trust fund for her two children. If Onassis died first, Jackie was to receive $150,000 a year for life. This was the deal that Teddy put to Jackie, and she gave her consent.

Ari flew to London to break the news to Maria Callas of his impending marriage. When he returned to New York, a friend asked how the meeting had gone. 'I won't tell you what happened,' Ari laughed. 'But I will tell you I hope that what happened to me never happens to you.'

Callas said: 'She did well, Jackie, to give a grandfather to her children. Ari is as beautiful as Croesus.' Later, she was sad: 'First I lost my weight, then I lost my voice, and now I've lost Onassis.' Elizabeth Taylor supported Onassis. She and Richard Burton had enjoyed his hospitality on several occasions, she said, and she had found him charming, kind and considerate. 'Jackie has made a good choice,' she said. Doris Lilly, who was also fond of Ari, reflected: 'Jackie always seemed to have been attracted to older men, possibly because you don't have to shoot them in the legs to keep them home at night.'

While the American press dredged up damaging stories about him, Onassis sent Johnny Meyer on a mission to buy the silence of former lovers, among them Gloria Swanson. The actress, who was living in New York, simply refused to believe what she was hearing. Using all his powers of persuasion, Meyer finally convinced her that Onassis really was going to marry Jackie Kennedy. Gloria controlled herself with great difficulty. 'And what makes Mr Onassis think, Mr Meyer, that our very brief friendship a long time ago is a matter I would wish to rake up now?' she said icily. She instructed him to impress upon his boss that she regarded the suggestion as 'a compliment to my memory and an insult to my dignity'. 'She's quite a dame,' Meyer told Onassis. 'I never even got a chance to offer her the money.'

One former lover who needed some cash was Veronica Lake, who was working as a barmaid in a hotel just off Park Avenue. A tabloid newspaper discovered her there and paid her a few dollars to recount her affairs with Howard Hughes and Onassis. Her once glamorous life was tacked on as a postscript to Ari's latest adventure.

The two people who should have mattered to him most, Christina and Alexander, weren't even consulted about the wedding. Ari knew in advance that his offspring were capable of hating Jackie even more than they had loathed Callas. When Christina had met her, she had lapsed into a moody silence and remained insolently uncommunicative. She still prayed that her father would change his mind. Alexander had never met the Widow, as he called her, but reason told him the only thing she was attracted to was his father's wealth. Like Christina, he knew Onassis was really just three months short of entering his seventieth year, and his health had noticeably declined.

When Onassis first introduced his son to Jackie at Artimus's villa in Athens and informed him of their wedding plans, Alexander had jumped into his Ferrari and sped off into the night. 'It's a perfect match,' he confirmed later. 'My father likes names, and Jackie likes money.'

Despite the public outcry and private dismay, the wedding of the year went ahead as scheduled on 10 October 1968, in the little chapel under the cypresses on Skórpios. Reluctantly, both Christina and Alexander had turned up after Jackie was reputed to have written a letter to them that said, 'Don't worry. I love only my poor dead husband, and your father loves only your mother.' Alexander gave the letter to Tina, who revealed its contents to friends. One absentee guest was Rose Kennedy, who refused to attend the Greek Orthodox service. It was a rainy, blustery day, but the weather didn't prevent an armada of press craft from buzzing *Christina*. The yacht was moored at Skórpios, and its crew forcibly repelled would-be boarders. 'Telis' was too elated to care about the newsmen or to notice that the gods on Olympus were angry. He had found the ultimate Desirable Woman who, after the traditional passing of the wedding crowns, would be his.

Part of Jackie's physical attraction for him was that she had large, round, brown eyes set wide apart – the same as Penelope, the mother he had lost as a six-year-old boy. And when he made Jackie his possession, her dark hair was combed high, and her neck was enclosed in a collar of fine lace. Christina and Alexander knew she bore a striking resemblance to Penelope in their father's favourite picture of her. However, Jackie was not intended as a mother substitute, but as a new Penelope, wife of the modern Odysseus. 'Five times a night and twice in the morning,' he boasted to Costa

Gratsos shortly after the wedding. 'She surpasses all the women I've ever known.'

Onassis knew that Man could displease the gods in two ways, either by offending against the moral law (in which case he incurred their wrath), or by attaining too many riches or too much happiness (in which case he excited their jealousy). In his all-consuming pride, he seemed to have forgotten that after hubris came nemesis.

When the couple made their first public appearance in Manhattan they chose the celebrity hangout, P. T. Clarke's, as the venue. In a private back room, they munched cheeseburgers and then deliberately moved to a table fronting the street in the restaurant's public section to take their coffee. 'The worst thing that can happen to a man is to become a celebrity,' Onassis moaned. 'It's as though there was a law that you have to walk naked in public and no matter how well built you are, they make you look ridiculous.' Jackie gave her Sphinx smile and said nothing. Before long, she would have made Onassis look more ridiculous than he would ever have believed possible.

TEN

THE STING OF THE CENTURY

TO HIS CONSTERNATION, Onassis discovered that Skórpios was uncomfortably well named. He had purchased this 500-acre, scorpion-shaped islet as his own earthly piece of paradise in 1963 but had not found much peace here. Fatally stung by his vision of dynastic grandeur, he had chosen to drop anchor at 'this wild little rock', as he called it, for reasons of sentiment as much as pride. He believed that owning a piece of land within sight of Ithaca, homeland of Odysseus, would somehow memorialize his own questing. It would make him an aristocrat of sorts, ennobling the adventurer so often spurned by others of higher birth as nothing more than a vulgarian. More immediately important, it would place the colossus in elevated shoes once again on an equal footing with his greatest enemy, Stavros Niarchos, who had his own island retreat, Spetsopoúla, in the Aegean.

Onassis had bought his speck of pale olive-grey rock and dark cypress two miles east of Nidri bay for $100,000, planting with his own hands 'all the trees and shrubs of the Bible', among them almond, pine, laurel and fig. But, first, he had sent in crop-dusting planes to spray the landscape with chemicals to kill off insects and snakes, and then covered the scorched wastes with shiploads of rich soil from Corfu. For a time, he set aside the wheeling and dealing of the marketplace. Stripped to the waist, he would sit at the same table as his workers, drink retsina and listen to tales as old as antiquity.

Marrying Jackie Kennedy, the ultimate Desirable Woman in his eyes, had been a means to an end; one more ritual in the rite of passage to godlike immortality. 'He had Fabergés, he had yachts, planes, he bought divas – why not the most famous widow in the world?' said Taki Theodoracopulos, the shipowning columnist.

There was also Niarchos to consider; there was *always* Niarchos to consider. His brother-in-law had divorced Eugenie and married Charlotte Ford, the glamorous elder daughter of the motor magnate Henry Ford II. Ari had countered with Jackie, whose mannequin chic was the perfect showcase for his wealth. Perhaps he should have noted that Niarchos's marriage to Charlotte (his fourth) had ended virtually before it had begun – and he had returned to Eugenie even before his young wife had given birth to the child she was expecting.

The trouble with Ari was that once he owned something, it suddenly lost its splendour, and he sometimes wasted huge amounts of money on buying things of doubtful provenance. His splurges into the art market, where Niarchos was rightly considered a connoisseur, were a good example of this extravagance. At one point in the early sixties, Onassis had 40 paintings secretly going under the hammer at Sotheby's in London as 'the property of a gentleman'. According to the Onassis Papers, the sanctity of the saleroom guaranteed his anonymity. 'Sotheby's advise that the large number of so-called El Grecos might be sold separately as Dalmatian Primitives,' an aide reported to him in a memorandum. 'They would not fetch very much, but it would be better than nothing.'

So even the fabled El Grecos in *Christina* were just that: fables. When Emery Reves had challenged the authenticity of *Madonna Supported by an Angel*, the 'El Greco' that hung in the saloon, Ari had replied: 'If people wish to believe it to be genuine, why spoil their pleasure?' The same doubts applied to *Boy Lighting a Candle* in the master suite. 'Niarchos had a very discriminating eye – it was the perfectionist thing in him – whereas Onassis didn't give a damn about possessions,' said Alecko Papamarkou. 'Paintings were just trophies to him, external signs of success.'

It was the same with Jackie, the most expensive trophy he had ever purchased. 'He wanted to show the world, as well as Stavros

Niarchos, that he could buy anything or anybody,' said Doris Lilly. In one sense, however, Onassis had been the victim of the Sting of the Century, which would ultimately bring Jackie around $11,000 a day in cash for the duration of her marriage. The first year of married life was estimated to have removed $20 million from the Onassis exchequer, according to Pulitzer-prizewinner author Fred Sparks – a spending rate of $384,615.38 a week. Jackie had squandered $300,000 on clothes compared to $30,000 as the President's wife. But this seemed insignificant compared with the $5 million Ari had lavished on jewellery for her from Van Cleef & Arpels, Cartier and Tiffany.

Not counting personnel connected with the running of his businesses, there were 202 people on the payroll, which cost him another $1,030,992. There were houses to maintain in Athens, Monte Carlo, Montevideo and Paris, as well as Jackie's Fifth Avenue apartment and permanent hotel suites in London and New York. *Christina*'s annual upkeep was $1.4 million, and on top of all that were insurance premiums at an annual rate of $2 million. Under the prenuptial agreement, Jackie had received $360,000 in cash at the rate of $30,000 a month, but she had also recouped thousands more from the sale of many of her new clothes to a New York store that specialized in second-hand designer labels.

However, neither jewels, clothes nor cold hard cash was enough to buy Jackie's love. Even while she was on honeymoon, she had written to her old admirer Ros Gilpatric: 'Dear Ros, I hope you know all you were and are and will ever be to me. With my love, J.'

Ari knew nothing about the letter at this stage, but he knew things weren't going according to plan. His greatest folly had been to involve himself with the Greek Premier, George Papadopoulos, in a 10-year, $400-million investment project called Omega, which involved the construction of an oil refinery, an aluminium plant, shipyards and air terminals. The deal had foundered after Ari had renegotiated the terms so often that the Greeks threw up their hands, withdrew the offer and gave the package to Niarchos. Ari took his troubles to Maria Callas, who listened dutifully while he complained about his business problems and the shortcomings of his new wife.

Although they slept in separate beds, Jackie used sex to placate her husband whenever she felt he might be losing interest in her. She would spray herself with perfume and vamp around in front of him in harem pants or a slinky negligee irrespective of whether guests were present or not. One night John Karavlas, *Christina*'s second captain, found the couple having sex in a fishing boat tied up to the yacht during a visit to Corfu. 'As I peered in, I could make out a man's nude posterior rising and falling, rising and falling,' he said. 'The man heard me and looked over his shoulder. It was Onassis. He was on top, and Jackie was beneath him. They were making love.' But sex without the aphrodisiac of love soon became as meaningless to Ari as everything else in his life. Although she spent a fortune on clothes, Jackie dressed mainly in jeans and T-shirts, which did nothing to enhance her skinny figure. Maria Callas's secretary, Nadia Stancioff, told us she had seen Onassis place his hand in the diva's lap in Paris in 1969 and say: 'Ah, that feels good! It's great to feel Maria's big fat thighs again. I've really missed them. Jackie is nothing but a bag of bones.'

The only member of the entire Onassis family who had found any semblance of a normal relationship was Alexander. He had fallen in love with the former model Fiona Campbell, who was divorced from Baron Heini von Thyssen. The two lived quietly and happily together despite several attempts by Onassis to drive them apart.

Alexander was anxious to return to his loved one when he and two other pilots boarded *Christina*'s ageing Piaggio seaplane at Athens airport on 22 January 1973. The Piaggio had recently been serviced by mechanics from Olympic Airways, but as the plane took off, it banked sharply to the right and crashed into the ground. Alexander's brain was destroyed by the impact, and he died after Ari had reluctantly agreed to switch off his life-support machine. An enquiry showed that the cables that controlled the Piaggio's flight rudders had somehow been reconnected the wrong way round during servicing, and the more the pilot had tried to correct the amphibian's course the more it had veered out of control. Onassis believed that the plane had been sabotaged by his enemies in the CIA, and he vowed to prove it.

After his son's funeral on Skórpios, he took a long cruise in *Christina* across the Atlantic and down to the Caribbean, but he could find no peace anywhere. He bombarded his staff at Olympic Airways with phone calls seeking any fresh developments in the investigation he had ordered into the tragedy. When none was forthcoming, he secretly ordered a new base to be set up for him in Italy.

His son had called Jackie 'the Widow', but Christina began referring to her stepmother as 'the Black Widow' after her brother's tragic demise because, she said, 'everyone around her dies.' Ari picked up on the theme, and whereas he had previously heard only the tinkling of Jackie's little-girl laughter, now he seemed to notice only the wails of her complaints. Jackie hated the food on Skórpios, loathed the heat and found the company tedious. As there was no TV reception, she preferred to watch newly released movies flown in from Hollywood than sit under the starry sky with her husband.

'I never got on as well with Jackie as I did with Maria Callas,' said Nigel Neilson, Ari's imagemaker. 'She had a whining voice and would sulk if she didn't get her own way. Maria and Ari would have a shouting match and then make up. It was a fiery, more Mediterranean, relationship, but much easier to live with than Jackie's precious behaviour. Once on Skórpios, Ari and the rest of his guests were on the verandah of the chalet enjoying a fabulous moon. Jackie said, "I've had a movie sent across from the States. It's set up in the boathouse. Come and watch it." Onassis protested, "But Jackie, it's so beautiful out here." Jackie sulked, and Ari turned to me. "Neegel (he always called me Neegel) will sing us a few songs, and we'll all be happy." I could see I was being set up, so I said, "I don't have a guitar." "I'll have the guitar sent up from the yacht," said Ari. He did – and I strummed away until Jackie was placated. She requested songs like "Danny Boy" to show that, even though she hadn't watched her movie, she was really getting her own way after all. She was like that.'

The contents of Jackie's letter to Ros Gilpatric became known after it was removed from his office and offered for sale in New York. When Onassis had verified that the letter was genuine, he went searching for a lawyer with the qualifications to tackle Jackie and the Kennedys. He found his man in Roy Cohn, Joe McCarthy's former hatchetman and a sworn enemy of the Kennedy family. One of the first things Ari told Cohn was that he had secretly plotted with an Italian member of the paparazzi to catch Jackie sunbathing in the nude on Skórpios. When the pictures appeared in print under the headline THE BILLION DOLLAR BUSH, Jackie had abandoned Skórpios and began to distance herself from everything to do with Onassis except his money. Like a Trojan horse in reverse, she stuffed her empty self with everything that stores, from Harrods to Cartier to Bergdorf Goodman, could offer. 'I accompanied her on one of those shop-till-you-drop sprees,' said Truman Capote. 'She would walk into a store, order two dozen silk blouses in different shades, give them an address and walk out. She seemed in a daze, hypnotized.'

As the bills from these expeditions rolled in, Onassis became more and more disgruntled. 'The only place she'll find sympathy from now on is between shit and syphilis in the dictionary,' he told Johnny Meyer. He made an appointment to see Roy Cohn to discuss a divorce. 'Cohn was a despicable and unsavoury man,' said a respected Wall Street attorney. 'He waved wills in front of the dying and got them to sign – that was the type of man he was.'

Ari met him at the El Morocco and spilled out his feelings over the Black Label scotch. 'Among the things that infuriated him was Jackie's habit of sending both her maid and her secretary Nancy Tuckerman to his office at the end of each month with shopping bills for such vital necessities as the purchase of 200 pairs of shoes at one sitting for a total of $60,000,' said Cohn. 'He threw the bill on the table and clutched his throat. "I've had it up to here with her," he said. "I cannot understand her. All she does is spend, spend, spend – and she's never in the same place as I am. If I'm in Paris, she's in New York. If I go to Skórpios, she goes to London."'

Ari's greatest rancour was centred on Jackie's spending. 'I am an enormously wealthy man,' he told Cohn, 'but I still find it hard to understand why I should receive a bill for 200 pairs of shoes. It isn't as though I don't provide her with a generous expense account – I do. What's more, the shoes are only one item. She orders handbags, dresses, gowns and coats by the dozen – more than enough to stock a Fifth Avenue speciality shop. This woman has no conception of when to stop squandering my money. I'm fed up with her, and I want a divorce.'

Onassis paused to allow the import of his words to sink in. Then he returned to the theme that Cohn believed 'was the real reason behind his wanting a divorce – not her spending, which he could afford, but her coldheartedness'.

'She's never with me,' Onassis said sadly. 'If she goes to Elaine's, Le Cirque or the Persian Room, or Lincoln Center or the Metropolitan Museum of Art, I find myself alone in Paris in Maxim's and Régine's, or in London at the Savoy, the Dorchester or the Ritz. She wants my money but not me.'

'He discussed in detail his desire to spring the divorce action as a big surprise before Jackie could launch an effective counterattack in an area where it would hurt him most – the pocketbook,' said Cohn. 'He didn't want her to get wind of it because he feared she might end up with a larger share of his property than she would through a routine divorce proceeding. He admitted that the year before, while they were cruising off Haiti, he tried to convince her to sign a divorce agreement; he told her they could remarry secretly 24 hours later. A divorce without alimony, he said, would convince the public that she wasn't interested in his money. Of course he had no intention of remarrying. But Jackie didn't fall for it; she was far too intelligent.'

'This time the centre of the action is going to be in Greece, where I can take care of myself,' Ari had said. 'But I'm worried what she can do to me in Paris, in London and in New York, where I have major buildings. That's why I need you. I have already retained lawyers in Paris and London, but I want someone like you to protect me here.'

After a miserable holiday in Acapulco, Jackie and Onassis argued on his private Learjet during the return flight to New York. When he claimed that all she wanted from him was his money, she lost her temper and told him that she expected nothing from him. That, he replied, was precisely what she was going to get. Retiring to a quiet corner of the Learjet, he wrote his last will and testament in his own hand, as required by Greek law:

> I, the undersigned Aristotelis Socrates Onassis, wishing to settle my estate after my death, and being of sound mind, am proceeding with the present handwritten will containing my last wishes and order as follows: *Article 1:* Should my death occur before the creation of a Public Benefit Foundation in Vaduz, Liechtenstein, or elsewhere, under the name 'Alexander S. Onassis Foundation' to provide, *inter alia*, for the establishment, maintenance and operation of the Foundation, and to assist in the fields of medicine, education, literature, religion, the sciences, research, journalism, arts; to provide also for the establishment of international or national awards, with monies similar to the Nobel Foundation in Sweden, I hereby direct and order the executors of my will listed below to establish this Public Benefit Foundation in Vaduz (Liechtenstein) or elsewhere, with the above-mentioned purposes, as well as similar and other such purposes at their absolute discretion, determined by a majority among them, and also to draw up the articles and by-laws of the said foundation, in accordance with the law for the operation of the same.

Continuing in the same neat, even Greek script, he set up two new holding companies called Alpha and Beta. All his assets, including his shares in at least 70 companies, the Avenue Foch penthouse, the villa in Athens, the Learjet and a private helicopter, would be held by Alpha. Beta would contain only shares in Alpha. Christina was to get all the assets in Alpha as well as an allowance of $250,000 a year and, if she remarried, $50,000 a year for her husband. The controlling interest in Beta of 52.5 per cent would go to the Alexander S. Onassis Foundation, which would be run by a board of directors. Christina would get the income from 47.5 per cent of the entire estate.

> Having already taken care of my wife Jacqueline Bouvier, and having extracted a written agreement through notary in the USA, by which she gives up hereditary rights on my inheritance, I limit the share for her and her two children John and Caroline to a lifelong income of $150,000 [per annum].

These bequests would be declared null and void should Jackie contest his will, and he urged his executors to fight any changes 'through all legal means'. His sisters, Artimus, Merope and Callirhoe, would each receive $60,000 a year for life, considerately indexed against inflation.

'My yacht, the *Christina*, my daughter and wife, if they so wish, can keep for their personal use,' Ari wrote. Otherwise it was to be given to the Greek state. Jackie was given a 25 per cent share in *Christina* and Skórpios. As chief executor of the will, he named 'Athina *née* Livanos-Onassis-Blandford-Niarchos, the mother of my son Alexander'.

In drafting his will, Ari's aim had been to make amends for the life he had led. He had reached the summit of his own Olympus only to find that when he looked at the view, there was no future. All he could see was the past with its echoes of faded glory. The legacy he had outlined in his will would give the Onassis name a role in the world for time immemorial. It would create a legal entity to provide unborn generations with the tools to build a better society. The foundation's future vice president, Paul Ioannides, put it succinctly when he said: 'A legal entity doesn't fall in love or get divorced or have mistresses.' It was the most foolproof scheme Onassis had ever devised – and one that told Jackie exactly what he thought of her.

PART TWO

THE LEGACY

ELEVEN

GIRL IN A GILDED CAGE: THE FRIEND'S STORY

IN FEBRUARY 1995, Alecko Papamarkou looked out of the window of his apartment on the 29th floor above Fifth Avenue in New York City. Lunchtime skaters in gaudy attire criss-crossed the rink in Central Park like the winter figures in one of the Four Seasons murals that had adorned the dining room of Aristotle Onassis's yacht, *Christina*. His gaze shifted across the park to the horse-and-buggies plying for hire beside the Plaza Hotel and then on to the hotel itself. 'When Christina turned three in 1953, we were in New York,' he said. 'We went with one of her aunts from the Plaza to F. A. O. Schwarz and bought her a big yellow giraffe. It was a lovely toy for a child, but what she really wanted were her mother and her father.'

The baby who had given her first plaintive cries in New York on 11 December 1950 had grown into a little girl with curly black hair, a swarthy appearance and panda-like circles around her eyes. Right from birth, she looked more like Aristotle than Tina, a point her mother constantly made to friends in front of the child as she was growing up. Christina lived in a limbo of luxury at the house in Sutton Square or in a suite at the Plaza, surrounded by wealth, indulged by paid retainers but starved of parental love. It was to her enduring sadness that she had been born at all. 'Why did God give me so much pain?' she once asked a friend. 'It would be better if I had never existed.'

Sensing that she was unlovable, Christina picked up her survival skills from her unruly older brother, Alexander, who showed every sign of being just as rebellious as his father had been at the same age in faraway Smyrna. Alexander had developed a wild streak, which none of the servants dared to contain. He taught his little sister how to throw food at the walls, break toys and throw screaming fits until they got their own way. When one harassed nanny threatened to report them to their absent father, the children were secretly delighted. Even punishment at his hands was preferable to being ignored. They also knew that Onassis invariably arrived home from his travels crackling with electric merriment and laden with gaudily wrapped presents.

Although she always ran to greet him, Christina was otherwise a shy, withdrawn child who recoiled from normal human contact. 'Sometimes you would suddenly notice her sitting there on the sidelines, watching, not saying a word,' said a visitor to the Onassis household. 'But very little escaped her. You'd see a glance between her and Alexander. People said they didn't get on, but I think they understood each other and what was going on perfectly.'

Christina's life changed for the better after Ari moved the family to Monaco in 1953 and the following year took delivery of the yacht he had named after her. He realized that his young family were an asset among the rich in the golden grottoes of the Côte d'Azur. They gave him an identity and a role beyond that of the businessman-buccaneer for which he was famous, even if he failed miserably to carry out his fatherly duties. By the time of her fifth birthday, Christina had learned to put on masks like an accomplished little actress. Among visitors, she played the adored daughter, accepting her parents' hugs and kisses as though they were a normal part of her life. At other times, she knew it was wiser to be invisible and just watch from the periphery.

'Christina would always be sent for to be introduced to guests,' said Nigel Neilson, who often visited the family in *Christina*. 'She was an absolutely sweet child with no airs or graces. She was never a tomboy; she would rather play with dolls than get involved in dangerous pursuits. Alexander was the tearaway, crashing speed-boats and getting into scrapes.

'Christina's favourite toy was a wooden horse on wheels. It towed a pianola which played nursery rhymes. She loved music. At parties, she always wanted me to play a Greek folk song called "Theo Prasina Matia", which is about a girl with green eyes.'

Neilson was the recipient of the 'adored daughter' treatment during a visit to *Christina* in August 1956. He was in the saloon with Ari when Christina ran in and jumped into her father's lap.

'Where have you been today, *chryso mou* [my golden one]?' Onassis asked.

'To get my hair cut,' replied Christina, shaking her head to show her trimmed curls.

'What was the hairdresser's name?'

The little girl shook her head shyly. She had no idea.

'Then tell me what he was like,' Onassis persisted.

Christina lowered her head, and tears welled up in her eyes.

'You ought to know,' chided her father. 'Next time you go, ask him about his family and where he lives. You can learn something from everyone, no matter who they are.'

In front of his guest, Ari was imparting some fatherly advice but at the same time highlighting her shortcomings in front of one of his employees. 'He was devoted to his two children,' Neilson maintained, 'Alexander possibly more so because he was the heir, but Christina was his little princess.'

However, sessions such as the one Neilson had witnessed had a harmful effect on Christina's confidence, and she retreated further into herself. For a time, she stopped talking altogether. Tina took her to a child psychiatrist in Zurich, who diagnosed her condition as 'mercurial mutism', an attention-seeking silence often associated with insecure and over-protected children. When she had gained the parental attention she craved, Christina started speaking again as though nothing had happened. She had discovered that sickness – preferably one that didn't cause physical pain – gave her power over her parents. She also learned that they showered her with presents every time she made them feel guilty.

By the time she was seven, she was showing off the latest birthday additions to her jewellery collection. 'I sometimes wonder if I can avoid spoiling the children,' Tina sighed. 'Christina is not so difficult, I suppose, because girls are more practical than boys.' In other words, little girls could be bought off with yet another diamond tiara to parade in front of the latest crop of guests.

Christina was back in New York for her ninth birthday in December 1959, but there was no sign of her nomadic father. Onassis was flitting about Europe with Maria Callas but found time to tell a reporter that he had spoken to his daughter on the phone. 'She said she missed me,' he said, 'and I told her I was going to see her soon. I don't know where yet. I asked Christina what she wanted for her birthday. She wasn't sure, so I told her to go out in New York and pick anything she wants.' She went back to F. A. O. Schwarz and bought a doll to add to the nursery full of yellow giraffes, wooden horses and pianolas, which were the most steadfast things in her life. Then she went to bed and cried herself to sleep.

Her parents' marriage ended in the divorce courts the following year, and as a child the only time Christina saw her father after that was either in Monaco or at the Avenue Foch penthouse when she and her brother went to visit him under a joint custody arrangement. They became friendly with the Michard-Pellissier family, who lived on the first floor of the apartment building. Jean and Gisèle Michard-Pellissier had three children, Florence, Hubert and Caroline, and they knew Ari and Tina well. In fact, Jean Michard-Pellissier, a lawyer, represented Ari's interests in France. 'He used to go with my father to a night club called the Elephant Blanc and, of course, to Maxim's where he had the same table in the big room at the end on the left,' Florence told us. 'I was the oldest child, and I met Christina when she was very young. Alexander was exactly the same age as my brother, and my sister was exactly the same age as Christina. When they were very young, Hubert and Caroline used to go sailing in *Christina*, but as Christina grew older she became closer to me.'

Christina was 12 when she moved to England after Tina married John 'Sunny' Spencer-Churchill, Marquis of Blandford and heir to the Duke of Marlborough. The family lived at Lee Place, a country house in Oxfordshire near the Marlborough seat of Blenheim Palace. She found that her new half-brother, James, and her half-sister, Henrietta, warmly welcomed the presence of an older sibling into the household. She also mixed with other girls of her own age at a private girls' school, Headington.

When she was 16, she had her nose remodelled by plastic surgery, and the dark circles were removed from under her eyes. Onassis immediately cast around for a suitable husband and decided that a match with Peter Goulandris would consolidate the fortunes of two famous shipping families. But although Christina and Peter liked each other and dated for a while, Christina had no intention of settling down at the same age as her mother had taken up with her father. 'How could I fall in love when I have a father like mine?' she asked. 'As soon as I meet a boy, I immediately compare him with my father, and my father comes out best. Whenever we go to a night club together he makes everything come alive.' Her life had become a succession of night clubs, restaurants, theatres and private parties, at which she was always on show as the daughter of Aristotle Onassis. The real Christina, the little girl in need of love, was rarely seen and never heard.

This illusion of happiness on the night-club circuit was short-lived. Soon after midnight on 4 May 1970, Christina's beloved Aunt Eugenie was found unconscious on Spetsopoúla after she had taken an overdose of alcohol mixed with barbiturates. She had died before medical help could be summoned to the Niarchos island. When Christina learned that her uncle had slapped his wife to try to revive her, she was inconsolable. The Greek authorities accepted that Niarchos had struck the comatose Eugenie only to save her life, and he was cleared of any criminal intent. Christina's response was to look for a stable relationship that would give her life some permanence away from her family.

'Christina had a little flat in Reeves Mews near Claridge's,' said Alecko Papamarkou, who was then a handsome, 40-year-old bachelor. 'She had a twentieth birthday party, and I went. She was so excited. She kept saying, "Daddy's coming, daddy's coming." Onassis came for a little while, then left. It was very sad. She said to me, "Alecko, I want you to marry me." "But I'm too old," I said. "No, you're not – you're the nicest person I know," she said, and she proposed again. She was looking for a father figure, and her first husband, Joe Bolker, was just such a man. But the main problem was that Christina was really crying for affection all her life. It was very sad.'

However, Christina took several detours with young lovers in her search for an older man. Shortly after her 20th birthday party, she was introduced to Luis Basualdo at the Corviglia Club in St Moritz. Basualdo was the archetypal Latin lover, a darkly handsome Argentinian polo player who turned out for Lord Cowdray's team in England. Basualdo had styled himself on the legendary playboy Porfirio Rubirosa after meeting his idol at the Jockey Club in Buenos Aires. As the former husband of the heiresses Doris Duke and

Barbara Hutton (among others), Rubirosa had lived a charmed life in the boudoirs of rich women. His nickname was 'the big-dame hunter', and he was described in the 1959 edition of the *International Celebrity Register* as 'an intermittent husband and frequent co-respondent'. He was a lover of Eva Perón (with whom Onassis had had a one-night dalliance) when he served in Buenos Aires as Dominican ambassador to Argentina.

He and his friend, the automotive millionaire Gunther Sachs, later collaborated on a playboy's guide entitled *How to Seduce Women*. Rubi, as he was known, had acquired large sums of money, a house in Paris, sports cars, jewellery and a string of polo ponies from his conquests. 'Rubirosa taught me things about life and love,' said Basualdo. 'He said chubby, homely heiresses were a better bet than beautiful, slim girls with nothing. They would always look after a man, and I could still bed pretty girls in the afternoon.'

Christina qualified as a 'chubby heiress', while the 'pretty girls' in Basualdo's life included Lord Cowdray's daughter Lucy and an American girl, Justine Cushing. Basualdo had a fling with Christina that started that Christmas, spanned the New Year and ended only in spring after Christina had returned to London. 'She was sexually very demanding,' he said, 'but for a while at least she was happy.'

Aware that her weight caused a problem in attracting eligible men, Christina booked into a German clinic and lost 25lb. She was fit and slim when she met Joe Bolker, a 48-year-old Jewish building and real estate millionaire based in Los Angeles, in May 1971 at the indoor swimming pool her father had built at the Hôtel de Paris in Monte Carlo. After some initial skirmishing over the obvious problems – an age difference of 28 years, her status as an Onassis heiress, her possessive father – they started an affair at her Mayfair flat. Twice-divorced and the father of four daughters, Bolker was flattered by the attentions of this hot-blooded young woman, but he returned home prepared to dismiss it as nothing more serious than a holiday romance. Christina, however, had other ideas. Bolker was not only an older man but he also bore a noticeable resemblance to Onassis in that he was small, dark and silver haired. In a series of transatlantic phone calls, the love-lorn heiress made it clear to this 'dinky American millionaire', as she called him, that she wanted to be free of her father's influence and that she saw him as the means of escape.

Suddenly, Bolker realized that Christina was talking about wedlock. Although he had no personal knowledge of Onassis, he knew enough about his methods from what Christina had told him to realize that he had entered dangerous territory. He told her that while he found her attractive and enjoyed her company immensely, he wasn't in love with her, and marriage was out of the question.

'I remember seeing Christina in the old Jimmy's near La Coupole in Paris,' said the Danish model Kirsten Gille. 'She must have been 20. She wanted to marry this man – the American Bolker – and she was crying because he didn't want to marry her.' In July 1971, Christina flew to California and turned up uninvited on the doorstep of Bolker's condominium apartment at Century Towers West, LA. Alarmed that her parents knew nothing about her movements, Bolker insisted that she call her mother.

The American was utterly bewildered when Tina suggested to him over the phone that he should do the honourable thing and marry her daughter. Tina had her own reasons for wishing to divert her former husband's attention away from her own affairs. She had recently filed for divorce from Blandford and had secretly agreed to marry Stavros Niarchos. She urged Bolker to make 'an honest woman' of her daughter, knowing that Onassis would move heaven and earth to prevent such a union taking place. In the meantime, she would be free to carry out her own switch of partners with a minimum of interference.

Bolker might have been unaware of the Byzantine world into which he had stumbled, but he was no fool. He refused to marry Christina. 'What's the matter?' she asked. 'Aren't I good enough for you?' No one had ever denied Christina anything she had ever wanted, and she resorted to her old attention-seeking behaviour. She went into the master bedroom of the apartment and stuffed a handful of pills into her mouth. When Bolker found her, she was unconscious. Fortunately, one of his neighbours was a doctor, and Christina received immediate treatment to save her life.

Bolker's resolve collapsed under this pressure, and he married Christina in Las Vegas on 29 July 1971. Onassis was celebrating Jackie's 42nd birthday on Skórpios when he heard the news. 'He was furious,' said an aide, 'and he did not hide his anger.' The Bolkers were subjected to extraordinary pressure. Christina was cut off from a $100-million trust fund she was due to inherit on her 21st birthday, and their phone lines were tapped by Johnny Meyer. The American spy invited Christina and her husband to lunch at the Polo Lounge of the Beverly Hills Hotel and, having listened to their pleas to be left in peace, he promised to file a sympathetic report to Onassis. In fact, he did the opposite. He orchestrated a telephone campaign against Bolker, in which anonymous callers warned Christina that he was a gangster and a womanizer. When that failed to unnerve her, vicious rumours were spread among their friends. Finally, Bolker was threatened with physical harm unless he ended the marriage. However, it was Christina who made the break, although her decision had nothing to do with her husband's well-being.

When Christina found out that her mother had secretly married Niarchos in Paris on 22 October, she decided that her rightful place was with her father. The family's blood ties had proved stronger than the attractions around Rodeo Drive. After her 21st birthday at the Bistro in Beverly Hills, she declared that the marriage was over. 'I'm too Greek,' she told Bolker, 'and you're too Beverly Hills.' Meyer and two armed bodyguards arrived in LA with instructions from Onassis to escort Christina safely back to London, and the marriage was dissolved the following year. Bolker had some harsh observations to make about his erstwhile father-in-law. 'He used his children, his family, he used everybody,' he said. 'He would publicly say, "I love my daughter, I love my son," but there was no love; he had no feelings, no conscience. He was a user of everybody.' The divorce was barely a year old when Christina embarked upon a love affair with a man who was the antithesis of Joe Bolker. His name was Thierry Roussel.

TWELVE

YOUNG
ELVIS OF THE
CHAMPS-
ÉLYSÉES

AS A TRAINEE boulevardier, the young Thierry Patrick Roussel kept a cuddly toy gorilla and a set of weights in his bedroom. The gorilla had the words RODNEY NEEDS LOVE inscribed on its T-shirt; the weights were to build up his muscles. After a strenuous workout, he would soak in the tub of an adjoining bathroom, throw back his head and shout, 'YES! I'M THIERRY ROUSSEL!' Above anything else in life, he was determined about two things: he would find a love that knew no bounds, and the world would know his name.

Roussel was just over 6ft tall with an athletic build and long, dark blond hair that swept back to reveal a handsome, chubby face. In the manner of Elvis Presley and other great rockers, he had bushy sideburns, and he liked to dress in flashy clothes, which were liable to get him noticed. His eyes were a piercing shade of blue, and only a thoughtful expression and a religious medal, which he wore on a gold chain around his neck, belied an otherwise tough, streetwise exterior. Women threw themselves at the pharmaceutical heir. 'He was one of *les branchés* [literally, the plugged-in], and he had a different girl every night,' said a close friend of the family. 'They were sexy, aggressive, well dressed and high class.'

Thierry's father, Henri Roussel, had been a 19-year-old pharmacist in the family business when he had fallen in love with the beautiful 20-year-old Francine Grinda, older sister of the tennis-player Jean-Noel Grinda, who would later represent France in the Davis Cup. The following year, they were married after Francine became pregnant with her first child, a daughter whom they named Christine. Thierry, the second child, was born on 16 February 1953, in the fashionable Neuilly district of Paris, where the family lived in a big house with an indoor swimming pool. 'He was born, as we say, with a silver spoon in his mouth,' the friend told us. 'His grandfather had founded the Laboratory Roussel in 1928, and it became France's largest pharmaceutical company.' A couple of years later, a second daughter, Patricia, became the last addition to Henri and Francine's family.

Although they wanted for nothing material, and there were servants to take care of the house and the children, the Roussels did not enjoy a happy home life. Francine, just 21 when she married, had grown into a difficult woman and an indifferent mother. 'Henri told me he suffered a lot at the hands of his wife,' said the friend. 'She was a very domineering woman, and she found ways to be mean to him and the children.' Thierry was placed in the care of a nanny; her name was Ellen, known as Nen. She was remarkably small, and she had started work as a 13 year old in the Grinda household. Nen had brought up Francine's mother, then Francine and, finally, Thierry – three generations of the same family. But the child she loved the most was Thierry, who was a very sensitive boy in need of a lot of attention.

'Henri and Francine often went out in a group, a foursome, with a rich man called Bauche and his wife, Marceline, and Henri eventually started an affair with her,' said the friend. 'He left Francine when Thierry was around 10 years old, and he later saw a big fight between his parents, though not over custody of the children. Thierry was a very difficult child, so his father sent him to his own mother, Madame Roussel, in Paris. He got on very well there and lived with her for two years until something unfortunate happened. She was in a chauffeur-driven Mercedes with her notary when the car was involved in a crash with a lorry. They were all killed. Only the notary knew the secret of where Madame Roussel had kept her money in Switzerland, and he was killed with her. So the family were going crazy trying to find out where all the money was.

Obviously, the Swiss never said anything. There was a big fight in the family about this, and Thierry remembers it very clearly. Within two days, he was packed off to boarding school.'

The school Henri had chosen for his son was Ecole des Roches, one of France's leading boys' schools, which was noted for its strenuous, character-building curriculum. There, Thierry mixed with the sons of the nobility, European royalty and great industrial families like the Citroëns and the Renaults. He was a popular boy, although he showed off to overcome his feelings of inadequacy. When he turned up among his classmates in an outlandish rabbit-fur coat looking like Rocky Racoon, he was making a statement: Look at me – I'm Thierry Roussel. Academically, he was bright, but he found outdoor pursuits far more appealing than book learning. The Roussels were a very physical family in that regard. Henri, one of France's leading marksmen, taught his son how to handle a shotgun on the family's sporting estate, Bonneville, near Beaugency in the Sologne, 120 miles south of Paris, and he also took him big-game hunting on another estate that the Roussels owned in Kenya. At Marbella, where the family had a 5000-acre ranch, he learned horse riding, water-skiing and power-boat racing.

However, the apparent intimacy between father and son turned into an intense form of rivalry after Thierry reached the age of puberty. 'Thierry told me his father had been very young when he was born, and there was always competition between them,' said his close friend. 'It was a lot more noticeable from Thierry's side then, but Henri had made Thierry feel this way because he was only 19 when he and Francine started going together. He didn't get married until he was 20, but the first child was already on the way. He felt he had sacrificed a lot for his family.

'Henri had been trained as a pharmacist in the family business but hated the work. He was a great sportsman and wanted to spend his time hunting and chasing adventure. When he left Francine, he sold his part of Roussel to his brother, Jean-Claude Roussel, who was also a very active man. He was a very good helicopter pilot who used to fly very close to the ground chasing rabbits and killing them with the runners of the helicopter. But one day he went up and hit some overhead power cables and was killed in the crash. Twelve years later his son, Alain Roussel, died in a helicopter crash in Switzerland. He was very close to Thierry and a very good friend of mine.

'Henri is a very generous person, especially with his family.

Francine had this beautiful apartment in Paris, and he made sure she wanted for nothing. In that way, he respected her absolutely. He had been with Marceline ever since he left Francine, but only married her after his wife died. Thierry's older sister, Christine, married the Duc de Chevreuse, who is half French and half Argentinian. They have a magnificent château near Paris. The younger sister, Patricia, is a very sweet girl who works for Thierry. She finds apartments and studios in Paris for him to buy for renovation in his property-development business.'

Thierry's first connection with Christina Onassis had come at the 1964 wedding of his uncle, the dashing Jean-Noel Grinda, to her Parisian neighbour Florence Michard-Pellissier. Thierry and Christina had both attended the wedding, but neither paid any noticeable attention to the other. 'I'm sure they were both there, but I don't remember anything else about them on that day,' said Florence. 'I was only 21, and my parents had invited a lot of people to the wedding.'

While he was still a student, Thierry formed a strong attachment to Odile Rubirosa, former wife of the Dominican playboy. 'Rubirosa had fallen in love with Odile like Lolita when she was only 19, and he was in his fifties,' said a friend. 'She was a very pretty young French girl with blonde ringlets and a slim figure. She was born Odile Berard, but she called herself Odile Rodin when she started work as an actress.' A satirist of the period had quipped after Rubirosa's 73-day marriage to Barbara Hutton was dissolved that his next bride would be Fort Knox, but instead he fell for Odile after they met at the Bagatelle polo field in 1956. The following year, Odile had become the fifth – and last – of his wives. At Odile's insistence, he gave up motor racing but continued to play polo. Ironically, his grey Ferrari clipped a parked car in the Bois de Boulogne in the early hours of 5 July 1965, while he was driving home after celebrating a polo victory. The Ferrari crashed into a chestnut tree, and he died from his injuries.

'After his death, Odile lived with Alexander Onassis in Monte Carlo for a while – she was only 27, and she was his first serious affair,' said the friend. 'She was always in our group; she was a lot of fun and terribly jet set. Thierry met her when he was 15 or 16 years old, and he used to take his little motorbike and ride to her house at Marnes la Coquette near Paris.' Thierry's aunt, Florence Grinda, said: 'He was very young when he was seeing Odile, only about 16.

He was very good looking then, but he became a bit fat.'

Odile already had an admirer, a handsome Italian, who was peeved to discover that he had a rival for her affections. For his part, Thierry was too preoccupied with a headful of dreams about sports cars and beautiful women to pay much attention to the other man's jealousy, a mistake that would later cost him dearly.

After leaving school, Thierry worked in the advertising department of Roussel Uclaf before striking out on his own. Henri had sold the big house at Neuilly and decanted into a smaller one in the same area of Paris and, after living with his father for a time, Thierry moved into an apartment in the fashionable sixteenth arrondissement.

One night in Le Castel, a popular Left Bank nightspot, his uncle Jean-Noel introduced him to two Swedish models who had recently arrived in Paris. Thierry liked the look of one of them, a winsome blonde with a cute face and showgirl legs, and he started to date her. Her name was Marianne Landhage, but she had started to use the professional name of Gaby in her work. 'When they met, he was 18, and she was 20,' said the friend. 'He had led quite a lively life until then, and Gaby was exactly the opposite of everything he had known, but strangely enough he fell in love with her. He rented an apartment for her and spent a lot of time with her. Gaby was quite pretty then – she looked like a glamour girl.'

When Gaby Landhage first became a Parisian model in 1971, a reporter had asked her the routine question: 'Would you like to marry a rich man?' Candidly, she had replied: 'No, I will save my own money.' But she soon discovered that earning a living as a model meant taking some of her clothes off as well as putting them on. In September 1972, just a year after she had started her professional career in front of the camera, two photographs of her – one naked, and the other semi-clad – appeared in her home-town newspaper, the *Gothenburg Post*. 'No one thought it was daring,' said a Scandinavian friend, 'because nudity or semi-nudity isn't considered obscene in Sweden.'

Gaby had been born Marianne Landhage into a working-class family in Gothenburg, Sweden's second biggest city, in November 1951. Her mother was a seamstress in a textile factory, and her late father had been a printer. She was raised in a terraced house in the suburb of Västra Frölunda. 'You can hear Gaby's background when she speaks Swedish,' said the friend. 'She has quite a heavy accent. In England, you have cockneys, and it's the same thing here. She comes from a very simple family; that can happen – it's not a bad thing at all.'

Marianne was well liked at school, gaining good marks in English, and her first ambition was to become a translator. She had little interest in modelling. Staff at her first school remembered how she sewed a dress in class but, when the teacher asked her to model it, she refused. At high school, she continued to study languages.

According to a classmate, Marianne's modelling career began after she was approached by an agent who had spotted her in a school photograph. After leaving high school, she began modelling properly, including work for local women's clothing stores. 'I remember her as a very likeable person,' said Hans Tranberg, one of her hairdressers at the time. 'She was a relaxed and gentle woman without any prima-donna behaviour.' At the age of 18, Gaby was discovered in Gothenburg by the Danish photographer Gunnar Larsen, who was based in Paris. Describing her as 'beautiful, nice and talented,' he said he had asked her to come to the French capital to work for him. It was in Paris that she changed her name to Gaby after a new agent told her the name Marianne was too common in France.

Larsen, a tall man with long blond hair, blue jeans and a flowing scarf, had struggled with an artist's tenacity to make his mark in the cut-throat business of fashion photography. Always a member of avant-garde circles, he liked to hang out at Café de Flore in St-Germain-des-Prés with the existentialist writer Jean-Paul Sartre. When the fashion world failed to appreciate his skills, he staged his own clothes show with a panache that owed more to show business than the couturier salons. In one of his collections, models marched along the catwalk wearing jackets pockmarked with 'genuine bullet holes from the Vietnam War'. In another, two girls dressed as cats made love to each other on the catwalk.

However, it wasn't all a gimmick; Larsen got results and acquired a nickname: 'the man who gave girls with a dream a chance'. He had a reputation for decency, which meant that newcomers to the Paris scene such as Gaby Landhage could safely lodge at his modest set of chambers off Rue St-Denis without compromising their virtue. In the same unassuming manner in which he had helped hundreds of other models to get started in their careers, he warned Gaby that modelling was a lot of hard work, but he also demonstrated how exciting it could be. 'She was extremely lucky to meet Gunnar Larsen,' said her friend. 'He did a lot for all the Scandinavian girls at the time.' Gaby was staying at Larsen's flat when she met Thierry Roussel at Le Castel. She had just signed a contract with the new Elite agency, which guaranteed her an income, and felt confident enough to make a long-term commitment to one man.

'Thierry wanted to marry Gaby then,' said Larsen, 'but his family were against it because she wasn't considered good enough.' The couple had frequent arguments about this and went for weeks without speaking. It was during one of these separations in 1973 that Thierry was introduced to Christina Onassis, who had been grieving over the death of Alexander since January.

She and her brother had shared the same careless upbringing and, even though Alexander had been known to describe his sister as 'a spoiled brat', the bond between them had had a psychic quality, which enabled them to know exactly how the other felt. Thierry was lover and replacement brother rolled into one, and her attraction for him was immediate and obvious. At 22, Christina had considerable sexual experience to draw upon, but she found him to be innovative and passionate. As well as consolation, there was excitement in the arms of this tall, blond Adonis with the chubby face. Her eyes sparkled, and she started to enjoy herself for the first time in a long while.

'Christina's dream was to marry a blond Frenchman and to have blond children,' said Florence Grinda, Thierry's aunt. 'He had to come from a good family because she wanted to be loved for herself and not for her money. She wanted to marry Thierry. She said to me, "Come to see my father and tell him Thierry is fantastic." So we were invited by Ari Onassis to go to Skórpios for that reason. There was me, Hubert and Caroline, Thierry, and Marie de Luynes, who was Christine Roussel's sister-in-law.'

Although Christina was ecstatic at the prospect of a second betrothal, she was determined not to make the same mistake as she had with Joe Bolker. Outsiders were not welcome in the Onassis family. Indeed, she and Alexander had contrived to drive away Maria Callas and Jackie Kennedy because, in their eyes, no woman, no matter how famous or glamorous, could replace their mother in their father's life. Their reactions to 'the Singer' and 'the Widow' had contained all the pent-up emotions of a silent scream. Tina's marriage to Stavros Niarchos after the death of Aunt Eugenie had violently underscored the children's suspicions that dark and dangerous forces were at work in their family.

But if Christina had been grieving for her brother, the loss had hit Ari immeasurably harder than anything else in his life. On Skórpios, he visited Alexander's tomb every day and wept openly. At one point, he had wanted to have the body deep-frozen and stored in a cryonic-care unit until medical science could discover the requisite neuro-surgery to rebuild his shattered brain. Ari had given up this scheme only after his friend Professor Ioannis Georgakis had convinced him that locking his son into an Arctic time warp would 'impede the journey of his soul'.

Ari's supertankers were earning a profit of $15 million a month during these boom times, but no amount of money could give him back the one thing he wanted: his son. As a peace offering, he even invited Tina and Stavros Niarchos to visit Alexander's grave with him. Jackie had sulked during the visit and slipped off to the Pink House, which Onassis had built for her on the island. She had left the island by the time the young 'wedding party' had arrived from Paris. 'Ari had a little room next to the living room in the Pink House, and he was living very simply,' said Florence. 'It wasn't a big house because he actually preferred to spend his time on the yacht.'

Ari had resorted to bouts with a bottle of Johnnie Walker Black Label and sang mournful Greek songs to his guests. He often walked alone on the pebbled shore throughout the night, ending up with a dawn vigil at his son's tomb. It was against this melancholic background that Thierry Roussel, in his twenty-first year, made his entrance as a potential son-in-law.

At first, Ari responded to the young man's presence with the wariness he reserved for fortune hunters, but as soon as he saw Thierry's enthusiasm for sailing, he started to take an interest in him. When the sailboat that Thierry had been using went missing one morning, Ari ordered a similar craft to be lowered from the deck of *Christina*. 'It began to take on water because it hadn't been serviced in a long time,' said Roussel. Nothing could have been contrived to drive Onassis into a greater fury. The air crash that had killed Alexander had happened immediately after his seaplane had been serviced by mechanics from Olympic Airways – badly serviced, according to an official report he had received that summer – and even though Ari preferred to believe his own sabotage theory, here was an inexcusable example of negligence on the part of his crew. 'Onassis snapped off a series of orders to his men, and in a few hours they had plugged all the leaks,' said Roussel. To ensure that the boat was seaworthy, Ari had insisted on accompanying Thierry on its first voyage, and they had sailed around Skórpios together.

Ari was far from displeased that the young Frenchman had slipped into a romance with his daughter. The Roussel name was highly respected in France and, although he would have preferred a Greek son-in-law, Ari saw the possibilities of a wider merger. If Christina would not carry out his wish that she marry Peter Goulandris, this energetic and presentable heir provided a thoroughly acceptable alternative. He was astonished when the Michard-Pellissiers sounded a warning note. Florence, who had divorced Thierry's uncle Jean-Noel over his philandering, knew that her nephew came from the same rakish stock. 'We didn't say very nice things to Ari about Thierry,' she told us. 'I liked him, but I knew he wasn't going to be right for Christina. He was too much of a playboy. I knew he had been going out with Gaby since he was very young, finishing with her, then going back to her. I said to Christina, "Forget about it. He will never leave Gaby."'

If Christina had paused for a moment, any doubts she might have felt about this piece of intelligence were swept aside when Thierry invited her to visit him at his father's estate in Marbella in September. Back in Paris, she consulted Odile Rubirosa, whom she knew through her father and brother. 'She wanted to know what he was like with other women,' said a friend. As for the Roussel family, Christina knew that penniless Swedish models rated nowhere in terms of eligibility among the *haute bourgeoisie*.

But she was sadly disappointed when she arrived in Marbella to claim her prize. Her eager young suitor of a few weeks earlier had lapsed into a solemn mood, which she had not seen before. Thierry told her that he had changed his mind because he was too young to make a lifelong commitment. When Christina asked him about the other woman, he admitted he was in love with Gaby and that he was not prepared to give her up. He had enjoyed their romance, but he would have to pass on the wider issue of marriage. Florence had been right.

Christina returned crestfallen to Paris, where Onassis, realizing for the first time that although he had lost a son he still had a daughter, decided it was time for her to learn more about the shipping business. He sent her to New York to learn at the knee of Costa Gratsos, who was president of Victory Carriers, the tanker arm of the Onassis empire that had been set up in trust for Christina and Alexander as a tax-avoidance device back in the fifties. He also gave her Eleni Syros, the maid who had worked for the Onassis family in Athens, Skórpios and Paris with her husband Jorge since 1962.

Onassis kept in touch with Christina's progress and, when he felt the time was opportune, he started to introduce her to important people in the oil world. She joined him in London for a visit to the headquarters of British Petroleum.

'I remember Onassis brought his daughter to lunch to introduce her to the experts,' Sir Eric Drake, who was BP chairman between 1969 and 1975, told us. 'Christina kept her mouth firmly shut; she didn't utter a single word. It happened to be my son John's birthday that evening, and Christina had known him since they were babies in the South of France. Onassis and Christina came around to our flat to celebrate the birthday, and she was chattering away like a magpie. I asked her, "Why have you changed since this morning? You didn't say anything at lunch." She said, "Father said I must listen to every word and keep quiet." Onassis did a lot of business with us, and I suppose he was a rogue, but as far as I was concerned he was a very decent chap. I found him very straight in my dealings with him.'

Back on the boulevards, Roussel probably wondered about the possibilities that the Onassis millions would have opened up for a budding venture capitalist like himself. 'He became involved in home furnishings, an advertising agency and a publishing house, but it was really hard going,' said a former friend. 'He was also connected with a modelling agency called First, which was run by his friend Paul Hagnoer. Thierry told me he went to a party one night expecting a roomful of beautiful girls only to find that all the models were young men. It wasn't what he had expected at all.' It was later reported that he sold out his interest in the agency at a loss of between $3 million and $4 million.' However, Paul Hagnoer told us: 'I was a director and general manager of First, and it never lost money. Thierry wasn't my partner officially; he was my partner through some other company. It's totally ridiculous to say he lost $3 million – an agency cannot make such a loss.'

Altogether, Roussel was with Gaby for seven years, although they didn't live together for much of that time. 'She would be off working somewhere, and he would be off with other girls,' said his former friend. 'He wasn't faithful to her – Thierry didn't know what it was to be faithful. Gaby would go off maybe for three months and come back – they were always having big fights – and she was always saying, "I want to get married." Always "I want to have children." Like a lot of Swedish girls, the main thing was to get married, have children, and afterwards the husband could do whatever he wanted. It was typical. But I can't say she was not in love with him; she probably was. Then she gave him this ultimatum. She said to him, "I'm going off to America to work for three months. We'll meet at Christmas, and you can tell me whether you've decided to get married or not."

'So she went to New York and tried to give the impression that she was all alone. However, I know she wasn't because an acquaintance of mine had an agency there, and he said she had a boyfriend, which was normal, but she always played the madonna.'

While Gaby was in New York, Roussel started to court Danish model Kirsten Gille, whom he had met in St Tropez during the first year of his liaison with Gaby. The first thing Kirsten had noticed about him was that his swimming trunks were inappropriately brief – 'They weren't swimming trunks at all but very vulgar bikinis,' she said. Kirsten was the well-bred daughter of the United Nations diplomat Halvor Gille and his Swedish wife Inger, but she had few feelings of sisterhood for Gaby. In Kirsten's eyes, Gaby had broken one of the few taboos of the Parisian carousel by making a play for her previous boyfriend while they were very much à deux.

'I had been living with a very good-looking Italian man for several years, and Gaby saw him on a plane,' she said. 'They started talking, and he found out who she was. He invited her out, and she accepted. They flirted. The reason from his side was that he had been angry with Thierry over his previous girlfriend, Odile Rubirosa. They had been together for two years when she had a fling with Thierry, who was very young at the time. So my Italian took Gaby out, and she played the game, but being a good Italian, when it came to going further, he just said, "No, thank you." He told me she had replied,

"Well, you know, it could have been something very serious for me."

'I didn't appreciate what she had done. I was *living* with this man, and she knew me. She was suffering because Thierry was being unfaithful to her, yet she went out with my boyfriend knowing I was with him. After that, she came up to us every time she saw us in a restaurant to say hello. I used to feel so annoyed because she was so boring, and she would always speak to me in Swedish, which I can speak because my mother is Swedish.'

Gaby had given up on the Italian Lothario, but she did not give up on Thierry Roussel, even though she had moved back to Sweden and was living in a flat in Malmö. 'She would call every six months to speak to him, and she would send a picture of herself in a cheap plastic frame,' said Kirsten Gille. 'She sent it not so much to make me jealous, but because it would touch him since she had always said that she wanted to marry him and have his children. She would call him when her birthday was approaching, and beg him to go and see her. Thierry wouldn't say anything to me, but I always sensed it; it was a sort of game for me to find out. So he would go to Sweden to see her for four days and come back a day and a half afterwards because they always had a big fight.'

Thierry and Kirsten had set up home in his rented apartment at 32 Avenue Pierre 1er de Serbie, near the George V hotel. There were three bedrooms, two living rooms, one of which Thierry used as a *bibliothèque*, and a dining room. The decor was lacquered eggshell white with black, modern furniture. Kirsten, a *Vogue* model who also had a successful career in Italian films, had a good eye for fashion, and her lover's appalling taste in clothes was not limited to tango-style swimsuits.

'When Thierry and I started our affair, he was 25, and he had no idea about clothes,' she said. 'He would dress like Elvis Presley in white leather, which he thought was very cool. I took him out and bought him tasteful outfits, and every morning I arranged all his clothes on the bed and dressed him. He's got very curly hair, and he always put gel or something on it to keep it in place. At that time he was earning a bit of money, and he would get up very early in the morning to go to work. He walked the short distance to his office at 55 Rue Pierre-Charron, near the Champs-Élysées. I would make phone calls to organize things for him. I love riding, and I had one horse at that time which I would ride at Chantilly. The rest of the time I was organizing things like a business lunch at the apartment or dinner for up to 50 people in Sologne, where he had a staff of Moroccans. He liked to go there at the weekend for the hunting and shooting.

'In Paris, we didn't go out that much because he was getting up so early, but if we went out it was to Régine's. Thierry had an advertising agency, and it worked well. He sold 50 per cent of it for 10 million French francs, so he was very pleased. I'd say it's the only time in his whole life where he's been in a business in which he's earned a bit of money. Thierry bought me a car when he did the deal. At that time, he was living on money he had earned. He was not very rich – he was normal; he was trying. I think it was his best time, his most stable time. He was not always faithful to me, but he was the most faithful he had ever been in his whole life. It was the most normal time he had ever had. For one thing, we both liked animals, horses in particular, and he also had a beautiful German shepherd dog called Vedocq which lived with us.'

Early in the relationship, Kirsten realized that something was seriously wrong with her young lover. 'I'd wake up in the middle of the night with a feeling of anguish,' she said. 'I would think, Why am I so depressed? This was the beginning of our relationship, and I had no reason to be depressed. I realized it was him. This aura was so strong that it would come on to me. I'm not sensitive, and I don't believe in those kind of things, but it was so strong that it affected me. He was a depressive. He didn't know how to be happy. He would be well and suddenly – phttt! – go down for three days and then come up again. He wasn't a drinker, he would only drink a bit if he were tense. When he started to get grumpy, I'd say to him, "You've got to get out of this," and he would stop and get better. He worried a lot about money – that was the No. 1 concern. He was a money lover, and he wanted to be a somebody. His dream was to be a really big businessman who had arrived by himself in the style of Aristotle Onassis. He wanted to show people that he was a good businessman; that he had made his own money. He wanted a kingdom with everybody down there looking up at him.

'He cried only once in the time we were together – over money. He lost one million dollars in Singapore, where he had set up a business, and the man with whom he associated did something wrong. Thierry didn't only cry; he hid himself away because, you know, he was very proud and had a lot of ego. His ego was so big it could nearly kill him. But we managed to deal with most things.

I wasn't with him with the idea of getting married; that's not the way I see life. I just want to be happy in myself. Thierry was two years younger than me, and I decided to continue the love affair for as long as I was happy with him. The day I was unhappy, I would leave him.'

After three years together, Kirsten did leave Roussel but not without some resistance on his part. 'He had some good ideas, but in the end he started to lie to me and plan trips with other girls. I caught him on the first one when he went to Marbella with four models. I packed his suitcase for him as I always did, but when he arrived in Marbella and opened it, all the Elvis outfits came out. He hadn't thrown them away, and I had packed them to let him know how I felt. He was very angry when he phoned me, but he was laughing at the same time.

'His father, Henri, said I'd been mean to him to pack such a horrible suitcase, but what did he expect me to do? – he had gone off with four women. That was it; I left him. I was fed up with him and his family.'

The split was followed by phone calls from a contrite Thierry, who was hoping for a reconciliation. The calls continued for nearly a year, then suddenly stopped. A decade after they had become lovers, Christina Onassis had come back into his life, and he knew this was his chance to make up for all the failures of the past. 'Thank God I've found her again,' he told a friend.

THIRTEEN

THE CIA, SEANCES AND SEX: THE PRIVATE EYE'S STORY

IT HAD BEEN on Skórpios during the summer of 1973 that Christina had realized her father was close to cracking up over Alexander's death. As Jackie seemed incapable of providing the love and support he needed, Christina began to welcome the renewed presence of Maria Callas in his life. Onassis had started to see Callas again on a regular basis, deliberately taking her to restaurants in Paris and Athens where they would be seen and photographed. His intention was to make Jackie jealous, but he also needed a shoulder to cry on.

He complained to Callas about his wife's overspending and her coldness towards him. The criticisms were music to the diva's ears, but the fault was not all on Jackie's side. She had always known that Onassis was different from other men, and she had rapidly learned after marrying him that he was very peculiar indeed. 'He even checks under the bed for evil spirits,' she told a friend.

Callas, however, shared Ari's concern about the supernatural, even believing that the curse her husband had put on them had been responsible for many of their troubles. Her career had been blighted ever since she had moved in with Onassis in 1960. Since then, she had appeared in only three operas, *Norma*, *Médée* and *Tosca*. She had consulted clairvoyants and spiritualists to try to revive her career, but the curse had remained firmly in place. Before making a film version of *Médée*, she visited the Parisian astrologer Joelle de Gravelaine to check that the omens were right, but although the production went ahead, her performance was widely panned.

Callas wasn't the first woman to notice Ari's superstitious nature; his former lover, Ingse Dedichen, had been astounded by some of his beliefs. 'He retained superstitions from his childhood which were to me bizarre,' she said. 'He even resorted to "charms" to protect me from evil. In Athens, he offered me a blue stone worth a few pence to keep away the evil eye.'

His former aide Frank Monte claimed that Ari resorted to spiritualist methods to make contact with the dead. 'Onassis did try to get in touch with Alexander through mediums,' the private eye told us from his office at the Rockefeller Center in Manhattan. 'The second night after I met him in mid-1973 we went off to a seance in Milan. I stayed outside the address as the bodyguard, and he was in there for about an hour. He had been into magic or the supernatural for a long time. It wasn't just that he had started to have seances because he wanted to reach his son. Callas had got him involved in ceremonial magic, and he had taken to it. He had a little temple with an altar and candles in a small room in his house just like a Christian might have a picture of the Virgin Mary somewhere. He would go in and say certain things to empower himself. It wasn't satanic. There's a great difference between ceremonial magic and Satanism – this was nothing to do with Satan. It was a spiritual thing about his inner self, and it had started to become his form of meditation. He had been doing that for a long time, all this mind-over-matter stuff to make his will stronger than the will of his enemies.

'He had a cloak which he wore, and he had a bell to call the spirits. It wasn't a joke, and it wasn't malevolent; it wasn't voodoo, it wasn't pagan, and it wasn't sacrificing anything or drinking blood or any crap like that. It was quite respectful. He had books he used for reference purposes and, luckily enough, they were in English so I was able to read them. One was called *The Golden Dawn*, and he was doing stuff out of that. It was his way of relaxing to get ready for some of the meetings he had to attend about the supertanker he was building and other deals which were in the pipeline.

'His favourite spiritualist – he called her a witch – was a very old

Italian woman called Antonietta Allessandrelli in Rome. He had an apartment in Via Cavour, and we used to walk around the corner past the Victor Emmanuel monument to her place. She was in her eighties and quite well-to-do because she had been seer to the deposed Italian king and the dictator Mussolini. He went to see her quite often. I was very impressed by the whole set-up at her home; she was a very impressive woman. He paid her well, and he said she was accurate about things. Sometimes he would ring her at one o'clock in the morning, and her helpers would get her out of bed, and we would walk around to her apartment for a seance.'

A well-built man with brushed-back black hair, Monte provided a vast amount of detail to back up his claims. Born François Ferdinand Montenari at Alexandria, Egypt, in July 1945, Monte said he worked for Onassis between mid-April and mid-August 1973. The tycoon had introduced himself to Monte after he had described some of his undercover work at a meeting of leading businessmen in Milan. 'I had been making a lot of noise as the up-and-coming private eye in Australia,' Monte said. 'Onassis had always been interested in little toys and bugs, and here I was with a bagful of them, and I knew how to use them. I could also break and enter, and speak Italian.'

Onassis approached the young go-getter and offered him a bodyguard's job, but he made it plain at the outset that his real work would be in the field of industrial espionage.

'Onassis had based himself in Rome after his son's death, although he would slip off to Paris in the middle of the night without telling anybody, and I went to Skórpios with him a couple of times,' he said. 'He had a villa at Castel Gandolfo 20 minutes outside Rome. In Via Cavour, he had the entire third floor of a five-storey building, and sometimes he would work from there. The Rome thing was about completing a couple of very big oil deals with the Saudi Arabians who, I understand, he had done a lot for, and finishing off his latest supertanker, which was being constructed by the Japanese.

'Italy was the base of operations for a short time because it was unexpected. Many of the things could have been done much quicker in Tokyo, but he said he didn't trust the Japanese. He was quite spooked at the time. It was no joke that two of us used to taste his food in restaurants, and it was no joke that he had a trusted house-keeper cooking for him at home. While I was with him we moved twice. Removalists would just pick up all his furniture and other belongings and move from one villa to another villa practically overnight. One of my jobs was to make sure that the rooms he used for meetings were debugged and, within reason, I knew every piece of furniture in those rooms. We wired metal detectors around the doorways, but anything like a pen or some loose change would set them off. We were playing all those sorts of games to keep sterile rooms for him to do business in.

'He was particularly paranoid about the telephone, and we were forever changing lines. I would come in to find technicians wiring phones with new numbers. He really believed that everybody was after him, and I found out that people *were* after him. I didn't know at the time if it was the Italian secret service or the CIA because you don't catch them and find a badge in their pocket. But he was being bugged, and he was being followed, although nothing ever happened to him. I found in a couple of instances that there were wire-taps on the line. I took them off, but they were back on a few days later. We also changed cars from a stretch Fiat to a stretch Mercedes to throw off the tail. Everybody was trying to find out what he was doing – not only to spy on him for business reasons but also to put him out of business. The Americans were really after him with a vengeance: they wanted to send this guy nuts and put him out of business.'

Monte had no doubts that the CIA was Ari's main enemy and that the tycoon was the target of a covert operation. 'He believed that the CIA were definitely out to try and kill him,' he said. 'He would get up like a mad drunk in the middle of the night saying, "They're here, they're here. They're out there. The CIA are breaking in." After his experiences in Monaco, he didn't think much of the French, but he said if they were going to kill him, they would just walk into the room and do it. "The Americans will never come face to face with you," he said. "They will try to get your best friend to get you." In fact, three different guys from the CIA did approach me in the street and offered me money, not to kill Onassis but to spy on him. I told him about it, and we started feeding them information, some of it correct but the rest completely false. I know they were genuine agents because I have since met members of the CIA in America who have confirmed it.

'I wasn't a personal bodyguard in the sense that I stood next to Onassis in the toilet, but that was my title. He could hardly say, "This is my industrial spy. This is my bug man." I was armed, and Onassis carried a pistol – a very small .25 automatic – for protection. He was a very suspicious character, and although he had a couple of serious bodyguards who could kill in a second without a gun, he took me with him around Italy because I spoke Italian. He would ask me to check up on somebody, and I would find a pretext to ring them. I would tell them a story or talk to their secretaries and do some intelligent digging. The targets were mainly Arabs and Japanese he was doing business with, and he was out to get them.

'For example, some Japanese came to see him, and they were trying to sell him some turbines for the supertanker for $5 million, but he knew he should be able to get them for $2 million. However, he was caught in the middle because they had some of his money, he had credit with them, and he couldn't go elsewhere. They were shafting him, and he wanted to get the goods on these Japanese to shame them. He wanted them followed back to their hotel bedrooms and bugged and watched. What I did for him was the spying thing of finding out where people were conning him. He wanted to be able to sit down in front of them the next morning and say, "Well, you said to your office in Tokyo last night that you're prepared to sell it for $2 million. Your own bosses told me it was going to be $2 million so why waste my time? It's $2 million or nothing – take it or get out."

'He was trying to protect himself by dirty deeds, even setting them up with prostitutes for blackmail. I felt morally OK with that because they *were* trying to do him in at his worst moment when he had all these responsibilities, and he was feeling very bad about Alexander. I felt it was moral, even though it was sometimes illegal. These people were definitely screwing him on prices or lying about things or trying to rip him off.

'I wasn't with him 24 hours a day, although we lived in the same house. I would be away 10 hours a day shadowing or watching some Japanese or Arab businessmen. The Arabs were all Saudis, and quite a few were ministers in the Saudi government. They would come to see him about oil deals, and he would want them followed back to the Excelsior or wherever they were staying. We had rooms at the Excelsior, the Boston and the Eden so that we had access. The Arabs and the Japanese would stay at these hotels, and therefore I had to be able to get in and out without arousing suspicion. Sometimes they would mention where they were staying during some idle chit-chat at a meeting with Onassis, and we would go to the place and wire it before they got back. The locks were all fairly old and could be picked or plasticked or jemmied quite easily. At the Eden, the Boston and a couple of other hotels we had some of the management on side.

We had passkeys from one or two of the boys there, and we gave them $500 or $600 every time we wanted to do something. Onassis would be quite neurotic about money, depending on his mood. He would blow up over a thousand lira to buy a newspaper, yet hand me $10,000 to pay some guy for information.

'I had 20 or 30 identical bugs – battery-powered transmitters that go on to a frequency, and you sit down the road listening or transmitting on to a tape recorder. Sometimes I put a microphone and a tape recorder into the bed of a hotel room if there was enough time to rip it open and staple it up again. You put a tear in the cloth and have the microphone very close to that tear, and you can have the recorder on long play for 12 hours. We were only after snippets of information – like when a man walked back into his room after a meeting with Onassis and called Riyadh for an hour – that was the hour we wanted. Onassis wanted to know what they were plotting against him.

'The tapes were handed to Onassis, and he gave them to a translator, a balding little Italian guy called Umberto. He was a professorial sort of guy, walking around with a briefcase full of tapes and transcripts, and making a heap of money. Onassis wouldn't sit there and listen to the tapes himself; he would read Umberto's transcripts. There were a lot of problems in the oil industry at the time, and that was why he was anxious to get his supertanker out.'

Apart from commercial information, Onassis also gathered evidence of sexual peccadilloes. 'There was no one he didn't do business with, and he set up many of them with girls,' said Monte. 'He would give me a big quid to find, not prostitutes, but girls who were fairly attractive. I would pick up girls, take them shopping and make sure they arrived at his parties dressed the right way. He didn't want that bored Italian prostitute look; he wanted non-professionals – amateurs who would be spontaneous, like shop assistants, secretaries and perhaps a few housewives. I would give them so much money that they would come around and have a few drinks with the Japanese or the Arab businessmen. They would mingle and pretend they just worked for the company. Quite a few male movie stars also turned up at these parties. I remember David Niven and Richard Burton being there a couple of times. Burton drank and drank – he cared more about booze than the women, even though I had got the longest legs and the biggest boobs around. I had the names of 19 girls in my book, all flirty with a cute edge to them.

'Onassis was always present at these parties because he liked the games. He liked to see how vulnerable the Japanese were; he would try to catch them out. He also liked the power his money had over these women; he wanted to corrupt them. Physically, he wasn't ailing, but he was mentally ill. There were some nights when he was with it all; he was doing business, he was talking, he was a bit sad, but he wasn't moping in his room and crying. Altogether, we gave about 15 parties either at the villa at Castel Gandolfo or the Rome apartment. He would get into it in front of the Japanese guys and tell the girls to take their tops off. He would throw money at them – it was done to embarrass the Japanese; to show them that he had the power.

'In those days, a couple of hundred bucks was a lot of money to a girl who was working behind a counter somewhere. It was my job to find the right girls. I would say straight out, "We want to fill up the room with beautiful women, and you're one of them. We'll pick you up and you're going to be home by 10 or 11." We were not trying to line them up with the Japanese for sex; he was just trying to tantalize them. He was trying to rope these guys in, then send the girls home. It was part of the power trip. In the middle of the party, he would say to me, "OK, that's enough. Get all the girls out." I'd haul the girls into the kitchen and get them off into the car and drop them off in town again. He would then throw prostitutes at them later on for sex, and we would bug them.

'I saw him being quite sexual with a couple of girls, and I remember one instance when he got carried away with the girl who had worked in the tobacco shop at the Excelsior. Once she dropped her clothes, he sort of lost it and wanted to drag her off into the bedroom. I wasn't going to stop him, and I wasn't there to help her. A woman who takes a couple of hundred upfront and arrives in a see-through dress at a place she doesn't know – I'm sorry, she's got to expect it. I had just arrived in that world, and I was trying to please to get my leg up in the business world and understand what the hell was going on.'

Although Monte worked closely with Ari, his boss clung to his mania for secrecy. 'He always had this thing about nobody knowing everything he was doing,' he said. 'I was a newcomer, and that was my strength. I had been picked out of nowhere and hadn't applied for the job so he trusted me for a short time. A lot of people would ring, and he wouldn't so much use codenames as not mention their names. He would call a lot of people himself or have me call people for him. It wasn't a very formal thing. He used to do a lot of his own work because he didn't trust his assistants; he was very suspicious of everybody.

'He knew the stuff I was doing, and he knew how to work the gear. He wasn't an idiot; he would ask pertinent questions. I gave him a gadget known as a VSA [voice stress analyser], which was also known as a PSE [psychological stress evaluator]. This had been developed by the CIA to be used in Vietnam during the interrogation of prisoners to find out whether they were lying or not. They had just come on the market as a prototype, and I was one of the few people who knew how to use them. They do work if you're very good with them. It has a lot to do with the questions you pose to get answers as close to yes and no as you can, and you check them on a graph. You can tell stress more than you can tell a lie. The one I gave Onassis looked like a pocket calculator with a series of pinprick lights plus a numerical counter. He fed a roll of graph paper into it, which printed out while he was talking on the phone. It was a toy, and if you relied on it too much you lost other nuances in the caller's voice. He also used to speak into a voice changer, a box with a dial on it, which he attached to the phone line with a couple of alligator clips. He would twist the buttons to change the frequency and thus distort his voice, but he was kidding himself – no one could ever mistake him for anyone else.

'When he went to Paris, I would look after the integrity of the premises in Rome. We taped the doors, the rooms were not cleaned, and we made sure nobody broke in. We used little tricks, from sprinkling talcum powder on the floor to setting up voice-activated tape recorders in the rooms. It was important that he could arrive back and walk straight into a meeting. He would tape-record conversations he was having with people and, while he was away, I would replay those conversations down the lines between the villa and the apartment. It caused utter confusion to anybody who was listening; they would think he was in Rome when he was still in Paris. He was out 24 hours a day to confuse and distract; that was the game he was playing.'

More than anyone else has ever dared, Monte was able to cast a searching light over the dark side of Onassis's character. 'He wasn't a nice guy,' he said. 'He certainly destroyed a lot of people by holding back monies or making their life difficult in other ways. One particular vendetta was against a businessman in Turin who had upset him some years earlier. He was always telling me to get up there and put him out of business. "Let's see how good you are," he would say. "Buy out his stock, get his sales girls to leave, cut his phones, screw his wife . . ." He really was into settling scores short of cutting someone's throat. I never heard him order anyone to be killed. This particular fellow in Turin had told his ex-wife about one of his business deals to ingratiate himself with her, and Onassis had found out. So when he heard that the guy had surfaced in Turin and was doing quite well, he wanted me to ruin him, but with everything else going on I was too busy. The feud with Niarchos was a much bigger thing. Onassis felt intimidated by his panache; he saw himself as a peasant, whereas Niarchos had style. And, of course, he hated him for marrying Tina; he thought that was pretty dirty pool.'

Monte confirmed that Ari's relationships with Jackie and Christina were abysmal. 'Christina was in and out of the villa making a lot of noise and acting a bit crazy,' said Monte. 'He was very angry that she wouldn't take much notice of what he wanted her to do. He hated the fact that she was crawling after these good-looking, blond, playboy types like a little Greek girl. According to him, they were all bums. He started making insinuations to me about her. "Next time she's here, you must take her out," he said. "Or isn't she good enough for you? She's a rich girl, you know." A couple of times she came to talk to me, and she was quite rude and pushy. She was spoiled, but nobody dared to tell her that anything was wrong with her. With Jackie, it was a no-win situation. Any time he spoke to her, he was fighting. He would half blame her for things that were happening in his life.

'Secretly, Onassis was bisexual. There was a guy called Julio, a 22-year-old Italian, at the villa, and although I never saw them kissing or hugging, I had the impression they were lovers. I did catch them sort of in bed. Onassis was in bed, and this guy was on top of the bed with his shirt off, as if comforting him more than anything else. I do have some knowledge that he was bisexual because he definitely put it on me a couple of times. He got drunk one night and kept telling me, "I love you. I really love you." I was much slimmer then. He would also try out other men. Every now and then a waiter would come up to serve us in a restaurant, and Onassis would casually reach out and grab his balls. That was supposed to have been funny to everybody, but it wasn't funny to the waiter, and it was embarrassing to some of us who were straight. Once again, it was his power trip.

'He told me straight out he would trust me more and let me do more things if we were together. But I must admit he didn't push it after I showed him pictures of my children as babies. Nor did he regard himself as homosexual; it was just part of the camaraderie among boys and men.'

Monte said that much of Onassis's frantic business activity was to cover up the grief and guilt he felt over Alexander. He clung to his belief that his son had been the victim of a conspiracy because, if there had been no conspiracy, then the blame for the crash lay with the repair engineers whom he had hired to service the plane. Onassis had kept the Piaggio in service even though Alexander had pleaded with him to replace it with a modern amphibian. Enjoying the comfort of the old plane, he had refused to part with it. No one was more to blame for Alexander's death than Onassis himself, and that was a truth he couldn't bear to face. His obsession drove him to offer a $1 million reward to anybody who could prove that his son had been murdered.

'The way he talked about it convinced me that somebody had, in fact, killed the boy,' said Monte. 'I knew about the interrogation of the other two pilots on board the seaplane, and something was terribly wrong. Onassis believed it was the CIA, and I believe he was right.'

Onassis was so paranoid about the presence of the CIA that he needed safe addresses. 'He ordered me to find a tailor's shop in a quiet spot where he could make secret phone calls,' said Monte. "When I go in, it will look like I'm being fitted for a new suit," he said. "I know the hayseeds from Ohio are following me, but they won't see through this ruse." He thought everybody in the CIA and the FBI was from Ohio, and he thought they weren't clever enough to know the difference between one of the great sartorial menswear stores on Via Veneto, where we usually shopped, and a back-street tailor's. I found a suitable place six blocks from the apartment towards Via Nazionale, and we paid the tailor $1000 to have a secret phone put in. Onassis wanted to be absolutely sure that he wasn't bugged, and he didn't want anyone to know the number. So we didn't have it fitted by the guys we were bribing at the telephone exchange. Instead, I rang up posing as the tailor and said I wanted to have another phone put in. We actually unplugged the handset and took it away when he wasn't using it to avoid it ringing in his absence. We would also go down to the store and walk out with a parcel that looked like a suit or some shirts to keep the cover.

'Onassis went there fairly frequently throughout the time I was with him. He would go down to that store and sit in the back room with bolts of cloth everywhere and talk on the phone. All the machines would be switched off to make it quiet. They were serious calls but not the usual business ones. He never took any papers with him; he just sat there and made calls. I would go in from time to time to make sure no one had shot him. There was a bodyguard in the front, one in the back and one in the car. I could hear him talking, and he just wanted to be left alone in there. He was mainly in there for an hour so it looked like a fitting for a suit, but he was once in there for four hours, talking on the phone and then waiting to be called back.'

One of the people Onassis called was Howard Hughes, who had been one of his son's heroes. Alexander made no secret of his admiration for the former daredevil pilot's achievements in aviation. He had read everything written about Hughes, from the making of the 1930 Hollywood epic *Hell's Angels* to the plane crash that almost crippled him for life, to the adventures of the Spruce Goose, a plywood flying boat that Hughes had designed to carry 750 passengers. Whenever he got a chance, Alexander pestered his father for details about his meetings with Hughes. The reclusive millionaire had always been well disposed towards Onassis, even though he envied the tax-free position he had held in Monaco, which he described to Robert Maheu as 'the ideal set-up'.

Hughes had been driven out of Vegas by the fear of contamination from a nuclear-test explosion in the Nevada desert. He had settled in the Nicaraguan capital of Managua until an earthquake had sent him scurrying from his hotel in December 1972. Badly shaken, Hughes had made a dash for London, even though he had no valid passport. Nevertheless, he was admitted to the country and had checked into Suite 901 at the Inn on the Park on Park Lane. Onassis contacted Hughes on his private line, which was connected to a specially amplified receiver to overcome Hughes' deafness.

Maheu had been able to assure Hughes that the CIA was innocent of any involvement in Alexander's plane crash, and Hughes advised Onassis to forget about it: there was no conspiracy. 'Maheu claimed they had nothing to do with the kid,' confirmed Frank Monte. 'He approached me in 1978 after Onassis had died and said he had some things he wanted me to know, so we traded, and that was one of the things he told me. There were a couple of times we had disappeared off the face of the earth, and he wanted to know what had happened. He was fairly knowledgeable about what had happened in Rome; for instance, he reckoned he had sent the guys who had approached me. Therefore, I believed him about his involvement. With all our shenanigans, the CIA had been keeping up with half of what Onassis was doing, but they couldn't put the pieces of the puzzle together – and that's the whole idea.

'I realized how right Onassis had been. Maheu was the one who said to me straight out that the CIA had orders to scuttle him and stop his business. He had screwed the American secret service at some time, and this was a long-standing pay back. They had orders to do anything they could do to make sure that an American company got the business instead of Onassis. I have since had a drink and a chat with other former agents, and they told me in no uncertain terms that the orders were to fuck this guy up.'

The time for Onassis to stop playing games once and for all came on the morning of 10 September 1974, when Tina was found dead in Niarchos's Paris residence from a drug-induced oedema of the lung. At 45, the emaciated figure on the bed was a shadow of the beautiful woman who had once graced the world's finest salons. Ari was conscience-stricken. He had outlived his much younger wife as well as their son. His vague hope that she might one day leave Niarchos and restore his honour had disappeared for ever.

Once again, Christina turned her venom on her stepmother. 'Christina was highly distraught,' said Costa Gratsos. 'She felt Jackie was somehow to blame. Death was never very far from "the Black Widow". Christina feared her. She felt Jackie had magical powers. Everybody around her had perished.'

The effect on Ari's health was plainly visible. His muscular body had shrunk, he ate only with great difficulty, and alcohol no longer provided the desired escape. His face resembled a death mask, and he couldn't keep his eyes open. He had been diagnosed as suffering from myasthenia gravis, a degenerative muscular disease brought on by stress, alcohol and fatigue. His doctors explained to him that a defect in the body's chemical process prevented impulses being transmitted between nerves and muscles. This loss of control was progressive and incurable, but it could be treated with drugs.

Christina taped her father's eyes open with strips of Band Aid, and he endeavoured to carry on as though nothing was wrong.

'Ari was charming, wonderful, full of life,' said Florence Grinda. 'He hated everything chichi and lived a very simple life. I remember once we were going out of Avenue Foch with Odile Rubirosa and the actress Elsa Martinelli to a night club. Ari started giving money to all the photographers who were waiting there for him. He told them, "I feel so terrible for you waiting for me all the time. I'll give you some money so you can go and have a good time, and at the same time leave me alone." He was a very generous person. He was loved by everybody. He was fantastic. My ex-husband, Jean-Noel, was a partner in a very fashionable night club called Le Privé. The last time I saw Ari Onassis was at a party called the Fabulous Fifties, which we gave at the club, and everyone came dressed in fifties style. Ari was with Christina, who was dressed in socks, and [her hair in a] ponytail. He had one eye almost closed from his illness. It was one of the last events when people saw him in public. He was fun, Ari, he loved the good life.'

On 15 January 1975, Onassis lost a long and bitter struggle with the Greek government to retain ownership of Olympic Airways. He no longer possessed the stamina to sustain his old technique of arguing over every point, agreeing a deal and then changing his mind at the next negotiating session. Exhausted, he relinquished control of the airline like a drowning man letting go of a liferaft. The loss filled him with a compulsive fear that everything he had toiled and schemed to create was about to crumble into dust. Calling Christina to his side, he made her promise that she would marry Peter Goulandris to protect the rest of the Onassis fortune. When Christina went skiing in Gstaad with Goulandris a couple of weeks later, the talk of marriage was revived, and Onassis seemed relieved. But on 3 February Christina received a call from Artimus telling her that her father had collapsed at his Glyfada villa with severe abdominal pains.

Christina flew to Athens to find that 'the Black Widow' herself had arrived from New York with a heart specialist, Dr Isidore Rosenfeld. A liver expert, Professor Jean Caroli, had also been summoned from Paris. Ari complained that he had a problem eating. 'I find it hard to chew,' he told the doctors. As well as a heavy dose of influenza, the doctors diagnosed gallstones and, while they agreed that Ari's infected gallbladder was poisoning his system and should be removed, they couldn't agree on the time or the place for the operation. Jackie insisted that her husband should be flown to the American Hospital of Paris rather than to New York. 'He's my husband,' she snapped, 'so let's not argue about it.'

Ari reluctantly agreed to leave Athens and was bundled into a limousine clutching a red Hermès cashmere blanket, which Jackie had given to him, and a copy of a book called *Supership*, which predicted the advent of the first million-ton tanker. Arriving in Paris in his Learjet with Jackie, Christina and Artimus, Onassis refused to go directly to the American Hospital in Neuilly-sur-Seine but instead ordered the car to take him to Avenue Foch, even though the press were camped outside in force. With great valour, he got out of the limousine unaided, crossed the pavement and walked down the path past the flowerbeds, through the door, under the archway and made it as far as the lift before collapsing.

After a night of broken sleep and nightmares, he received Johnny Meyer in his darkened bedroom the following morning. 'You didn't expect to see me looking like this, old friend?' Ari said, noting Meyer's surprise. 'A bag of skin and bones.' Meyer quipped: 'Don't worry, Ari, no one ever died of droopy eyelids.' Onassis responded with a joke of his own: 'It's God punishing me for always biting off more than I could chew.' They both knew that he was dying. All the bravado had gone, and his great wealth counted for nothing. 'His whole life from the cradle to the grave was there on a tiny table – a goddam calculator and a crucifix,' Meyer later recalled in his unpublished memoirs.

At 11.50 the following morning, Ari left his penthouse for the last time, in a blue Peugeot that shot out from the underground garage and crossed the press lines with horn blaring. At the American Hospital on Avenue Victor-Hugo, he tried to slip unnoticed through the chapel, while photographers were distracted snapping Jackie and Christina at the canopied front entrance. But a paparazzo spotted him and snatched the last picture, a portrait of a fallen idol. The patient was taken upstairs to the first floor and given a private room in a wing named after Eisenhower, one of no fewer than six presidents who had presided over Onassis's long battle with America.

The tension between Christina and Jackie boiled to the surface almost immediately, but Onassis was too tired to care. Rather than sleep under the same roof as Jackie at the penthouse, his daughter moved into a suite at the Plaza-Athénée. With her aunt Artimus, she remained steadfastly at her father's bedside. When Artimus had to return to Athens to look after her ailing husband, Christina took an adjoining room at the hospital, returning to the hotel only to change her clothes and make phone calls. The prognosis was dire. Doctors told Onassis that if his gallbladder was not removed immediately he would be dead within a week. They needed authorization from next of kin to carry out the operation and, in Jackie's absence, Christina gave her permission.

Onassis said to the surgeon: 'You understand, doctor, the meaning of the Greek word *thanatos* – death? You know that I will never come out of hospital alive. Well, please practise *thanatos* on me.'

Nothing of the sort occurred. After the operation on 9 February, he was placed on a respirator and a kidney-dialysis machine. Jackie visited him frequently at first but did not deny herself the pleasures afforded by her favourite city. She dined at Café des Deux-Magots on the Left Bank with a friend, shopped in the *grands magasins*, went to the cinema and had her hair done.

On 22 February Ari was still grievously ill, and one of the surgeons who had taken part in the operation said: 'Our last ally for saving him is his pride.' But he had rallied surprisingly well by the end of the month. When the hospital reported he had made 'a slow but progressive improvement,' Jackie flew back to New York and telephoned every day.

In a considerate show of support, Peter Goulandris moved into Christina's hotel suite. Together they went to Onassis's bedside and told him that they intended to marry. But although Onassis received the news gratefully, he could talk to Christina only about joining her brother. 'I'll soon be on Skórpios with Alexander,' he said. Maria Callas was admitted to the sickroom for a final visit, after which she left Paris and flew to Palm Beach, where she went into seclusion in a rented house at 12 Golf View Road, near the Everglades Club.

Christina was at his side when his life quietly slipped away during a rainstorm on Saturday, 15 March 1975. The moment she realized her father was dead, Christina lost control and, grabbing a surgical instrument, slashed at her wrist. She managed to make a cut before she could be overpowered. In Florida, Callas received a phone call to say that Onassis was dead. Over the next few days she received so many letters and telegrams of consolation that she said: 'Suddenly, I am the widow.' Nadia Stancioff said: 'He was definitely going to divorce Jackie, and he would have married Callas if he hadn't become ill. He had even proposed to her again.'

Onassis seemed to have written his own epitaph when he said, 'I'm just a Greek kid who knew how to do his sums,' but for once in his life, he was guilty of reckless understatement.

FOURTEEN

A FUNERAL
AND FOUR
WEDDINGS

NOW ONLY THE Legacy remained, much of it uncountable in dollars and cents. 'The last time I saw Aristotle Onassis he was dressed in black,' said Alecko Papamarkou. 'He had a black suit, black tie and a white silk shirt. His eyes were shut from his illness, but he was still gripping. God had allowed him to go to dizzy heights and then gave him all these other things to make up for it.'

In death, the mantle of 'these other things' had passed to 24-year-old Christina and, on a bleak, overcast day in March 1975, she wore the tragedy and the suffering with the look of a woman possessed. Less than six months after she had lost her mother, she was on her way to bury her father. Shock and grief were visible in her glazed expression as she stepped from the Olympic Airways 727 that had borne Aristotle's coffin from Paris to Greece. The plane had landed at the Greek military airport at Actium at two o'clock in the afternoon and, beyond little knots of mourners, a hearse waited to carry the body to the fishing port of Nidri on Lefkas island for the final stage of the journey to Skórpios.

In black leather trench coat and black Valentino dress, Jackie had been the first to step from the aircraft, presenting the waiting photographers with that fixed, Sphinx smile and an exterior of cold steel. She was followed by the man she had chosen from the very beginning of her Onassis odyssey to represent her interests, Senator Edward Kennedy. Beefy of build and flushed of face, the liar of Chappaquiddick showed no signs of recognizing the fact that his very presence at the funeral of a man who had grown to loathe him bore all the hallmarks of parody. Among relatives, friends and business associates, Aristotle's three sisters, Artimus, Merope and Callirhoe, stood rooted to the tarmac like three silent sentinels.

When Christina emerged from the hatchway, she had stumbled down the steps as though walking in space. She wore no make-up, and her hair was windswept, but she paid no heed to the impression she might be making. As she reached the ground, Jackie had taken her firmly by the arm and guided her across the tarmac to the leading limousine. As flashbulbs popped, and Jackie smiled again, Christina said to her in disbelief: 'Oh, God! Even now . . . how can you?'

'Hang on,' Jackie replied. 'Take it easy now. It'll soon be over.' Christina climbed into the vehicle with Jackie and Teddy Kennedy, and the motorcade began its slow procession through the countryside towards the launch dock at Nidri.

On a stretch of road lined with mourners and the merely curious, the limousine suddenly jerked to an unscheduled halt and, in a flurry of arms and legs, a distraught Christina emerged through the open door and jumped on to the roadway. Moving as fast as she could on rubbery legs, she joined her aunts in the following vehicle, and the cortège resumed its grim forward movement. According to Costa Gratsos, Teddy Kennedy had chosen that moment to discuss his former sister-in-law's share of the Onassis inheritance. With an insensitivity that would have stopped even a Bostonian wake, the senator had said, 'Now it's time to take care of Jackie.'

On Skórpios, the coffin, which had been made from one of the island's walnut trees, bore a brass plate inscribed simply: *Aristotle Onassis 1900–1975*. So there it was for the privileged few to see: the secret of his real age, which Ari had literally carried to his grave. His body was carried up the hill to the tiny chapel and, after the briefest of services, each mourner kissed an icon placed on the coffin before it was lowered into the vault close to Alexander. The mourners included Peter Goulandris, and the sight of her friend at this crucial time seemed to give Christina new heart. As the funeral party retired to *Christina* for refreshment, she addressed the crew and her father's employees from the deck of the ship. 'This ship and this island are mine,' she said in Greek. 'You are all my people now.'

Arriving back in Athens, Jackie managed to read a statement to the press without breaking into a smile. 'Aristotle Onassis rescued me at a moment when my life was engulfed with shadows,' she said. 'He meant a lot to me. He brought me into a world where one could find both happiness and love. We lived through many beautiful experiences together, which cannot be forgotten, and for which I will be eternally grateful.' Then in words that could not have been more calculated to distress Christina, she added: 'Nothing has changed both with Aristotle's sisters and his daughter. The same love binds us as when he lived.' Christina had only to read those words to know that the Black Widow intended to squeeze every last cent out of her poor, wasted father.

Asked at a court hearing not long before his death how many ships he owned, Onassis had snapped, 'I have no idea. Do you think I have time to sit down and count them?' In truth, Onassis's death had left his empire in a state of confusion, despite a review he had ordered as a matter of urgency before succumbing to his final illness. He knew that his fleet, which totalled 5.2 million tons deadweight even if he couldn't remember the exact number of ships, was far from immune to the problems confronting other tanker owners during the Arab oil crisis of the mid-1970s. For that reason, said a Wall Street corporation lawyer who worked within the Onassis complex, a process of reorganization had already begun. 'Onassis was well aware of the managerial shortcomings of his company system,' he said. 'A few weeks before his death, he asked his close associates to "make use" of his passing on to restaff and reshuffle the management and modernize the administration of his business empire.' The intention was to transform the company into 'a strong, centrally directed, modern, worldwide corporation'. However, the suddenness of his demise had forestalled this objective, and it had been left to lawyers to unravel the legacy – and the disarray – he had left behind.

Christina dashed to Geneva, where a meeting had been hastily convened to tackle the problem of how to control the empire now that its creator was no longer alive. While some of the tankers carried rich, long-term charters with major oil companies, the majority would soon fall idle. But Christina had been fortified by the tragedies surrounding her. 'If they think they can walk in past me and take away what my father built up, they are in for a shock,' she declared. Brooking no argument, the heiress took her place at the table and was named as 'consultant' when a four-member committee, presided over by Eliot Bailen of the New York law firm of Holtzmann, Wise and Shepherd, was set up in New York to examine the business over which Onassis had exercised dictatorial powers.

In June 1974, Onassis had owned 56 ships, of which 44 were tankers and 12 were bulk carriers. A total of 55 were operating under the Liberian flag and just one under the Greek flag. In addition to the Olympic fleet, there was Victory Carriers, the trust formed in the mid-fifties for Christina and Alexander. This company controlled four tankers, or 200,000 deadweight of tanker tonnage, which operated under the US flag.

A Swiss source estimated that at the time of his death, the Onassis empire was worth 'well above a total $900 million'. Deducting a collective mortgage upon these holdings of $400 million, 'the value goes down to the $500 million bracket'. A breakdown of the empire in May 1973 showed that Onassis controlled 70 companies and also had a 'considerable interest' in four multinational corporations. Companies registered in the United States were involved in land development, house building and industry as well as shipping and transport. In Western Europe, they covered banking, industrial concerns, construction, tourism and transport. In Latin America, there was shipping, transport, agriculture, construction and tourism.

Intriguingly, a market source said that Onassis had purchased one million ounces of gold at between $42 and £43 an ounce. At the time of his death, gold had risen to between $172 and $173 an ounce, giving his estate a profit of $130 million. The exact location of some of the gold was a mystery. In his last months, Onassis had salted away a million here and there in safe-deposit vaults in various cities.

Apart from Christina, the two major figures in the Onassis empire at the time of his death were Costa Gratsos in New York and Professor Ioannis Georgakis in Athens. Gratsos was president of Victory Carriers and also ran the rest of the business in New York. Olympic Maritime, which supervised the ships, was based at 17 Avenue d'Ostende in Monte Carlo. The Springfield Shipping Company, which was responsible for hiring crews and provisioning the fleet, was based in Piraeus. But as well as the muddle, Christina had inherited a great deal of goodwill. 'Onassis ships were happy ships,' said a shipping source. 'Accommodation standards are recognized as high and, for years, he paid well above the agreed union rates. He also introduced a wide range of supplementary pension benefits. In 1974, all Onassis seamen and officers were brought under a non-contributory life cover scheme against death or incapacitating accident while in company service.'

The biggest headache facing Christina was that her father's will stipulated that her holdings were to be administrated by the board of the Alexander S. Onassis Public Benefit Foundation. Even though she was to be made Life President of the foundation, she had no control over any of the companies and, therefore, no control over her own money. Fortunately, many of the Greek directors realized from the outset that it would be preferable to have an Onassis at the helm rather than a group of largely unknown businessmen. To achieve this, Christina would have to break her father's will. She consulted one of the directors, Ari's friend and lawyer Stelio Papadimitriou, who came up with an ingenious solution. Under the *nomimos mira* clause, Greek inheritance law ruled that surviving members of the immediate family should receive no less than 50 per cent of an estate. Greek law also made it practically impossible to disinherit a widow, which meant that Jackie was entitled to a 12.5 per cent share of Onassis's wealth, even though she had waived her rights under this clause by signing a prenuptial agreement.

With the Onassis estate valued at around $500 million, this would entitle Jackie to $62.5 million. If Christina could dispose of Jackie's legal claim, she would be able to argue in court that, as the sole surviving beneficiary, her 47.5 per cent should be raised to 50 per cent. It was imperative for her to reach a once-and-for-all settlement with Jackie.

Her hopes that this might be dealt with smoothly were sabotaged on 12 April 1975 when the *New York Times* revealed that Ari had been planning to divorce Jackie at the time of his death. 'Jackie called up Christina in Monte Carlo, threatening that unless Christina put out a statement saying that everything had been lovey-dovey and wonderful between her father and Jackie, she was going to make no end of trouble over the estate, and everything else,' said Roy Cohn. Christina issued a statement through her Paris lawyer saying that the marriage had been a happy one and that reports of an impending divorce were totally false. This denial enabled Jackie to go to

Skórpios three days later for the memorial service that was traditionally held 40 days after a death. Jackie picked up her personal possessions from *Christina* and the Pink House. She also souvenired Ari's priceless amethyst Buddha inlaid with rubies.

The following month Christina flew to London and, using her flat in Reeves Mews as a base, met directors of BP and Shell to discuss the charter contracts they held with Olympic Maritime. She told the oilmen: 'In future, if anyone wants to do business with our companies, they will have to speak to me.' Sir Frank McFadzean, Shell's chairman, left the meeting describing Christina as 'a most impressive and very charming lady'. Nigel Neilson, whom Christina had retained as her public-relations spokesman, told the press: 'Everyone now knows Christina is definitely the boss.'

The other purpose of the trip was for Christina to meet Jackie on neutral ground to negotiate a buy-out of her claims on the estate. Pursued by photographers, Jackie had booked into Claridge's after arriving with her New York attorney, Simon Rifkind. Claiming press harassment, she cancelled the meeting with Christina and sent her a dozen orchids as a peace offering. As Christina had been on the receiving end of an equal amount of media attention, she found the gesture meaningless. When the two women did meet, Christina used her father's tactics of always pleading hardship and offered Jackie a paltry $8 million, which was immediately rejected.

The meeting broke up two hours later with Jackie insisting that the minimum she would accept was $20 million. While Christina seemed to regard such a sum as daylight robbery, she was secretly delighted. She later told friends that she had been prepared to go much higher. After stalling for time to check the figures with her financial advisers, Christina flew to New York and saw Jackie at her Fifth Avenue apartment. No lawyers were present, and she emerged 15 minutes later with a settlement: the $20 million Jackie had demanded plus an additional $6 million for taxes. Jackie also received another undisclosed amount for her quarter share in *Christina* and Skórpios.

But 15 months of legal wrangling over the fine print would pass before Christina finally scribbled her signature on a cheque. 'Jackie is the most mercenary person I've ever met,' she said. 'She thinks, talks and dreams of money, nothing but money. What amazes me is that she survives while everyone around her drops. She's dangerous, and she's deadly.'

Taking the agreement to the Greek court, Christina invoked *nomimos mira* and was granted 50 per cent of the proceeds of her father's estate. As his bequests had been deducted from the foundation's share, she automatically became the majority shareholder, free of any control from the foundation's board or anyone else.

The ships were divided equally between Christina and the foundation by the simple process of a lottery. Christina said she wanted to keep the shares that remained in Olympic Tower, the 51-storey office-apartment building that Onassis had built on Fifth Avenue, because it was a monument to her father's achievements in America. Then in a move worthy of Onassis himself, she visited the American embassy in Paris and renounced her American citizenship to avoid paying US taxes. As the beneficiaries of Victory Carriers had to be American, she named the American Hospital of Paris as the nominal recipients of its dividends.

'She is going to be one of the most expert shipping people in the world in a few years,' said Costa Gratsos. 'She will be capable of running all of these things without the advice of old, dilapidated men.'

Christina was, however, planning to share her responsibilities with a new partner. True to her promise to Aristotle, she had decided to marry Peter Goulandris. Immediately after the funeral on Skórpios, he had flown to his mother's house at Lyford Cay on New Providence Island in the Bahamas to make his intentions known to his family. But when Christina arrived a few days later, she had argued with Maria Goulandris, and the wedding plans were cancelled. 'I am tired of everyone trying to marry me off,' she said. 'It isn't because it's too soon after my father's death, but because I don't have plans to marry him or anyone else.'

Christina had been taking the anti-depressant drug imipramine ever since the funeral, but the side-effects had made her weak and tired. She had turned to amphetamines to wake herself up and, very shortly, needed barbiturates in order to sleep. 'After a while, the pills were not having any effect,' she said. 'To get off this vicious circle, I had to have shots. I even hired a private nurse to take care of this for me. She accompanied me everywhere.' A sure sign of her addiction was the suddenness with which she changed her mind about getting married.

The second of her whirlwind unions took place after her aunt

Artimus decided that Alexander Andreadis, second son of the Greek tycoon Stratis Andreadis, would make her an ideal husband. The Andreadis family owned ships, five merchant banks, insurance companies, a fertilizer factory and the Athens Hilton. Alexander, 30, was in charge of the family shipyards, although he was temporarily serving in the Greek army as a conscript. After Papadopoulos had been ousted as premier in 1973, the new regime had investigated tycoons who had profited during the Colonels' years of power. Seizing three of the family's banks, the Greek government accused Stratis, Alexander and eight others of embezzlement. In 1975, the Andreadis family needed $20 million to avoid punitive legal action, according to sources in Athens.

The matchmaking Artimus had arranged for Christina to meet Alexander at the coffee shop of the Athens Hilton. 'I was very near suicide that night,' Christina admitted. 'But the moment I met Alexander, I felt alive again. I was thunderstruck the moment he said hello. I know it sounds ridiculous, but my heart skipped a beat.' They took a cruise in *Christina* with Artimus acting as chaperone. 'I asked Alexander to marry me when I told him I couldn't live without him,' said Christina. 'He said very naturally, "Then why don't we get married?"' Soon after the ship returned to Athens, the couple announced their engagement – just eight days after their first meeting. The wedding was set for 22 July 1975, four months after the death of Onassis. 'I have suffered too much grief,' said Christina. 'I have no close family left, and despite the help of my aunts and Peter Goulandris, I was at the end of my rope when I met Alexander.'

'Everything was so sudden,' said Artimus. 'Christina is very happy because, for the first time, she has found a man who really loves her.' Miraculously, Jackie was invited to the wedding – and she accepted. Arriving in Athens, she said: 'I do love that child, and I'm happy she has found love. At last I can see happy days ahead for her.' The wedding was held in a Byzantine chapel at the foot of Mount Hymettos in the seaside resort of Glyfada. Shortly after the wedding, however, Alexander broached the subject of financial aid for his family. Instead of helping, Christina held a press conference to say that her fortune would not be merged with the Andreadis assets in any way. After that, it was open warfare.

In the Hôtel de Paris in Monte Carlo Christina was enjoying a late-night game of backgammon when Alexander picked up the board, threw it across the lobby and dragged her up to their suite.

Not long afterwards, he broke his leg in a motorbike accident on Skórpios. Christina wrote on his plaster cast, 'Too bad, Alexander, better luck next time.' The marriage was dissolved in July 1977 after their lawyers read prepared statements in court. Christina claimed that Alexander was 'despotic, foul-mouthed, blindly jealous and yet a womanizer, and fanatically self-centred'. Andreadis claimed his wife had 'a peculiar and dictatorial character and didn't really care about me. She also called me a peasant. Due to the short time between our engagement and marriage, I never got the chance to understand her nature.'

The following year, the Andreadis family were acquitted of the charges against them, and Alexander spent the summer with his new friend, the actress Koo Stark. Christina had resolved to take a new direction in life. 'I'm through with marriage and romance,' she said. 'I won't let anything stand in the way of running my business now. That is the one major goal in my life.'

It had been while she was pursuing that goal during her separation from Andreadis that she had met the man who was destined to become her third husband, the 35-year-old Russian Sergei Kausov. She had met him in October 1976 when she had gone to Moscow to lease some of her idle ships to the Russians and had called on the Russian Maritime Department's tanker division, Sovfracht. Kausov, who spoke English and French as well as Russian, was the head of the division. Although only 5ft 4in to Christina's 5ft 6in and with thinning fair hair, gold teeth and a glass eye, he charmed Christina at that first meeting, and they began an affair after he was transferred to Paris a few months later. Christina's navy-blue Mercedes was often to be seen parked outside the Sovfracht offices in Neuilly-sur-Seine.

Kausov's salary was only $235 a week, but he enjoyed fine wine and gourmet trips into the French countryside as correspondent of the Paris-based *Moscow Star*, a publication for expatriate Russians. He entertained Christina to lavish meals, after which she took him home to Avenue Foch for more intimate moments. Kausov had told Christina that he had a wife, Natasha, and an eight-year-old daughter Kayta, in Moscow, and for that reason the affair had to be kept secret.

However, first reports of a romance between the heiress and the Soviet shipping agent leaked out in February 1978 after Christina took Kausov to Rio for the carnival, and they stayed together at the Copacabana Palace. Kausov was immediately recalled to Moscow, where he was interrogated by Major-General Oleg Kalugin, head of counter-intelligence for the KGB. 'It was a genuine love affair,' Kalugin confirmed. 'He said to me, "I have never met in my life such a lady who I wanted to sleep with right away. Oh, what a woman!"' Answering suggestions that Kausov had been working for Russian intelligence all along, Kalugin said: 'Sergei was never a KGB mole.' However, Kausov's marriage to Natasha had broken up, and he had been forbidden to contact his Greek inamorata.

When Christina learned that the Kausovs had separated, she got in touch with the American oil millionaire, Armand Hammer, through an intermediary. Hammer, who had cordial relations with the Kremlin, claimed he convinced the Soviet hierarchy that Russia had everything to gain and nothing to lose if a Greek shipping heiress with access to millions were to marry a Soviet citizen. 'It was I who let them marry,' said Kalugin. 'I was the godfather. I remember going to see Andropov [the KGB chairman] and saying, "Some day she will bear him a child – maybe a boy, a Soviet citizen – and he will inherit billions of dollars from the Onassis family."' A visa was promptly granted, and Christina travelled by train from Paris to Moscow on her own.

She stayed at the Intourist Hotel on Gorky Street in a $200 a night suite overlooking Red Square. Costa Gratsos flew to Moscow to talk some sense into her, but found she would not listen to reason. She moved into the two-bedroom flat of Kausov's mother, Mariya, in the Lenin Hills, and the couple were married at 9.45 am on 1 August 1978, at the Youssopof Palace of Weddings in Moscow. But Christina did not tarry long. Three days later, she turned up in Athens alone and went to Skórpios with a dozen friends for a honeymoon without her husband. On 10 August, she flitted off to London for business talks with the directors of BP but surprised everyone by returning to Moscow four days later to face the harsh realities of life behind the Iron Curtain.

For $150 a month, Kausov had secured a seven-room apartment at Tyopoly Stan on the edge of the city near the botanical gardens. Christina flew in her friend, the interior designer Atalanta Politis, to redecorate it, taking great bundles of hard currency to the UPKD and other *berioska* stores that sold furnishing and luxury items to diplomats and privileged members of the Communist Party. However, the marriage did not even survive half of Christina's first Russian winter. In November, she told Kausov she wanted a divorce, and she spent Christmas without him at St Moritz.

Unexpectedly, the couple were back together again in August 1979 when they appeared on the beach at La Jolla, California, with Alberto Dodero, grandson of Aristotle's first mentor, his wife Marina and their two-year-old daughter. In gaucho hat, bathing trunks, shoes and white socks, Kausov strolled along the beach like a refugee from the Black Sea. He flashed his gold-toothed smile at chic Californian sunworshippers, while Christina winced in embarrassment. 'Everybody loved the Russian,' said Florence Grinda. 'But Christina used to say, "The Russian, I can't take him to dinner. He's not from a good enough family."'

Christina did not return to the Soviet Union with Kausov after the holiday. Instead, she had dinner in New York with Mick Jagger and, soon afterwards, ordered Stelio Papadimitriou to begin divorce proceedings against her husband for 'irreconcilable differences'. Christina bought the Russian two ships, a 60,000 ton tanker worth $4 million and an 18,000 ton bulk carrier worth $3.5 million, as a settlement. He was given a Soviet exit permit to develop his business interests in the West and remained devoted to Christina for the rest of her life.

Mindful of what she had missed during what she came to describe as 'my Moscow nightmare', Christina embarked on the life of a sybarite. She invited dozens of guests to Skórpios, where she held court with a fund of amusing anecdotes about her adventures. 'She told me the whole story,' said Alecko Papamarkou. 'How she had to clean the apartment, and she had no idea how to do it.'

Whenever Christina met anyone who knew Thierry Roussel, she cross-examined them about him. 'We went to Skórpios every year,' said Florence Grinda, 'and Christina used to tell me and my daughter Geraldine, "It's your fault I didn't get married to Thierry. I would have been so happy. It would have been a dream. I would have lots of children. Now everything's awful." She would tell us the same thing every year, and she would be half-laughing, half-serious.'

'She changed Skórpios completely. She had her own house, and she had a lot of little houses built for guests. The small living room became a big living room; she made everything big. She also installed a pool. She didn't change the Pink House; she just made it a guest house.'

Grumblers among the guests complained that as Christina didn't rise from bed until one o'clock in the afternoon, they were left hanging around the pool. Then launches would be laden with servants, food, wine and furniture for a visit to a nearby beach for a late picnic lunch. In the evening at the main house, there was dinner followed by dancing to music of Christina's choice, inevitably tedious disco renditions that reminded of her favourite night clubs. If she were bored, she yawned and retreated into herself as she had done as a child; a spectator on the sidelines of her own life.

Florence's perception was quite different. 'We used to have such a good time on Skórpios,' she said. 'Christina was a charming girl, a divine girl. She couldn't have been nicer. She was full of life and liked to have fun. She was a very good friend.'

The guests included Marina and Alberto Dodero and the new shipping tycoon, Sergei Kausov, who was on his way to making a $25 million fortune with the two ships Christina had given him. Two of the others were Luis Basualdo and his girlfriend Clare Lawman, a tall English blonde. 'After a couple of weeks we were bored and wanted to leave,' said Basualdo. 'So Christina offered me the job of *homme d'affaires* to stay with her.' He was paid $20,000 a month to provide company and entertainment for his employer and be her occasional lover. At times, Christina was too wound up to relax, and she had great difficulty getting to sleep. She told Basualdo she needed nine Nembutal tablets to knock her out at night. 'We used to fake it and only give her five along with four totally innocuous pills,' he said.

'Christina was always very generous with her friends,' said Florence. 'I don't just mean with giving big presents, but with her time. When we were going to Skórpios, she would send her plane to get us and then be there to greet us when the helicopter brought us across from Lefkas. But she never wanted to know when you were leaving. Normally when you go to a house, you stay a week or 10 days, but Christina just wanted you to stay as long as you chose and never wanted you to tell her when you were leaving. She hated goodbyes.'

Claiming she knew the disposition of her tanker fleet by heart, Christina took to running her empire by remote control. 'Every day I telephone to my directors in Monte Carlo,' she told guests. 'We speak of our plans, of business. To this I must devote two hours daily.' But she spent the majority of her waking hours in the pursuit of meaningless pleasure. Mostly in London but in Paris, Monte Carlo and New York as well, she earned a reputation as a manhunter. 'She had these young guys, very young – what they call in England deb's delights – and she had one a night,' said a friend.

By 1982, Christina was moving about so much that she had lost all sense of belonging to a single place. If she were at the Avenue Foch for a few weeks, the Learjet would be based at Le Bourget should she wish to fly elsewhere on a whim. 'I no longer have a fixed idea of having a home,' she said in New York. 'There is nothing ahead for me in that. Ahead isn't the poor little rich girl the magazines write about, but a woman who is suddenly sure of herself.' Then she went off to Studio 54 to dance the night away on amphetamines.

The reunion between Christina and Thierry had its origins at an upper-crust housewarming party in Paris. 'Christina met Henri Roussel at a dinner in Paris at the new home of the Countess Michèle de Ganay in 1983,' said Florence Grinda. 'He said to her, "Why don't you see Thierry again? You must get in touch with him."'

Henri, a rakish sportsman, had seen much of his fortune go the way of good living after selling his 20 per cent stake in Roussel Uclaf to his brother for cash. But he did not burden Christina with his own money problems. He knew that she and Thierry had enjoyed a fling 10 years earlier, but that Thierry had dashed her hopes of marriage by returning to Gaby Landhage. He let slip that his son remembered her with great fondness and always spoke kindly about her. Asked how Thierry was, Henri confided that his son was recovering from a broken love affair, not with Gaby but with a Danish model he had been escorting for three years. Asked where he was, Henri had replied that he was spending Christmas at the family's estate in Kenya – and, he added with a wink, he was on his own.

In fact, Thierry had incurred heavy losses in Algeria, where a joint venture he had masterminded in the wake of the disastrous El-Asnam earthquake in 1980 had gone awry. Working on a commission basis, he had set up a consortium of 15 or so companies under the collective name of Batimex to rebuild the devastated area. Work had barely begun before one of the member companies, Seal Baticlub, had found itself in financial difficulties. Formed in 1976, the company was jointly owned by several big French firms and specialized in building youth clubs. Unwilling to see the project founder, Roussel had bought Seal Baticlub for a nominal payment of one franc. He brought in his cousin François Beraut as managing director, and the builders started work funded by a FF60 million down payment from the Algerian government. But the site never got past the initial stages of preparation, and Seal Baticlub lurched towards bankruptcy for the second time in 1983. 'In Algeria, Thierry might have gone to prison because he owed millions of francs,' said Kirsten Gille, who was living with him at the time. 'I don't know if he would have gone to jail, but he was saying he could.'

According to Kirsten, Thierry had already learned how to manipulate Christina for money. She had rewarded his teenage love-making on Skórpios with a generous financial gift. 'It's very strange,' she told a friend after her return to Paris. 'He keeps phoning me and asking for money.' When friends ribbed the trainee playboy that he was behaving like a gigolo, it didn't bother him in the slightest. 'He'd made so much money that I told him he must be the greatest gigolo in the world,' said one, 'and he just giggled.'

'I was in St Moritz with my daughter that Christmas, and Christina started the story again about how she should have married Thierry,' said Florence. 'I said to Geraldine, "Please find out where Thierry is staying because I've heard enough of this story." She found out Thierry's number in Kenya, they spoke on the phone and agreed to see each other. He said, "Before I see you, go to Marbella and lose some weight." Christina was happy with that, but I told her, "He's still going to see Gaby."'

Christina took up the challenge and booked into a health clinic. Thierry sent flowers every day of her incarceration. When they were reunited in Paris in February 1984, Christina had managed to shed 22 lb and looked slimmer if not exactly svelte. Her face had regained its sensuous glow, her long-neglected teeth were polished white, and her notoriously unwashed hair shone with vitality. The couple announced their engagement on 23 February at a party at the Palace disco in Paris. Christina was so proud of her fiancé that she took him to New York and, breaking a promise that she had earlier made to friends that she would never speak to Jackie again, took him to see her father's widow.

Returning to Paris, Christina agreed to move into Thierry's new apartment in Boulevard de la Tour Maubourg rather than stay in the Onassis penthouse in Avenue Foch. This was an important move to qualify the couple for a French civil ceremony, which Roussel insisted on going through in addition to the Greek Orthodox rites of Christina's church. As a Frenchman, he wanted to be married in the

Rising Star (*above*): Thierry Roussel, 21 in this picture, has enjoyed the company of beautiful women all his life. Born into a rich family, he courted Christina Onassis in 1973, but his love for Gaby Landhage kept them apart for the next 10 years. Thierry and Christina were finally married in March 1984, after his father, the sportsman Henri Roussel (*left*), told Christina at a Paris dinner party that his son still thought fondly of her. Athina, the last Onassis, was born in January 1985.

Model Mistress
(*above*): Thierry
Roussel with Kirsten
Gille, the beautiful
Danish lover who helped
groom him, ridding
him of the Elvis
Presley-style image
complete with bushy
sideburns he sported
when they first met.

Togetherness (*right*):
Aboard his yacht, the
Tritona, Thierry enjoys
a happy occasion with
his wife Christina
(second wife), mistress
Kirsten Gille (far right)
and two friends. The
dog is honey, a Cocker
Spaniel belonging to
Kirsten who says it was
part of her agreement
with Thierry that she
should sooth and
befriend Christina.

Just Married (*above*): Thierry Roussel and Gaby Landhage seal their wedding-day bliss with an embrace in May 1990.
(Agence France Presse)

Danish Gold (*below*): Kirsten Gille shows the Nordic charms that made her a successful *Vogue* model, but her relationship with Thierry Roussel brought her sadness.

Queen of Skórpios (*above*): Christina was happiest before her marriage to Thierry Roussel when she was sharing her holiday isle with friends. She is pictured here with Florence Grinda (née Michard-Pellissier, *left*) and Florence's sister Caroline in summer 1979. In the background is Christina's third husband, the amiable Russian, Sergei Kausov, and another holiday-maker.
(Gamma)

The Last Dance
(above): Her dark hair
dyed blonde, Christina
bops the night away
with her last boyfriend,
Jorge Tchomlekdjoglou,
at a party in the
Uruguayan Embassy in
Buenos Aires, only days
before her death at a
country club in
November 1988.
(Associated Press: La Revista del
Mundo Buenos Aires)

Mother Love *(left)*:
Christina watches her
beloved Athina ride a
Shetland pony during
an outing in the French
countryside during the
last year of her life.
Athina was still only
three when her mother
passed away in
Argentina, aged just 37.
(Rex Features)

Swiss Miss *(above)*:
Athina is presented
with a lavish cake
during her third
birthday celebration in
St Moritz. In her

mother's will she
inherited the Villa
Crystal in the Swiss
skiing resort.
(Alpha)

Golden Girl (*above*): Athina chose a white bikini for a set of magazine pictures taken in Ibiza in July 1995. The Roussel family then moved on to Skórpios to enjoy the delights of the Onassis isle. (Alpha)

Double Dynasty (*right*): Athina shows that she has found lasting happiness with her father, Thierry Roussel, her step-mother, Gaby Landhage Roussel, and her half-brother and sister, Erik and Sandrine, during the Mediterranean holiday in 1995. Christina's friends say the Roussels are a tightly knit, loving family. (Alpha)

Carefree Skier (*above*): Thierry Roussel wants his daughter to enjoy her childhood, and here they have fun on the ski slopes together. But the threat of kidnapping, hijacking or a terrorist raid is omnipresent, considering the trophies of wealth associated with the Onassis legacy. (Alpha)

Hidden Asset (*below*): Athina's fortified home, tucked away behind trees and a high fence at Lussy-sur-Morges in Switzerland, is a modern, Scandinavian-style house far removed from the grandeur of her two Avenue Foch apartments in Paris. The electronic protection system here at Bois L'Essert is worthy of a James Bond movie. (EPA)

Elegant Heiress: Flanked by bodyguards and snapped by paparazzi cameras, tiny Athina Onassis Roussel is never allowed to forget that she is the richest little girl in the world. This chaotic scene was photographed at a Livanos family wedding in London in June 1994. Aged only 10, Athina had already learned how to remain poised even in a crush of burly figures and exploding flashguns.
(Marina Garnier)

eyes of French law. The couple took their civil vows on the morning of Saturday, 17 March, and after lunch repeated them in a Greek Orthodox church. For the wedding feast, Christina chose Maxim's, her father's favourite Parisian restaurant, and flew in the singer Marie Wilson and a British band called Supercharge to provide the music.

'She was very happy because she thought Thierry was going to change,' said Florence Grinda, who was one of the guests. 'I understood that, because my husband was also a playboy and when I married him I thought he was going to change, but he didn't. Yes, Henri was happy about the marriage. The Roussels had money, but if you have money, you want more. Thierry had problems with his business, and Christina helped him to get out of it.'

Christina shouted over the blare of saxophones: 'I've had 10 terrible years since my father's death, and the last two have been the worst of all. I was so unhappy that I was getting fatter and fatter. I was cracking up. But now everything is coming right.' Seated next to the bride, the Arab billionaire Adnan Khashoggi listened, nodded and beamed like a godfather. 'That,' commented Alecko Papamarkou, 'was the kind of person Christina collected.'

Adnan Khashoggi was the man who had aspired to step into Onassis's elevated shoes as the world's most famous playboy. Apart from offering the hand of friendship to Christina and Thierry, Khashoggi had enriched both the Roussel and Onassis families through property deals. Henri Roussel had sold Khashoggi his *estancia*, La Barako in the Ronda Mountains near Marbella on the Costa del Sol, for a reputed £500,000. In New York, the Arab Mr Fixit had purchased a two-storey apartment in Olympic Tower. Valued at $25 million, the duplex actually occupied the space of 16 apartments, on the 46th and 47th floors.

In southern Spain, he had stocked the 5000 rolling acres of the Roussel ranch with 1000 deer and 70,000 pheasants. Rifle-toting sentries guarded the huge iron gates, and a staff of 60 kept the place in a permanent state of readiness for their master's arrival. Like a latter-day Onassis, Khashoggi would sail into Puerto Banus in *Nabila*, the name engraved on her hull in solid gold letters a foot high. He always disembarked on to a red carpet laid at the quayside and was flown by helicopter to his villa.

'Henri sold the Marbella property to Adnan Khashoggi in the

early eighties,' said Kirsten Gille. 'I went there with Thierry before Adnan bought it. The old house was on one floor and, in Henri's time, the decor was based on hunting, but that all changed after the new place was built with a huge swimming pool and marble terraces. I've been to two of Adnan's parties there, once with Thierry. Henri didn't actually let go of all the land. He kept a very nice piece at the bottom of the estate for himself, where he built an enormous house with the help of Marceline.'

However, Thierry Roussel severed his links with the Arab after he married into the Onassis millions. 'Thierry wasn't interested in Khashoggi or anybody who was richer than him,' said Kirsten Gille. 'He isn't interested in celebrities. He isn't a social climber.' Now that he had access to serious capital, Roussel was determined to glow far more visibly than any mere Arabian Mr Fixit as soon as he had returned from his honeymoon in the West Indies.

FIFTEEN

GENEVA CONVENTION D'AMOUR: THE MISTRESS'S STORY

THIERRY ROUSSEL'S FIRST priority in assuming his marital responsibilities was to rid Christina's life not only of 'social climbers' but of some of his critics as well, particularly his aunt Florence Grinda. 'He didn't like all her friends, that's true,' she said, 'and he tried to ostracize us because we were against him at the beginning. He was furious with me because I had told Christina not to see him. I disliked the way he treated her. However, we were at the wedding, and it took maybe a year to cut us off.

'But whenever Christina was unhappy she used to come to see me. She was not an easy person all the time. Sometimes he liked her very much; sometimes he was impossible. Every time I told her what to do, she went directly to Thierry and said, "Florence says I should do so and so." So Thierry would complain to my ex-husband.

'Thierry was good looking but not as good looking as Jean-Noel. I said to Christina, "Be careful because you know the way my ex-husband treated me with girlfriends after my marriage," And Christina went straight to tell Thierry, and he said, "I will never be like Jean-Noel." I said to Christina, "I tell you things because you're my friend, but don't go back and tell Thierry because it makes a mess

---

189

each time." I couldn't win because she was crazily in love with him.'

Roussel's second task was to take a close look at his wife's expenditure. Her income was conservatively estimated at $50 million a year, yet he discovered she was spending less than $10 million on herself and her friends. Roussel told her she was living well below her means and offered some advice on ways of rectifying the situation. He persuaded her to get rid of the six-seater Learjet she had bought to replace her father's plane and order a larger one. They consulted catalogues together and settled on a Falcon 50, which would normally seat 20, but after they had the interior custom-built to their requirements it would take half that number in twice the comfort. The cost of the aircraft, including the specifications, was $15 million – three times the amount Onassis had spent on making *Christina* the most luxurious yacht afloat exactly 30 years earlier.

The Avenue Foch penthouse had provided a fashionable address for many of Christina's jet-set friends, but she acceded to her husband's demand that she drop most of them as proof that she really had changed her ways. While he had no objection to living on one of the finest *belle époque* streets in the French capital, he urged his wife to buy an apartment they could call their own. Christina obliged by buying two at No. 88 – one on the first floor and one immediately above it – and converting them into a duplex at a cost of $5 million with the help of her long-standing decorator friend, Atalanta Politis. But she had a sentimental reason of her own for the move. 'The person Christina loved most was my mother,' said Florence. 'She called her Granny. After her father's death, she used to come down in her dressing gown to see her. She would come for breakfast or drop in at any moment of the day. After she married Thierry, she took the apartment next door so that she could be even nearer. They were very close.'

Just behind the Grosvenor House Hotel in London, Christina had a house in Reeves Mews, which had belonged to her mother, and a small apartment in the same little street. She paid £830,000 in May 1984 for a four-bedroom apartment at 15 Grosvenor Square – again, one that no other lover could claim to have shared with her. Although Christina went along with Roussel's plan, she quickly slipped back into her old insecurity. Her father had told her that no man would ever love her for herself, only her money, and she started to demand more and more attention from her husband. Asked to give greater affection than he was capable of providing, Roussel overplayed his hand. When Christina sensed his insincerity, she treated him with an arrogant disdain. The arguments that would mar their early married life had already started. They split up three times during the first year of married life.

Roussel's response had been to restart his relationship with Kirsten Gille. 'He knew my dream was to go into horses,' said Kirsten. 'My original plan was to start humbly at the bottom and work for a stable owner, but Thierry was in a position to offer me much more than that.' Over a cup of coffee in Geneva – he knew Kirsten never touched alcohol, and he drank little himself – he put forward a four-point proposal, a sort of Geneva Convention d'Amour.

1 She would become his business partner in all of his equine activities.
2 She would meet, befriend and soothe Christina in the manner she had previously used to sort out troublesome people for him.
3 They would resume their sexual relationship.
4 She would not have any lovers apart from him.

Kirsten entered into the spirit of the concordat, and the couple began to buy horses, which Kirsten helped to train and then rode in show-jumping meetings on the tough European circuit. Neither did the other three clauses provide any problems for the Danish model. 'After I met Christina, she respected me a lot,' said Kirsten. 'She knew I had absolutely no interest in her money. I couldn't care less. I've never been interested in money. I'm interested in a good life and living well and doing what I like to do as long as my animals are happy and well treated. Thierry would invite me to stay at Boislande for a few days with Christina, but we did nothing. I respected her, and it never, never happened with Christina around. Christina never knew that side. I wouldn't have liked that.'

One thing that surprised Kirsten about Christina was her attitude towards her family. 'We talked about her father because I was sure she had adored him, but she didn't. The Greeks are very close in the family, but they are very tough with one another, very hard, and she was quite tough. She felt like an ugly duckling, and her mother had made her feel like that. Those were her words, not what I've read. I grew to like Christina, and I scolded Thierry about his behaviour towards her.'

However, although clause 4 prevented Kirsten from liaisons with the opposite sex, there was no similar prohibition on her partner. If his arrangements with Christina, Gaby and Kirsten weren't complicated enough, they became infinitely more so with the arrival of Teresa Prater, the six-foot tall, 21-year-old blonde from California. 'Thierry doesn't like women with a strong character, and I was too strong for him,' said Kirsten. 'We were competing all the time, and he doesn't like that – he likes women to be under him. Christina had rented a house on the bay at Cap Ferrat, and they had this big boat, which Thierry filled with his male friends. It was supposed to be men-only, but one day they brought along a group of stunning girls, models, who included this American, Teresa Prater.'

The yacht was called *Hansa*, which Christina had chartered from the billionaire art collector Baron Heini von Thyssen for around £20,000 a week. After cruising the Mediterranean with Thierry and 10 friends, they had moored at Cap Ferrat, Christina ever mindful of her gynaecologist's warning that she should take things easy. Married to a pregnant Greek wife, devoted to a soon-to-be-pregnant Swedish mistress and attached to a critical Danish lover, Roussel suddenly decided he was partial to some Beverly Hills chic. 'One of the girls on board was Estelle Halliday, who was to marry David Halliday, the son of singer Johnny Halliday,' said Kirsten. 'Estelle was a very pretty girl, but he didn't even look at her. He was only interested in Teresa. She was taller than me, and I'm 5ft 11in, but blonde like all the girls Thierry liked. Yes, it all started there for this long, tall girl; very, very American, but with a bit of a long, horsy face. He took up with her and put her in a Paris apartment and, to keep her to himself, he told her she was too tall to be a model. That was the big affair; it went on for some years. What attracted him to her was that sexually he was crazy about her. She had a big bust and that was very important to him. For her, it was that he was good looking, rich, and he had certain charms.'

'He had girlfriends, not just Gaby,' Florence confirmed. 'There was even a boatful of girls that summer. He was on a yacht with a lot of models.'

Roussel far preferred this Riviera ambience to the heat, dust and boredom of Skórpios. He explained to Christina that he was not comfortable there because the Greeks seemed to have a problem in recognizing him as the new boss. 'He wanted to be the main person, but all the staff loved Christina,' said Florence. 'It never happened with the Russian; the Russian was fantastic. He was very low key, and he accepted the fact that it was Christina's island, but Thierry always wanted to put Christina down and be the master. We used to laugh a lot and go for picnics; it was really wonderful. When Thierry came along it was very heavy because all his family and friends were there. He wanted to make it his place.'

It was on Skórpios during this first summer that Christina felt unwell. For once, her malaise could not be put down to pill-popping for under Roussel's commendable direction she had managed to wean herself off amphetamines in the weeks prior to their marriage and all but dispense with sleeping pills as well. She was flown back to Switzerland in September, where she moved into a Geneva hotel suite to be near her doctors for the remainder of her pregnancy.

With his wife bedridden, Roussel flew Gaby Landhage from Sweden to Paris, moved her into his old apartment and made good his promise, made at the time of his marriage to Christina, that 'nothing has changed' by becoming a regular visitor. During her husband's frequent absences, Christina had to content herself with visits from relatives and the few friends she was still permitted to see. She summoned a representative of Christian Dior to create a set of designer baby clothes at a cost of $25,000 and took comfort in the photographs of work-in-progress at Boislande. The faithful Eleni never left her side. 'She was like a daughter to me,' the maid told us.

With an audacity that his Parisian cronies found awesome, Roussel managed to keep four women in his life at the same time. The logistics would have defeated a less dedicated aspirant: using a jet plane and a fleet of fast cars, he visited Gaby at Malmö, Paris or Geneva; Teresa in Paris; Christina in Gingins, Paris or St Moritz; and Kirsten in Paris, Geneva or Monte Carlo. As Paris was the common denominator, it was theoretically possible for him to have four women at different addresses in the French capital at the same time – a performance worthy of the *Guinness Book of Records*.

However, there was a sudden dramatic development. Seven months after he married Christina and four months after she became aware she was carrying his child, Roussel was informed by Gaby that she was also pregnant. Conscious of his new celebrity status and fearful of disclosure in the press, the father-to-be suggested that Gaby return quietly to Sweden for her term. He promised he would visit her in Malmö as frequently as he could, a pledge made all the easier by having Christina's jet to chauffeur him around Europe.

This arrangement progressed remarkably smoothly until Christina took Athina home to Boislande after posing with the baby for her first picture session in Paris in April 1985. The Onassis–Roussel alliance started to show signs of strain when Roussel made it clear that he had fulfilled his duties to Christina and now needed to concentrate on his business activities.

Roussel was often abroad working on one improbable venture after another, sometimes taking one of his mistresses with him. 'He gets all these most incredible ideas,' said Kirsten Gille. 'I mean, we all have ideas about how we can make money, but he really wants to do it, and he goes for it. One of his projects in 1985 was to launch a timber company in Africa. He told me all about it and even got me an identity card that named me as his wife so I could go there with him. I never made the trip, but Teresa went with him. He rented a forest in Equatorial Guinea, West Africa, and started chopping down trees to sell the wood. Christina financed all that – and he lost everything, although he got on very well with the country's president. As a surprise, he had Christina send over her helicopter to take the president sightseeing. It cost $150,000 to get it there, fly it around and take it back. Thierry got quite sick over there when he caught a virus from drinking dirty water. He was really bad, really sick, and Christina went over and saved him.'

More often than not, Christina was left at home with the baby and, distressed by her husband's frequent absences, she talked to her lawyers about a separation. Word of the rift passed swiftly around Christina's circle of former friends, some of whom were openly gleeful that their judgment about Thierry had been proved right.

Incensed by these rumours, Roussel invited *Paris-Match* to send a writer and a photographer to Gingins. But if it had been his intention to show that husband, wife and daughter were one loving family unit, then the exercise could not have backfired more spectacularly. On the second day of their stay in Switzerland, the *Paris-Match* team were telephoned at their hotel by Roussel, who told them not to return to take the promised pictures of Athina: he was divorcing the baby's mother. The issue of *Paris-Match* that hit the Champs-Elysées a few days later published an article showing just how horrendous it was to live with a woman like Christina Onassis. Without quoting Roussel directly, it specified the bizarre hours his wife kept and described her erratic moods and her wilful impulses – all the things he had complained about during their frequent rows.

However, the real cause of Thierry's unrest was that Gaby's child was due to be born the following month in Malmö, and he needed freedom of movement. 'Christina and I talked about it afterwards, and she was very upset,' said Kirsten Gille. 'Thierry had said he wanted to leave her, and she couldn't understand why. The reason was that he knew Gaby was pregnant, and he was dead scared Christina would find out. Instead, Christina said, "I'll do anything you want. I love you, and I don't want to get divorced." So he more or less stayed.'

The baby was a son, whom Gaby and Thierry named Erik Christopher François. His birth gave the mistress a measure of security she had never had before, and it also restored something precious to Roussel. Although the relationship was clandestine and his son had been born out of wedlock, the very fact that he had produced an heir without any help from the Onassis millions had reinforced his manhood.

SIXTEEN

THE MATERNAL TRIANGLE

JUST FOUR WEEKS after Erik's birth, Thierry was on Skórpios for Athina's christening in the living room of the Onassis villa in front of 60 friends and relatives. 'Athina cried a bit during the ceremony,' said the priest, Father Apostolos, 'and Christina and her husband were obviously moved by the whole thing.' The baby had been immersed in a silver font specially made for the occasion, he said, and had been christened by Christina's uncle, George Livanos.

Christina had tried valiantly to keep up appearances during the holiday, not a role to which she was well suited. Guests swam in the pool, took long lunches in a picnic atmosphere on the beach and wandered through the exotic gardens that Aristotle had created with the help of Churchill's daughter, Lady Sarah. Christina posed happily for informal pictures with Thierry, which showed the young couple in the company of their six-month-old daughter. But behind his easy-going smile, Thierry was fearful that the helicopter that dropped out of the sky each morning to deliver the latest newspapers would also bring news from Sweden about his secret double life.

He was relieved there was a major diversion to occupy his time on the island: the launching of his new yacht, *Athina R*, the largest fibreglass boat in the world. Styled along military lines and with a cruising speed of 30 knots, Roussel planned to set up a production line for the craft at the Italian yard, Azimut. As she had done many times before with her father's tankers in massive shipyards, Christina christened a prototype for the yacht with the traditional bottle of champagne.

'It's a fair judgment to say that Thierry was obsessed with money,' said Florence Grinda. 'They were fighting all the time, and it always seemed to be over money. I don't know why, but he wanted to have his own aeroplane. He wanted to be like Onassis himself, yet in a way he was scared of being married to Christina Onassis. But you don't marry one of the wealthiest women in the world without knowing what you're getting into. She didn't make him feel she was the boss; she was very nice to him, although she had a difficult character sometimes.'

Soon after Christina and Roussel had returned to Boislande, he realized the hopelessness of his position and confessed to reporters that his marital differences were insoluble. Asked for reasons, Roussel had blamed everything from Skórpios and the legend of his dead father-in-law to the security systems that invaded his privacy in every part of the Swiss home that was supposed to be his as well as his wife's. However, the main thrust of his argument seemed to be that Christina should be content with the child he had given her and allow him to lead his life as he pleased. In fact, he was indirectly preparing her for the news that was bound to emanate from Malmö, where Gaby's mother, Maj-Lis, was proudly showing off her grandson.

Christina was still in the dark about Gaby's baby, but Roussel knew he was living on borrowed time when he heard that word of his infidelity was high on the agenda during the summer season in Monaco. It was also the moment Kirsten Gille's attitude towards him began to change.

Kirsten said: 'I was at Jimmy's in Monte Carlo one night when a girlfriend said to me, "Do you know there's been a baby born in Sweden?" And straight away I thought, Eh, voilà! I had always thought that Gaby was going to get him somehow. So I called up Thierry and said, "What have you done? You've had a baby with Gaby." He said, "No, no – never." And I said, "Don't lie to me," but he insisted it wasn't true. Knowing Thierry, I could even hear in his voice that it was true. Then I called up his uncle, Jean-Noel Grinda.

I said, "Jean-Noel, the biggest mistake of Thierry's life is to lie to me because I like Christina." When you are married, you stay with whoever you're married to – you don't have kids with someone else unless you get separated and then go off and do it. I wasn't going to tell Christina because I wouldn't hurt her, but I was really, really furious. I said to Thierry, "If you don't tell the truth, I'm going to scream it around town." So Thierry owned up.'

Slowly, it dawned on Christina that no matter how much money she lavished upon her husband, it was never enough to bring him permanently to her side. To provide company for herself as much as her daughter, she invited local couples with young children to visit the Boislande estate. While Athina and her new friends played with the animals in the zoo, Christina hosted tea parties for their parents in the landscaped gardens. The people of Gingins were Vaudois whose first language was French, which Christina spoke fluently. Like their Roman and Burgundian forebears, they had a warm, humorous style, which set them apart from their more austere Swiss–German countrymen. They encouraged Christina to join in community events instead of languishing in her luxury home. She responded to their kindness by donating 20,000 Swiss francs to furnish and equip a new kindergarten. But the loneliness had set in and, with it, came the return of her old depression. 'She always looked very sad,' said the Mayor of Gingins, Marianne Fritsch, who often saw Christina walking along her regular route from Boislande to the village. 'She always had her daughter and a bodyguard with her but, no, I never once saw her with her husband.'

Roussel was spending a great deal of time extricating himself from the financial mire into which he had sunk in the aftermath of the Algerian earthquake. On 10 April 1986, the Public Prosecutor's Department in the Paris suburb of Nanterre had begun an investigation into the bankruptcy of Seal Baticlub, a subsidiary of his Paris-based Gradient Group. On 29 May 1984 – 10 weeks after he had married Christina – Seal Baticlub had been put into liquidation and was subsequently declared bankrupt on 17 December 1985, with liabilities of FF100 million. Reporting the case in April 1986, Agence France Presse quoted 'judicial sources' as saying that 'suspect operations' had been uncovered by financial investigators, including the transfer of seven million French francs into an account at the Union Bank of Switzerland (UBS) via a Panamanian-registered company called Niblan Holdings.

Although Roussel argued that he was personally unconnected with the collapse of the project, the Nanterre court was 'otherwise convinced and has decided to make him pay up part of it'. On 8 January 1987, Roussel was charged with 'bankruptcy caused by misappropriation of assets, misuse of company property and falsification of business entries'. Five days later, he declared: 'I have been drawn to make this statement after a number of articles which have thrown doubt upon my person. Seal Baticlub, in which I have invested and lost FF30 million, never paid me any commission in a foreign bank account.' A civil case against Roussel, who had given his address to the court as St Moritz, was dropped after he arrived at an out-of-court settlement with the aggrieved parties, including several French colonial *pieds noirs* who had acted as middlemen to broker the original construction deals. The official inquiry ceased in August 1988 when it was decided there was nothing further to be investigated, and the charges were dropped.

Christina sometimes took Athina to Paris in the hope of seeing more of her absentee husband. She was staying at 88 Avenue Foch in the summer of 1986 when her uncle, George Livanos, asked if he might visit her on a matter of some delicacy. As gently as he could, he told his niece not only about the birth of Erik almost a year earlier but also how deeply Thierry was involved with Gaby Landhage. The secret was finally out.

'When she found out about Erik, she was furious, and she went crazy,' confirmed Kirsten Gille. Christina was still in a state of shock when 'Mr Christina Onassis II', her Greek ex-husband Alexander Andreadis, telephoned to discuss the matter. Alexander was living in London with his third wife, the model Gemma Grace, and working as joint chief executive of the Commercial Bank of London. 'He heard about the baby at a dinner party where somebody goofed,' said Kirsten. 'He spoke to Christina all the time – every day – and he was surprised that she hadn't known about Erik until her uncle told her.'

But just as suddenly as Christina's anger had surfaced, it vanished. Roussel had admitted to his infidelity in a manner of a man who had committed an unavoidable act while serving the interests of his country. He told his wife he had been involved with Gaby for 13 years at the time of their wedding and, if anything, she had stolen him from her. He was quite prepared to sacrifice his marriage if Christina continued to be unreasonable. 'So Christina tried it the other way,' said Kirsten. 'She said, "I've got to be really nice to Gaby and her child and try to work it out." She started to send her plane to Sweden with gifts for Erik.' Gaby received the gifts graciously and was even more pleased when Christina consented to allow Thierry to use the Falcon 50 on flying visits to Malmö. Gaby's family had accepted her status as a single parent without demur.

'There is no stigma attached to being an unwed mother in Sweden,' said her Scandinavian friend. 'If Thierry hadn't been willing to support her and the child, the state would have taken care of them. The Swedish attitude is that having a baby out of wedlock isn't immoral, just a natural consequence of what we used to call "free love".'

In December, Thierry was missing from St Moritz, where Christina spent the Christmas festivities with Athina and the Livanos family. As there was no longer any need to make a secret of his second family in Sweden, he spent some time in Marbella before flying to both Malmö and St Moritz. 'There is no shame in admitting that one loves two women,' he explained to reporters. 'Christina is the fire, and Gaby is the calm. I love them both passionately.' He saw no advantage in enlightening reporters about the existence of his other two mistresses.

Virtually with Christina's blessing, Gaby was now free to accompany Thierry on his business trips abroad. While Christina remained at home in Gingins, they enjoyed a visit to Dallas, Texas. 'He suddenly had the idea he wanted to see oil spurting out of the ground,' said Kirsten Gille. 'I warned Christina several times that Gaby was going to have another child because one wasn't enough. I said, "Be very careful, Christina. She's going to do a second one – be sure of that." But she said, "No, no, no, she can't have any more children." One baby was acceptable on the grounds that it might be a mistake, but two would be evidence that he was raising a second family, and that wasn't in the agreement at all. No one thought it could possibly happen except me. Christina said that Gaby was being really nice to her, and that was when she sent the plane to take Thierry to Sweden because he wanted to spend seven days a month there. Which he did, but he was so bored he used to call everybody up. There was nothing to do over there, and he was going crazy. He called me a few times but not very much.

'We had a strange relationship. In some ways, it was like brother and sister, but sexually it was like lovers. Mentally, we had a very close rapport. I'd understand him very quickly, and I'd say I was not far from being the one woman who could make him laugh. I remember when he was in a foul mood he would call me to come, and in a few minutes I could put him in a good mood.

'When Thierry suddenly invited me to have lunch with him in Geneva in August 1987, I looked at him, and I knew what had happened before he had said a word. 'I said, "Gaby's had another baby." And he said, "Yes, three months ago – a girl. We've called her Sandrine." I was so shocked I went white. "What about Christina? Does she know?" "No," he replied. "I'm just on my way to tell her."'

An hour later, Roussel was driving past the bobbing yachts and prim mansions on the Geneva promenade. Knowing with certainty that his life was about to change, he turned on to Route Nationale 1 and headed east in the direction of Gingins. Ten minutes later, he passed the Hôtel de la Croix Blanche on the short, final stretch of his journey to Boislande. As he paused outside the gates, he knew that his time of walking in the shadow of his famous father-in-law was about to draw to an end. When he informed Christina that Gaby had given birth to a daughter, there were tears and tantrums. 'It was a big shock when she heard about the second child,' said Florence Grinda. 'I knew about it, but I hadn't told her, and she was furious with me for that. "I'm going to leave him," she said. They were fighting and getting back together because the thing she now wanted most was another child, and she did really love him. She was even trying to make him jealous – you know, with another man or trying to slim to be glamorous. She was in love with him, that I can't ever say to the contrary.' Christina exclaimed: 'I'm like an Arab woman, sharing my husband with a concubine.'

'Christina didn't throw Thierry out – he left,' said a close friend. 'I saw her quite a bit, and we talked a lot about it. She was very upset. He had hurt her very badly with all his games.' In September 1987, Christina secretly divorced Thierry. To avoid publicity, she filed the suit in the mountain village of Celerina near St Moritz.

As a divorced man, Roussel was able to take stock of the ungainly situation into which his two families had placed him. He had won his freedom and, had he wished, could have married Gaby at any time. Instead, he took a completely different tack. On visits to Malmö and Gingins, he suggested in the manner of a peacemaker that it was time for Christina and Gaby to meet to see if a compromise could be worked out to the benefit of all parties. Christina had been instantly converted to the idea. Gaby had assumed the proportions of a *femme fatale* in her imagination, yet reports from friends who had met her in the past suggested she was nothing of the sort. Christine was vastly intrigued by this home-making paragon who had such a sure and capable hold over the man they both loved. Gaby was less certain that such a meeting would serve any useful purpose. Above all, she was wary about facing Christina's fabled wrath. However, she decided to try out the bizarre idea if only to prove that Thierry's instincts had been incorrect. Having made the suggestion, she knew he wouldn't be satisfied until it had been given a chance.

Christina immediately seized a home-ground advantage by offering to throw a dinner party for 12 of her friends in a Geneva restaurant. Thierry and Gaby would both be invited, but they should each arrive separately. The other guests would be warned in advance of what was taking place and told to behave as normally as they usually did. Reports about that night from the inner circle later claimed that this was exactly what happened. Christina had gone out of her way to make Gaby feel welcome in the midst of a group of people who were known to her only by reputation. Gaby had felt disoriented and ill at ease, but she had taken her seat at the table with only one male guest separating her from her hostess. She realized that, in a sense, she was auditioning for a role that would set the course of her life.

As the two women started to chat, Roussel was said to have adopted the demeanour of a man who had nothing more pressing on his mind than which wine to order with his food. As with Kirsten Gille, Christina found she had uncovered a rich seam of fresh material about her ex-husband. She discovered that far from being competitors, she and Gaby actually complemented each other in a strange way. Thierry had been right and, much to his understandable relief, a friendship was struck up between them.

Having met Gaby, Christina had wholeheartedly accepted Thierry's line that, as the Swedish woman had had first claim to his love, *she* was the interloper, the home-breaker. Therefore, she was prepared to settle for the secondary role of being 'the other woman' in his life. For Roussel, the risk element in this arrangement was incredibly high. Christina or Gaby had only to pick up the phone to exchange gossip about him. But it was a risk he was willing to take. Gaby could offer him stability, Christina could help his businesses, and Kirsten and Teresa could provide the erotic stimulation he needed.

Christina was delighted when Thierry showed no signs of straying from his commitment. He rang her frequently from Paris and saw her and Athina regularly whenever he visited Switzerland. He rented a house for Gaby, Erik and Sandrine not far from Gingins, which enabled him to commute between his two families with as little disruption as possible. Whether he was present or not, Gaby took her children to visit Christina and Athina at Boislande. Meanwhile, Christina continued to support Thierry's business ventures. Estimates of the total amount he eventually received from her vary from between $50 million and $73 million. However, her family put the figure somewhere in between the two. 'Her grandmother, Mrs Livanos, told me that Roussel did very well out of making love to Christina,' said Alecko Papamarkou. 'He managed to get several million bucks out of her all told.' Living in nearby Lausanne, Arietta Livanos was much closer to Christina than any of her other Greek relatives and, therefore, in a better position to know. 'My poor Christina can never separate her money from her emotions,' Arietta told a friend.

One of the strangest aspects of Thierry's double life had been the attitude of Athina's other grandmother, Francine Roussel. 'Francine was very domineering, and she had done very strange things to me, very weird, when I was with Thierry,' said Kirsten Gille. 'I warned Christina many times to be careful, but she gave her a car as a present and was really nice to her. What Francine did was to manipulate the whole thing between Thierry, Christina and Gaby. She thought it was very amusing that Thierry had had a child with Gaby without Christina's knowledge. So she was pushing that side of Thierry's life and being really nice to Gaby, while playing the mother-in-law role in front of Christina but being a bitch behind her back. What really shocked me was that after Sandrine was born, she held the baby's baptism in her country house.'

When Christina tired of her solitary life at Boislande, she flew to Le Bourget in the Falcon 50 and moved into Avenue Foch for a change of scenery. Most of the staff from Boislande followed overland in a fleet of Mercedes. Christina, Athina, her nanny Monique and one of the bodyguards, a genial-looking giant called Archie, occupied the duplex, while the rest of the entourage, including Eleni and Jorge, went up to the penthouse.

One of the main purposes of these trips was for Christina to unleash herself upon the department stores in the grand boulevards and the fashion shops on the Rue du Faubourg-St-Honoré. For emergencies like this, she kept $100,000 cash in a safe at Avenue Foch, and her Paris cheque account never fell below $1 million for more than 24 hours. As soon as it dropped below that figure, it was automatically topped up from the Olympic Maritime office in Monte Carlo. A further $50,000 cash was delivered by special courier once a week to cover staff wages and the upkeep of the two households.

'The duplex was very modern, all white, and completely different from the penthouse, which was redone by Atalanta Politis,' said Florence. 'The furniture was mainly Ari's because Christina did not buy a lot of things. Neither she nor her father were like Niarchos, who bought a lot of works of art. Onassis bought one Monet, *Water Lilies*, but he didn't have a lot of other treasures.'

Once Christina had satisfied her immediate craving for shopping, she rang Paris-based friends to announce that she was 'at home'. Her visitors included Sergei Kausov, who always remembered her birthday with the gift of a new Mercedes-Benz. 'She even went back to Kausov at one point after her break-up with Thierry,' said Florence. 'I always thought the Russian was perfect for her.'

Christina entertained in the penthouse, where callers were met at the door by Philippe, the liveried butler, and handed flutes of Dom Perignon. As they nibbled pâté de foie gras and caviar, Christina dipped into boxes of her favourite Lindt or Godiva chocolates. Naturally enough, the centre of attention was Athina, dressed like a Hollywood child prodigy from the fifties in one of the 100 Chanel or Baby Dior dresses that were kept in her wardrobe. Christina often changed her daughter's clothes four times a day for different sets of guests. One visitor claimed that Athina had driven a miniature motor car around the apartment unchecked until she finally crashed into the dining-room table. 'Pieces of gold-encrusted china and crystal glass fell to the floor,' he said, 'but Christina just looked at her adoringly.'

Athina's bedroom on the upper floor of the duplex was connected by an intercom system to the adjoining bedrooms of Monique and Archie in case she stirred in the night. Apart from the little electric car, Athina's favourite plaything was a cheap doll called Chiffon and, at another time, it was a rag-tag-and-bobtail bunny called Molly. For breakfast, Athina had two glasses of orange juice, some flavoured yoghurt and a boiled egg. The servants, Michel and Vionisis, always dressed in black jacket and tie to serve the food from silver trays. Lunch, prepared by Marcel the chef, was fish from Prunier or meat from a butcher on the Rue Marboeuf. 'There were a lot of servants, that's for sure,' said Florence.

For outings, Athina climbed into the navy-blue Mercedes next to her mother to be driven down the street to the Bois de Boulogne. Monique and two bodyguards, Archie and another SAS-trained man called Peter, followed closely behind in a second car. The group boarded a little ferryboat and chugged across the lake to the Châlet des Iles, a restaurant situated on an island. In this idyllic setting, Athina chased red-crested roosters and bantam hens, which strutted among potted plants at the fringes of the open-sided restaurant. After lunch, Archie, an avuncular figure with a bald head and a walrus moustache, took the little girl to see the peacocks in the island's gardens or sailed a model boat for her in the lake.

For longer excursions, Christina took Athina to a country estate she had rented at Fontainebleau, where there was a small menagerie similar to the one at Boislande but including fluffy white rabbits. As soon as Athina missed her playmates Erik and Sandrine, Christina would ring Gaby, and the children would be reunited under the same roof, where they sat quietly watching Mickey Mouse videos. There were squeals of delight whenever their father put aside his business and called to see them. Visitors who had heard only second-hand reports about the amazing maternal triangle of Christina, Gaby and the man they both loved went away impressed by what they had seen. Secretly, they wondered just how long it would last.

SEVENTEEN

LAST CHANCE OF LOVE AT VILLA TRIANON

THE STATUS SYMBOL that aroused envy among Thierry Roussel's Riviera rivals was his three-masted schooner *Tritona*. A truly classic yacht riding at anchor off the Hôtel du Cap or tethered to the seawall at Cannes with a view of the Croisette was much more prestigious than any of the marine plastic and curved glass leviathans favoured by Arab princes and arms dealers. Roussel was justifiably proud of *Tritona*.

Originally built by the Italian designer Cantieri Codecosa in Viareggio, the yacht had been refitted and modernized in 1986. At 118-ft long, she might be only one-third of the length of Onassis's now discarded *Christina*, but she had more style and an impressive range. Two 450-hp General Motors engines could drive her for a distance of 2000 miles at a cruising speed of 10 knots. There was luxurious accommodation for Thierry, Christina, Athina, her nanny Monique, and eight guests as well as self-contained quarters for a crew of 13, including the bodyguards.

When Roussel and his ex-wife entertained, as many as 100 people could come aboard for a party on *Tritona*'s aft main deck. An air-conditioned saloon, furnished with soft brown leather sofas, two precious brier-wood tables and a refrigerated bar, opened out through glass doors on to an outdoor room with built-in tables and settees for lounging and dining. On the upper deck, Christina and her friends could sunbathe on loungers in an area open to the sky. The laundry could handle anything from Athina's swimsuit to a soiled dinner jacket, and the kitchen was equipped to provide meals of cordon-bleu standard. An unusual feature was the original wine cellar, which held more than 200 vintages.

The master bedroom, La Suite, was a 30-foot wide stateroom with separate dressing room. The other cabins all had colour television, high-fidelity stereo radio and a video-cassette recorder. On the bridge a satellite system allowed Roussel worldwide telephone and telex communication with his business interests.

Christina badly needed a holiday. She had endured a particularly onerous regime at the Buschinger Clinic in Marbella during the spring of 1988, and she was keen to show off her new figure to Roussel in the hope that it would tempt him into making love to her again. She desperately wanted to have another child by him – a brother or sister for Athina; she wasn't fussy about the gender, just the father. Having two children with Roussel would place her on equal terms with Gaby Landhage and show that, although she and Roussel were divorced in the eyes of the world, they still had eyes for each other. 'Thierry had been trying to get her to slow down and accept the situation between them, but she was just as determined to get him back,' said Kirsten Gille. 'On the boat she looked really healthy and I thought, My God, she's done it. I can still see her laughing with delight at herself.'

However, a healthy and energetic Christina presented Roussel with a problem. He was engaged in sexual relationships with three women – Kirsten Gille, his American sweetheart Teresa Prater and Gaby Landhage – and more or less had his hands full. Unaware of the extent of his commitments elsewhere, Christina viewed this reluctance to make love as a temporary setback and made alternative arrangements. In exchange for a $165,000 Ferrari, she persuaded him to set up a sperm bank from which she would make withdrawals at her most fertile time of the month and, by mechanical means, have his spermatozoa injected into her.

To take her mind off love-making, Christina sought other diversions with friends who had gathered on the yacht. Although the saloon was liberally stocked with parlour games such as Scrabble and

Trivial Pursuit, a comprehensive video library and a hi-fi system to play her favourite tapes in stereo, Christina was soon bored and turned her attention to the vast collection of glossy magazines and tabloid newspapers that were delivered to her in great bundles every day.

'She loved scandal and gossip so much that I said to her, "Why don't you start your own magazine?"' said Kirsten Gille. 'She suddenly had a brainwave. "Let's start a radio gossip show right now," she said. "We'll put on the radio and do the latest gossip show right now," she said. "You mean like the theatre, saying things we know about other people?" And she said that was exactly what she had in mind.'

The yacht's stereo radio was switched through to the aft-deck and, against a background of rock music, the guests took turns at providing shocking snippets about people whom Christina either knew personally or had read about.

'Every time it came to Christina's turn, it got very strange,' said Kirsten. 'She would say, "Dear Mummy, I've lost 50 pounds, and Thierry says I look terrific," or "Dear Daddy, You'll never guess who Jackie's seeing." It took several minutes to sink in that she was composing make-believe letters to her parents, even though they had both been dead for years. It made me realize she wanted their love so much that she was keeping them alive in her head.'

The *Tritona* was moored that summer off the tip of St Jean Cap Ferrat where Christina had rented a villa, Le Trianon, named after the Petit Trianon palace at Versailles, in which Marie-Antoinette had entertained her most intimate circle. She had also taken a smaller house next door for Gaby, who was due to arrive on 15 August with Erik and Sandrine. In the interval, Christina and Thierry were geographically, if not sexually, closer than they had been in several months.

This proximity had a profound effect on Christina's thinking. Watching Athina and Thierry playing happily together, she decided that this was the way things were meant to be. The absent Gaby and her children quickly became an irrelevance, an unfortunate error that had occurred because she had lost control of events. She decided that everything harmful that had ever passed between her and Thierry was due to the damaging effect her wealth and background invariably exacted upon her love affairs with men, whether she was married to them or not.

The pattern was unmissable. She fell in love with a man, her love was reciprocated – and then arguments over money sabotaged the dream. She now saw that she had robbed her husband of his pride and his dignity. If she changed her will to bind Thierry to her little girl legally, she would have proved to him that he had her trust. His pride would be restored, and he would start to view her not just as a bountiful source of mere money but also as his partner in an on-going enterprise: the rearing of their daughter. Acceptance of these fatherly duties would be the first step in a process of winning him back completely.

When Christina began to articulate this aberration, her friends stopped short of telling her otherwise. Lulled by fine weather and even finer wine, the house guests had slipped into an easy camaraderie, which no one wished to spoil with harsh realities. One argument after another had marred the earlier part of the year for Christina and Roussel, and the respite in hostilities was a welcome relief. Christina started to talk about remarriage and, when her friends picked up on the theme, she did nothing to discourage it. As proof that the relationship between her and Thierry had changed for the better, she told them about her efforts to have another baby. She saw nothing humiliating in describing in clinical detail her visits to the sperm bank. 'It proves that he really wants me,' she told friends. 'Wait till I tell Gaby I'm pregnant!'

By the beginning of August, Christina had convinced herself that she and Roussel were a couple again in every sense of the term. If the catalyst had been the obvious happiness she saw in her daughter's face whenever she was with her father, the deciding factor was a growing belief that this was meant to be. All Christina had to do was take charge of events and turn these few halcyon days into a lasting reality. When she decided to hold a lavish soirée for the friends who had supported her with varying degrees of loyalty since her divorce, what she really had in mind was not so much a party as a pre-nuptial feast. After establishing the reunion as fact, the wedding would follow naturally at a time to be announced. 'It's perfectly all right for divorced couples to remarry,' she told friends. 'My father would have remarried my mother if things had been different.'

Roussel immediately saw the danger in what was happening, but he seemed powerless to resist his headstrong ex-wife. Instead of objecting, he started to enter into the spirit of things. Invitations were dispatched to 250 people, many of whom were to be flown at

Christina's expense to Nice from London, Paris, Athens, New York and Los Angeles. It was no accident that the event was timed for the night of 14 August, the evening before Gaby's arrival. The last thing Christina wanted was for Gaby to turn up and spoil her fantasy. Mementoes of the occasion, such as paper napkins and matchbooks, were stamped by the hundred with the legend CHRISTINA & THIERRY. The society photographer Gérard Delorme was summoned from his studio on the Avenue Victor-Hugo to take photographs, which would be mounted in special souvenir albums to be given to guests after the event as proof that it had not all been a grotesque joke: Christina and Thierry really were together again.

On a matchless Riviera evening, uniformed retainers led the excited new arrivals through the mansion to a rear terrace, where they were greeted by Christina, Thierry and Athina. They made an attractive threesome. Christina's hair, streaked blonde, flowed down to her shoulders, and she inclined her head towards her ex-husband at every opportunity. She looked stunning in a short-sleeved white dress embroidered with blue and lilac ribbon. Around her neck was her $2 million emerald pendant, and she clutched a tumbler of her favourite Diet Coke. Towering over his ex-wife, Roussel was at his most handsome; his curly hair was swept back almost to the collar of his black tuxedo, and his smile gave no indication that he would rather be somewhere else. Athina was dressed in white and, apart from a ribbon in her hair, she was a miniature version of her mother. She had been allowed to stay up in order to feel a part of the proceedings.

As an orchestra played, the assembly walked down stone steps to a huge, flower-decked marquee, which had been set up under palm trees on the lawn with a commanding sea view. At the entrance, a sumptuous spread had been laid out on two long, white-clothed trestle tables edged in lilac ribbon to match Christina's dress. The chefs themselves were on duty to crack open hundreds of boiled lobsters, carve great haunches of roast beef and dole out mounds of seafood-laden pasta. Waiters in white tuxedos and black trousers dispensed the vintage wines that Christina had personally chosen. The guests sat in groups of 10 at round tables, which fanned out across a covered, Astro-turf surface the size of a playing field. Lighting the whole scene with a decadent Roman splendour were flaming torches in clusters of three, and on each table five lilac candles burned from a floral centrepiece of white lilies. It was the Côte d'Azur's party of the season, and it cost Christina $500,000.

After dinner, the guests rose to dance, always the high point of the evening for Christina, but all the more so tonight because she was newly slim and with the man she loved. As Christina and Thierry twirled around the floor, some people came to believe what they were seeing: the couple really were reunited. But others knew exactly what lay behind the masquerade and felt sorrow for their deluded friend. 'Christina was so happy that evening,' said Kirsten Gille, one of the guests. 'It was obvious from the way she behaved that she was trying to get him back. If he so much as put his hand on hers, she would take this as confirmation that he was back with her. She read something positive into everything he did; if he smiled at someone, it was because he was happy just being with her. It was touching but pathetic because I knew that Teresa was still in his life; she was always with him, although she wasn't invited to the party.'

From a third-floor window, Athina peered down at the festivities in the open-sided white tent until Monique put her to bed long before breakfast of scrambled eggs, red caviar and champagne was served at four o'clock in the morning. The orchestra stopped playing as the sun rose in the direction of Antibes, and the last of the marathon dancers crawled off the dance floor. Many of them would never see their hostess alive again. 'It was a fantastic party,' said Florence Grinda. 'It was great fun – and it was the last one before she died.'

While cleaners removed any trace of the party prior to Gaby's arrival, Christina joined Roussel for breakfast. When she reminded him that this was *their* secret from Gaby, he exploded over the crois-sants and coffee. Spelling out the true situation in language that could not possibly be misconstrued, he told her that the woman he loved was Gaby and that they were planning a life together. He had undergone the charade of the previous night for the sake of his daughter, but the game-playing would have to cease the moment Gaby and her children arrived. Christina was devastated. She had hoped Thierry would accompany her to Argentina for the 40th birthday party of Marina Dodero in October. If things had gone as she had planned, that trip would also have been their second honeymoon.

'Christina was so upset after that party,' said Kirsten Gille. 'The next day they had lunch at a bar because the boat was late in arriving.

They went on board and anchored off shore, so I swam out to join them. When I climbed on board, I could tell that things were tense. Thierry took me to one side and told me they had had a very big row, and he was about to leave. When he left the boat, Christina broke down and cried in my arms. She said, "Why does he treat Gaby like a princess and me like a whore?"'

After Gaby's arrival, the situation deteriorated even further, and Christina returned with Athina to Boislande in a state of deep depression. Her eating binges returned, and she took amphetamines to minimize the damage to her figure. She was on the old mood swings and roundabouts, and there was worse to come. If the consequences hadn't been so grave, the events that transpired in one 24-hour period would have had all the elements of a French farce. 'Thierry was still hiding that he was seeing this American girl Teresa, and Christina suddenly found out,' said Kirsten Gille. 'I think Thierry told her to make her realize he was serious about not getting back together. Christina called up Gaby, and said, "Did you know Thierry is seeing Teresa?" Gaby didn't know, and she rang Thierry and was furious with him over the phone. Christina then called him up and said, "Why are you doing this to us?"'

If ever a playboy found himself on the receiving end, it was Thierry Roussel when his complicated lovelife began to unravel with bewildering speed. 'Christina called me up, and I agreed to ring Thierry,' said Kirsten. 'I was screaming at him, "How can you do this?" I knew the whole thing, and I got very angry because Thierry had said to Christina, "If you continue to behave like this towards me, I'm going to marry Gaby." I said to him, "How can you marry that girl? What is she going to give you in life?" And Thierry had replied, "I will marry her." Christina kept saying to me, "Teresa is a problem for me." And I said, "No, Teresa is not the problem – it's Gaby. Teresa's American; she'll try, but she won't get him, but Gaby is Swedish." When I told Christina that Thierry had said he would marry Gaby, she was so upset that she went to Argentina with a broken heart.'

However, she did not depart immediately. Marriage to Gaby was the ultimate deterrent that Roussel could invoke against his ex-wife's wilfulness. The threat completely cowed Christina, and she agreed to go ahead with the changes to her will. One of the disputed points between them had been a large bequest she had intended to make to her uncle, George Livanos, the only surviving child of Stavros and

Arietta Livanos. Christina had wrested her mother's share of the Livanos fortune – an estate totalling $77 million – from the hands of Stavros Niarchos after taking legal action against him in 1974. Niarchos had agreed to a settlement under which he had kept $9 million in cash and one ship, and handed the remaining $68 million over to Christina.

Fully aware of what she was doing, Christina took a room at a Geneva hotel and handwrote a five-page document that substantially altered the terms of her will. The most significant change was that, in the event of her death, she appointed Roussel as one of the five trustees of her estate until Athina reached the age of 18. After that, the entire massive fortune would pass to her daughter. She cut her uncle out of the will completely and passed the Livanos millions on to her daughter as well. For Roussel, there was to be an annuity of $1.42 million for life, provided the revenue from Athina's estate did not fall below $4.5 million a year.

When the existence of the handwritten pages became known, the old Greek trustees in Athens were highly suspicious about Christina's reasons for such a major shift in direction. However, friends pointed out that, as Christina was about to embark on a lengthy return flight to Argentina, she had done nothing more dramatic than to bring her will up to date in line with the changing circumstances of her life. This view failed to appreciate the point that, despite everything that had foreshadowed those changes, including the fiasco at the Villa Trianon, she had successfully bound Roussel to her in life as well as in death in the manner she had planned in the south of France.

Her next move was to check into the Clinique Valmont, one of Switzerland's leading therapeutic centres, for some cosmetic repairs. Under anaesthetic, she had her thighs surgically reduced to remove unsightly bulges of cellulite, which had become more noticeable through her excessive dieting. She spent weeks in a wheelchair before the bandages could be removed from her legs, a picture of misery with only the love of her little daughter and prescribed medication to ease the emotional and physical pain.

During her convalescence, Christina poured out her problems to Marina Dodero in long-distance phone calls to Buenos Aires. Marina and her husband Alberto were familiar with every twist in the distressing saga, and they encouraged Christina to put her life in Europe on hold and come to Argentina as soon as possible and stay for as long as she liked. An unexpected bonus arose in the shape of

Marina's brother, the portly Jorge Tchomlekdjoglou. Christina had known him when they were both growing up, and he had recently paid her a courtesy call during a trip he had made to Europe in 1987. He had seen at first hand how Christina had been treated by Roussel and his family, and was only too willing to help. His own kith and kin were deeply indebted to Christina's generosity. She had loaned Marina and Alberto Dodero $4 million to rescue their textile business in Buenos Aires from closure, a debt that had led to some rancour between the parties over repayment, but the matter had been settled in a tearful reunion between Christina and Marina and had, in fact, brought the two women even closer together.

Jorge, who now ran the family business, was extremely grateful to Christina for this financial assistance and wished only to offer her a sympathetic ear and whatever support he could give.

Racked with self-doubt, Christina flew into Buenos Aires on 19 October 1988, on an Aerolíneas Argentinas flight with her maid Eleni and her friend Atalanta Politis, who had also been invited to Marina's party. She moved in with the Doderos but also took a $1000-a-day, two-bedroom suite on the sixth floor of the Alvear Palace, a few blocks from her friends' apartment. Using the suite as a base, she could make as many phone calls as she wished to Athina and her business associates without interruption. Although she pretended to be free of Roussel, preferring to talk about the social whirl that had instantly engulfed her, she had conceived yet another desperate plan to attract his attention. 'She started an affair with Marina's brother to make Thierry jealous,' said Kirsten Gille. 'It was done on purpose with that objective in mind.'

Jorge was an ideal candidate for this deception, although he was far from lacking an attractive side. An amiable, well-balanced soul, he also understood the machinations of the jet set. 'Jorge Tchomlekdjoglou was like an old slipper to Christina,' said Alecko Papamarkou. 'She had known him since he was a boy. He was educated in America, where his name created a problem. He once tried to place a collect call from a payphone to his home in Argentina. The operator asked him to spell out his name: "T for Thomas, C for Charlie, H for Henry etc, etc." He was cut off three or four times before he managed to get it all out. It's a family name, and he couldn't change it without losing the meaning. In appearance, he looks a bit like Andreadis, Christina's second husband.'

As the friendship developed a romantic edge in Christina's mind, she clung to Jorge night and day, even turning up at his office during working hours and reading magazines while he tried to concentrate on running a business. In the evening, they went everywhere in the same group, although Christina contrived to leave at the end of the evening with Jorge as though they were a couple. Photographs of Christina and her new escort were published in newspapers and glossy magazines throughout Europe. Realizing he was being manipulated, Jorge fell in with the arrangement until one evening when he said he would prefer to go out alone. He refused to take Christina to a diplomatic reception, the kind of event she usually abhorred but, because he was going, had suddenly expressed a fervent desire to attend. Jorge stood his ground. He said his aim was to protect her from newsmen, who were stalking her every move.

As gossip on a global scale was the object of the exercise, Christina became even more intransigent. She threatened to walk out into moving traffic unless Jorge relented. The safest course of action, he decided, was for him to fall in with Christina's scheme, even at the expense of becoming the butt of private jokes. The thought of being the cause of her suicide, however indirectly, was a powerful incentive for him to surrender to her every whim. If Christina had been serious about the threat of ending her life over a simple argument, it meant that drug-taking had seriously disturbed the balance of her mind. If she were merely being histrionic, it showed she was impossibly spoiled. Whatever the actuality, Jorge was not prepared to take the risk of finding out just how far she was prepared to go to get her own way. He gave in and allowed her to accompany him to the embassy.

Christina encouraged her friends in Europe to plant tempting morsels about her hot new affair in front of Roussel. She wanted him to eat, drink and sleep with the knowledge that she had found happiness with a man who desired her more for herself than for her money. The fact that Jorge wasn't tempted in the slightest by her wealth was of no moment whatsoever. The important point was that Thierry got the message that she was quite capable of replacing him as the dominant male in her life any time she chose. She let slip that she was looking for an apartment in Buenos Aires and, although she had spent $6 million setting up the Swiss home for Athina, she might well rebase in the Argentinian capital. It was, she pointed out, the scene of her father's earliest successes, and she had inherited numerous business interests here, which required her attention. Christina knew she held this trump card over Roussel, and she played it for all it was worth. 'She wanted to have men running after her, and she had affairs with one or two of them, but it was just to try to make Thierry jealous,' said Florence. 'Christina was letting it be known she might move to Buenos Aires to make him take notice.'

Throwing herself into plans for a new life, no matter how fictionalized it might have been, Christina embarked on a house-hunting spree that sent a frisson of excitement through the local real-estate market. The Onassis name was huge in Buenos Aires, and the prospect of sharing in profits that were usually divided between couturiers, jewellers, hoteliers, restaurateurs and hairdressers sent real-estate agents scurrying to Christina's side with offers of service. She combined the hunt for a home with sightseeing expeditions to her father's old stamping-grounds. Taken to the Boca down on the waterfront, Christina rhapsodized over the brightly repainted façades of the old working-class wooden houses that had given shelter to Aristotle as a hungry, newly arrived *émigré* back in 1923. In the Avenida 9 de Julio, she saw the obelisk that was used as the starting-point for measuring all distances. The significance of such a marker in her father's life was not lost on her.

Buenos Aires in the eighties had grown into a vast cosmopolitan city of 14 million people. At fashionable Palermo and Belgrano in the *Barrio Norte* she looked at luxury apartments with gardens and views of magnificent parks reminiscent of the Bois de Boulogne at the end of her own street in Paris, the Avenue Foch. Her hotel, the Alvear Palace – the Waldorf of Buenos Aires – was in La Recoleta, the cultural district that included the Museo de Bellas Artes and the new Municipal Cultural Centre. In traditional restaurants such as the Café de la Paix, La Biela and the Munich Recoleta, customers took their pleasure on terraces shaded by century-old rubber trees called *gomeros*. There were many memories of her father in the night-life area bounded by the Avenida Corrientes and calles Lavalle and Florida, where Christina found temples of international fashion as well as a proliferation of cinemas and theatres, and the night clubs that had started Onassis on his lifelong love affair with the *demi-monde*. The thought occurred to Christina that, as well as the sentimental attachment to her father, living in Buenos Aires would have many substantial advantages if she really were married to a man like Jorge.

Over dinner one night, Christina engaged a clergyman in a discussion about the meaning of life, which became the starting-point of a dialogue about a new spiritual direction she felt the need to take. She began to see clearly that holy matrimony meant a great deal more than merely turning a lover into her husband because she enjoyed their physical rapport. The notion that a husband might have another role to play, which was beyond sexual pleasure, stirred up some real feelings about Jorge. 'The old slipper' might just be the perfect fit.

When a reporter asked if she had found a suitable home in Buenos Aires, she replied that she was still house-hunting but confirmed that she would bring Athina with her on her next trip. Asked why she was often seen entering an apartment building on Avenida Montevideo, she replied: 'Because Jorge Tchomlekdjoglou, Marina's brother, lives there.' An open declaration like this actually worked in Jorge's favour in his main objective: to boost Christina's self-esteem and possibly save her life in the process. Her threat to throw herself under the wheels of moving vehicles came back to him like a recurring nightmare. He struck a bargain with her, which they solemnized in church: if she would cut her use of mood-altering pills by two-thirds, he would go on a diet to reduce his weight. Christina took the vow with a full heart, certain in the belief that only unhappiness had previously prevented her from kicking the habit. She had apparently had no comprehension whatsoever that the pills to which she was addicted were merely a symptom of a disturbance which had been buried in her psyche since childhood.

When Jorge made it plain that he had no intention of moving to Europe, she swept that suggestion aside by pledging to spend no more than two months a year away from Argentina. Not only would she have a home in Buenos Aires but she would also buy an *estancia* as a weekend retreat. Jorge realized that he needed to slow things down or he would be walking up the aisle as the fifth Mr Onassis before he knew it. 'Look, Christina,' he told her. 'I'm not like you, getting married every other year. To me, it's a very important step.' Christina interpreted Jorge's caution not as a delaying tactic but as a mark of respect for her position. If he were after her money, she reasoned, he would have jumped at the chance.

No one was happier than Christina at Marina Dodero's 40th birthday party at the small and exclusive Le Club. The select guest list contained 50 of the wealthiest people in Buenos Aires, but Christina was undeniably the star. When she entered the fashionable disco, the orchestra struck up the *Zorba* theme, and she fell in love with Jorge and Argentina all over again. Surrounded by friends and new admirers, her uncertainty melted, and a sense of belonging swept over her. With great difficulty, Jorge persuaded her to fly home to Europe, telling her that if she still felt the same way about him after six months, they would get married.

When Christina returned to Boislande, she found it impossible to settle back into her old routine of strolls along the country lanes with Athina and feeding the animals in the little zoo. While Athina splashed about in the indoor swimming pool, Christina talked endlessly to Jorge on the phone. While she had been in Buenos Aires, Gaby had given an interview to the French press in which she had confirmed their bizarre maternal triangle. 'Christina has invited me to many parties,' Gaby was quoted as saying. 'She buys my children presents. Everyone knows the situation, and it doesn't seem to bother Christina. I never got the impression I was her rival, though she loves Thierry.' Christina was so upset by the comments that Jorge agreed to the six months' cooling-off period being cut in half and then, in subsequent calls, whittled down to just two weeks. 'Just before she went back to Buenos Aires, she saw Thierry,' said Kirsten Gille, 'but I don't think it changed anything.'

Kirsten had been astonished to discover that Christina was about to leave so soon, taking Athina with her. She had phoned Boislande because her golden cocker spaniel, Honey, had just fathered puppies. 'I knew Christina wanted to buy a dog for Tina, and I offered her one of the puppies, half cocker spaniel, half Rottweiler,' said Kirsten. 'She thanked me very much and said, "No, I'm going to get a Labrador, but I'm going back to Argentina first, and I'll call you when I return." She never came back alive.'

EIGHTEEN

CHRISTINA'S FINAL HOURS: THE MAID'S STORY

ELENI SYROS HAD rarely seen her mistress in a happier frame of mind than on 9 November 1988, the day they arrived back in Buenos Aires for a new beginning. After the disappointments that had dogged her since she had divorced Thierry the previous year, Christina was determined to shed the past and reclaim her life. As always, her appearance set the mood she was in and, as she was noticeably slim, she faced this city in which the Onassis name was revered with a positive attitude.

'She had been on a strict diet because she wanted to become very thin,' Eleni told us. 'For three months, she had eaten very little, just a small salad and an egg. Normally, she had a big appetite and ate very well, but she had stopped eating, and she wasn't taking big pills. She was a good mother, and she had spent all her time in Switzerland with Athina. She was only three and a half years old, but they loved to go shopping together.'

The only sadness for Christina was that the little girl had not been able to accompany her on the flight to Buenos Aires. She had developed an ear infection from swimming in the indoor pool at Boislande and was too sick to fly. When she had recovered, Monique and a bodyguard would accompany her on the 14-hour journey to South America. The fact that Christina had not been prepared to wait for her daughter to get well, or to nurse her through her illness, showed how impatient she was to leave Europe and return to the emotional security she had found in Argentina on her previous visit.

Jorge greeted Christina more as a brother than a lover, to reinforce his wish that, if she were serious about marriage, they should proceed slowly. Christina's response was to have her hair streaked seductively blonde and to dress in a manner that reflected a liberated new attitude. She was single, thirtysomething and available for love, and if Jorge were not able to meet her needs, she would look elsewhere. 'She had a brief fling with a young man she met at a party,' said a friend. 'But I don't think she was trying to make Jorge jealous. It was just one of the things she did.'

When Christina wasn't attending to her appearance, shopping in La Recoleta or partying with Jorge and the Doderos, she resumed her house-hunting expeditions. She made an offer of $2 million for one apartment in the *Barrio Norte*, but the deal fell through after the owners changed their minds. She also asked her realtors to provide her with a list of suitable ranches that would serve as a country home once she had settled down in Buenos Aires.

In the middle of November, Christina attended the Greek Orthodox church in Buenos Aires and took her first communion in many years. She asked Archbishop Chrysoulakis, a family friend, to say a mass for her mother, father and brother the following Sunday. Although this outward devotion convinced the Doderos that she was taking life seriously, it was partly an illusion. Her real state of mind became apparent after she returned to the Alvear Palace a couple of nights later on Thursday, 17 November. She went to her bedroom but was unable to sleep. Dressing again, she put a favourite tape in her Sony Walkman and went down to the lobby.

It was four o'clock in the morning, and the reception staff were amazed to see one of the richest women in the world walking towards them in an apparent daze. The Walkman headset was clamped over her ears, and she was barefooted. When they managed to establish contact with her to see if she wanted something, Christina lifted the headset and declared she was perfectly all right. She was simply going for a walk. The staff protested that it wasn't safe in the streets at this hour, but Christina had replaced her headset, walked through the revolving door and disappeared into the night. Two hours later she still hadn't returned, and the staff were frantic with worry. They were debating whether to alert Eleni or call the police when Christina suddenly reappeared in the doorway. Bidding them goodnight, she returned to her suite as though a late-night stroll in a city where kidnapping was a constant fear among the wealthy was completely normal.

When the Doderos arrived at the hotel to pick up Christina and Eleni early on the Friday afternoon of 18 November, there was no sign that she had passed anything other than a tranquil night. At some time during that day, she had spoken to Thierry Roussel on the phone, and he later claimed she had been in high spirits. She chattered happily to the Doderos as they drove the 35 kilometres north-west from Buenos Aires to the Tortugas Club, their destination for a weekend of swimming, tennis and partying with the Buenos Aires younger set. Jorge was a regular at Tortugas and owned one of the 150 villas in the club's grounds.

After settling into her room in Jorge's villa, Christina decided to phone Boislande to see how Athina was progressing. She was missing her daughter and wanted to know how long it would be before she could join her. Despite the club's social prominence, the Tortugas management had to admit that no telephone on the premises was capable of making a transatlantic call. When Christina told Marina about this unexpected setback, her friend drove her to the telephone exchange in the nearby town of Tortugitas. However, the operator there informed Christina that overseas calls could only be made on weekdays and, as it was after 6pm on Friday, the weekend had already started.

The operator had failed to recognize the slim, blonde woman standing in front of her as Christina Onassis, and Christina, suffering from a sudden attack of nerves, had been reluctant to give her name. She wasn't used to a situation in which one of her requests wasn't treated as a royal command. 'It's very important I get through to Switzerland,' she said meekly. 'My little girl is ill, and I need to speak to her.' The woman at the switchboard suddenly realized who the stranger was. 'Are you Christina Onassis?' she asked. 'Yes,' replied Christina, 'and I really need to get through.' The operator immediately placed the call to Gingins and directed Christina towards a booth.

Within seconds, Athina had been brought to the other end of the phone, and mother and daughter were briefly reunited via the oceanic cable. Christina told Athina that they would soon be together again in Argentina and that she intended to buy a ranch with lots of ponies for her to ride. The little girl had been happy and excited when she put down the phone, according to a member of the household. It was the last time she ever spoke to her mother.

At the country club, Christina was in a good mood during dinner, a barbecue of the finest Argentinian beefsteak. 'She ate very little because of the big diet,' said Eleni, 'but she was very happy. She was talking and laughing, but she didn't eat. We were all together with the Dodero family and Jorge Tchomlekdjoglou and having a good time. She made plans for the following morning to go somewhere away from Tortugas for a trip.'

After midnight, Christina and Jorge went for a walk in the gardens and then, in line with Jorge's policy of separate beds, he retired to a guest house with other single men while she returned alone to her room soon after 1.30am. She had already said goodnight to the Doderos after agreeing to join them for an early-morning swim.

'At two o'clock I gave her two small sleeping pills which the doctor had given her,' Eleni disclosed. 'I said, "Do you want anything, Madam?" She said, "No, no." So I said, "I'm next door any time you want anything," and she said, "Goodnight, Eleni," and I didn't see her again. She went into the bathroom for a bath, and she stayed there. I really don't understand what happened because she was so happy.'

Police investigators were told that around 10am on Saturday, 19 November, Marina Dodero had expressed her surprise to Eleni that Christina hadn't appeared for breakfast. Eleni had answered that her mistress sometimes slept late if she had had a problem dropping off; it was best not to disturb her. However, Marina had gone into the bedroom and returned to say that Christina was out of bed, and the bathroom door was closed. Something triggered an alarm in Eleni. For one thing, Christina never took a bath until she had had a reviving cup of coffee. The two women were said to have looked at each other, then dashed into Christina's room and entered the bathroom. Christina was slumped naked in the tub, her body surrounded by about two inches of water. Her legs were bent at the knees, and her head rested upon them. While Marina screamed for help, Eleni ascertained what she feared was true. Her mistress was already dead.

The only medical help immediately available was the attendant at a first-aid station in the club grounds, but he could do nothing to revive the stricken woman. When a physician, Dr Arturo Fuentes, whom the Doderos had managed to contact, arrived at the villa, he found Christina lying on the bed. Her hair was wringing wet, and there was no apparent sign of life. The doctor later testified that when he learned she had been found in the bathroom, he had gone in there to search for pills but had been obliged to go back into the bedroom. Feeling frustrated, he had left the suite without making a proper examination of the body. Later, an empty vial, which was found to have contained amphetamines, was discovered in the bathroom. This crucial piece of evidence was dismissed as inconsequential on the grounds that Christina was unlikely to have taken uppers before going to sleep.

More than four hours after the body was discovered, Christina was taken to the Clinica del Sol, an exclusive hospital in Buenos Aires, where she was declared dead at 3pm. 'All efforts to revive her were useless,' said a physician. Judge Juan-Carlos Cardinali was notified that he had a case of 'questionable death' on his hands and ordered that an immediate autopsy should be carried out. This announcement alerted the press to the death of the most famous heiress in the world, and news-agency wires ran hot with the first reports. The post-mortem examination was carried out in the hospital morgue and, at eight o'clock the same night, the body was taken to the city's Greek Orthodox church, where people had already gathered for an all-night vigil.

Newsmen, photographers and TV crews from around the world descended on Buenos Aires to join local reporters and correspondents who had been keeping a close watch on Christina but had apparently lost track of her whereabouts in the last 24 hours of her life. 'The whole thing is a tragedy,' said Jorge. 'It has been a terrible shock for us all.'

After receiving the results of the autopsy, Judge Cardinali said: 'The pathologist's report, while reserving some elements for further study, gave the cause of death as acute pulmonary oedema.' He said he had turned his jurisdiction in the case over to a federal official, Judge Alberto Piotti, whose court in San Isidro included the Tortugas Club. It would be left to him to examine the question of whether a drug overdose, either accidentally or deliberately administered, had brought about the oedema, a dropsy condition in which the lung may fill with fluid. Judge Piotti ordered customs and border officials to prevent the transfer of the body from Buenos Aires until further notice. He said that a pill sachet belonging to her, but apparently missing, could provide important information.

Police who searched Christina's hotel room in Buenos Aires had found no fewer than 42 different medications in her name. However, Eleni was adamant in interviews with us that Christina had taken no drugs that night apart from the two small sleeping pills she had given her. 'She was on a big diet and maybe that killed her,' she said. 'But she didn't take any other medicine – nothing.' Within 24 hours of the judge's order forbidding removal of the body, the examiners had completed their tests, and a judicial release was signed granting permission for Christina to be taken back to Europe.

The official investigation into the fatality proceeded against a backdrop of near hysteria over whether or not the heiress had taken her own life. Christina had a history of suicide attempts, the most recent having taken place in New York City eight years earlier in 1980. As she had done on several previous occasions, she had swallowed half a bottle of barbiturates and been taken unconscious to Lenox Hill Hospital on the city's upper east side for treatment. When Jackie Kennedy heard about the incident, she asked her physician, Dr Henry Lax, to speak to Christina. Dr Lax visited the patient at Lenox Hill and tried to impress upon her the serious nature of her action. Christina had listened to his advice and been discharged from hospital, but she had been unable to shake off the symptoms that accompanied her drug addiction, such as irrational anger and free-floating anxiety attacks. A few weeks later, Dr Lax told Christina over the telephone: 'Now that you're out of the hospital, you're back to your old agitated self. You lose your temper too easily. You always yell at people. You shouldn't yell at people so much.'

Christina was contrite, but she remained excitable and erratic. She had been hooked on prescribed drugs since the late sixties, and only a period of complete rest and recuperation combined with long-term therapy could have overcome her psychological and physical dependence on mood-altering chemicals.

Her friends agreed that the problem had started in childhood. Christina had always been self-conscious about her appearance, a problem that was exacerbated every time she was seen in the company of her beautiful mother. Unkind comparisons were inevitably made between mother and daughter, and Tina only added to Christina's misery by harping upon her physical defects. She seemed to take it as a personal affront that her daughter should have been born in the image of her husband rather than herself. After Christina had had her nose bobbed in 1967, she decided to try chemical means to eliminate the puppy fat that had also marred her adolescent years.

'She told me the story of how she got started on drugs,' said Kirsten Gille. 'She went to see a doctor in New York – he was the big hit of the moment for ladies to slim down – and they gave her a little envelope. She left the surgery but went back again and said, "What's in there?" And they said, "Just take them." They were very rude to her. Actually, they were amphetamines, so then she couldn't sleep. So she had to take pills to get to sleep, then in the morning she felt so bad she had to take something else to try to wake up. But she never thought she might die as a result of what she was taking.'

Considering her family's medical history, Christina knew only too well that drug abuse as practised by her aunt Eugenie and her mother could have lethal consequences. During the seventies, she took so many pills and potions that she knew exactly the strength and capability of each tablet she popped. She called her strongest amphetamines *mavro mavros* (black black in Greek), which were powerful enough to keep her going for three days and nights of relentless partying. But not even Tina's sudden death in 1974 had given her sufficient pause to tackle her own addiction. Drugs had sustained her through the tragic death of Alexander, drugs had numbed her grief over her mother, and drugs had kept her going through the interminable nights in Paris while she waited for her father to die. Like Marilyn Monroe and many other celebrities before her, Christina was a tragedy waiting to happen.

Asked if she believed Christina had committed suicide, Kirsten Gille said: 'No, she loved Athina too much. She was crazy about her. Christina always took pills, and it was probably an accumulation. She was always fat. When she went down in weight, she would eat chocolate, cakes and sandwiches while Thierry's back was turned, then take pills to limit the effects of her eating.'

'I believe she died because she was taking too many pills, and she was always taking hot baths,' said Florence Grinda. 'She was found in her bath. Eleni came back and talked to us about it. She would never have killed herself because of her daughter. It was not in her character. She was too full of life. She used to take so many pills. I can see what happened . . . she must have taken, oh, I don't know how many sleeping pills, and got into a hot bath and died.'

While some of Christina's friends wanted a veil to be drawn over the dark side of her life to protect her memory, others felt it was important to get to the truth. The Livanos family, in particular, harboured deep suspicions about the events in Christina's bedroom on the morning of 19 November 1988. 'We need a pharmacologist, not a doctor, to tell us what really happened,' said Alecko Papamarkou, who had discussed the matter with the Livanoses as well as with Marina Dodero. 'Marina was telling me that Christina took so many uppers and downers,' he said. 'She would say, "Oh, I feel this way, or that way." It was shocking . . . one [pill] after the other. It was all extremes.'

Marina had the heart-rending task of breaking the news of his ex-wife's death to Thierry Roussel, who immediately made plans to fly from Geneva to Buenos Aires. But first he issued some very specific instructions regarding his three-year-old daughter. 'He was scared the Greeks were going to get Athina,' said Kirsten Gille, who spoke to him before he left.

Roussel confirmed this when he told reporters: 'I am going to fight to the bitter end to get Athina away from the Onassis family. Athina is all I care about, and I want her to have a proper family upbringing. The Onassis relatives must not get hold of her.' On his instructions Monique and two bodyguards boarded a commercial flight from Geneva to Paris with the little heiress. She was met by her grandfather, Henri Roussel, who drove her in his Mercedes to his country house in the Sologne. There, Roussel's elder sister, Christine de Luynes, was waiting to look after her. Athina had effectively been placed in the custody of the Roussel family until her father returned to France. When Athina enquired after her mother, she was told that she had gone on a long journey with the object of finding a brother and sister for her to live with.

Roussel's first destination on arriving in Buenos Aires late on Sunday morning was Christina's suite at the Alvear Palace, which was guarded by armed police. Christina's friend Mercedes Zavalia was in the suite taking phone calls from distraught friends and relatives who were not able to get through to the Dodero household. Mercedes had previously met Thierry in Europe and, she said, he fell into her arms and sobbed uncontrollably.

Friends said that Roussel discounted the rumours of suicide that had reached the Argentinian capital from the Tortugas Club. He maintained that, when he had spoken to Christina the day before her death, she had seemed happier than usual. That evening, he went alone to the Greek Orthodox church, where Christina's embalmed body was laid out in a glass-topped, ebony casket. She was dressed in a white tunic embroidered with flowers. Her hands were folded around a red rose. Roussel sat for an hour in the empty church, crying softly, and then he kissed her through the glass.

Four days later on Thursday, 24 November, police motorcycle sirens wailed to clear a path for the hearse bearing Christina's body to Ezeiza airport for the flight to Greece. In Athens, hundreds of mourners packed into the church of Aghia Fotina in the district of New Smyrna for the funeral service, while another 5000 people, braving heavy rain, blocked surrounding streets and crowded on to apartment balconies. Greek shipowners and Athenian dignitaries arrived to polite applause, and murmurs of approval greeted the Duke of Marlborough, the former Sunny Blandford. As Roussel arrived, jeers and whistles shattered the respectful hush.

'One part was all Thierry's friends and family, and the other part were all the Greeks and us,' said Florence Grinda, who attended with other members of the Michard-Pellissier family. 'The atmosphere was awful, awful, awful because the two sides were not speaking to each other.'

To reach the coffin, which was edged in silver filigree and covered with lilies, mourners had to file past a guard of honour formed by young men in grey flannels and navy blazers bearing the badge of the Alexander S. Onassis Public Benefit Foundation. It was fitting that some of the church's fabric had come from the Greek quarter of Smyrna, where her father had been born 88 years earlier. The largest wreath, more than 4ft in diameter, came from Roussel and Athina. After priests in robes of cream, gold and purple had conducted the prayer service, the coffin was carried out into the rain, where people surged forward to throw flowers on it. There was confusion about who was invited to go to Skórpios for the interment the following day.

'The one who was organizing it was Thierry Roussel,' said Florence. 'I asked somebody, "Are we going to go to Skórpios?" and they said that Henri and Thierry Roussel didn't organize for us to go. He knew that we could see through him. It's a very sore point. It was very mean for my mother not to be taken to Skórpios because Christina really adored her, and my mother considered Christina like one of her own children. For my mother, it was really hard that she couldn't go to the tomb. It was a big hurt for her and my brother. I even asked Eleni, and she didn't know what to say. People felt very embarrassed for us. We went back to Paris the same day; we didn't want to beg to go and, after that, we said we never wanted to see Thierry Roussel again. We said, "That's enough." Afterwards, George Livanos and the Niarchoses, who were very good friends of ours, called us and said, "Why weren't you on Skórpios?" When George and the others understood, they were shocked. George said, "Why didn't you ask me?" And I said, "Somebody else was organizing it." It was like the last stab. Henri was there like the father figure, the godfather, it was awful.'

As the funeral procession left Athens and headed for Skórpios via Nidri, the fishing village on neighbouring Lefkas, whole communities turned out to line the road in silent tribute. At Nidri docks, black-clad women who had known Christina since she was a child wailed and tried to touch the coffin as it was loaded on to a launch. The following morning Christina's coffin was carried up a red carpet into the chapel, where the Nidri parish priest, Father Apostolos, gave the final eulogy. 'You lived in tragedy, and you died in tragedy,' he said. 'Yet you gave us all so much happiness while you were with us. Your family, your friends, even the simple island fishermen who knew you, will always remember you for your kindness and generosity. Your memory will remain eternal in the mind of the world.'

A sobbing Thierry Roussel paid homage at the coffin and then, head bowed and clutching a candle, took his place with other mourners outside. These included Marina and Alberto Dodero, Jorge Tchomlekdjoglou, three of the Niarchos children, Philip, Spyros and Maria, and a representative of the House of Dior, which had not only dressed Christina and Athina but their dolls as well. Another mourner was Gaby Landhage, who had attended as much to support Thierry as to say farewell to her friend. In Gothenburg, her mother, Maj-Lis, was asked about her daughter's strange relationship with Christina. 'They were planning to go on a skiing holiday together at the Villa Crystal in St Moritz,' she said. 'They were true friends; there was no trouble between them.'

Then Jorge went inside the chapel and, when he returned, Thierry went back in again, still sobbing, as though the last tribute had to be his. 'Neither man spoke to the other,' said a witness. 'They exchanged just one telling glance.' The final tribute, however, came from Christina's third husband, Sergei Kausov. The Russian waited until the ceremony had been completed and the guests had departed before entering the chapel. Christina was entombed in a white marble mausoleum that held the bodies of her father Aristotle, her brother Alexander and her aunt Artimus. The fate of the entire Onassis family now rested with a three-year-old girl barely able to pronounce the name.

Christina's friends were openly sceptical about Roussel's grief, but his tears had been real enough. 'He was very attached to Christina in a way, and when he cried at the funeral it was not a fake,' said Kirsten Gille. 'He always had her to go to if something went wrong. He was attached to her. Thierry had one big quality, for if he had been in love with someone for a long time, like his nanny, he was very, very faithful to his history. He did everything for his nanny when she was very old, and he paid everything for her, and went to see her and worried about her. He was very attached to her, and it was the same with Christina.'

Although tributes to Christina poured in from all quarters, one voice remained conspicuously silent, that of her stepmother Jackie Kennedy Onassis. After settling with Jackie for $26 million, Christina had told friends: 'What she doesn't realize is that I would have given her 50 times what I gave her for the pleasure of never having to see her again.' Although still legally Athina's grandmother, as far as Jackie was concerned she was free of the Onassis family at last.

When the official report into the tragedy was eventually released in Buenos Aires, Judge Piotti declared that drugs had not caused Christina's death. He based this finding on the fact that tests had shown that although there were traces of amphetamines in her body, these were not in a sufficient quantity to have contributed to her death. He also stated there was no sign of barbiturates. Indeed, Christina had told Archbishop Chrysoulakis that 'for the first time in her life' she was able to sleep without the help of pills. However, our interviews with Eleni Syros proved that this simply wasn't true; Christina had taken two sleeping pills on the last night of her life.

The investigation report concluded that Christina's death had been accidental, the result of an acute pulmonary oedema of the lung, which had triggered a heart attack – the same cause given for her mother's death 14 years earlier. The judge was not able to provide any answer to the question of what had caused the oedema. In the absence of any evidence of foul play or a suicide note, his investigators had failed to shed any light on why Christina should have suffered the fatal cardiac arrest.

The most likely cause of pulmonary oedema in a known drug abuser is an overdose of barbiturates, such as the one that had ended Tina's life. It seemed highly suspicious that one report published in *The Times* soon after Christina's death claimed that the barbiturate drug Optalidon had, in fact, been found in the body, and another source claimed that a bottle of pills had been located near her bed. But the official investigation had apparently failed to confirm either of these points.

In her handwritten will, Christina ignored her uncle George Livanos, the rest of her family and all her friends, and she left nearly everything to 'my beloved Athina' when her daughter reached the age of 18 in 2003. The properties that went to the little girl until she decided what to do with them included Boislande, the Avenue Foch apartments, the Villa Crystal at St Moritz, other villas at the fashionable Greek resorts of Glyfada and Lagonísi, homes in London and shares in the Olympic Tower in New York as well as the Metropole Hotel in Monte Carlo. There was also the shipping operated by Olympic Maritime, although Christina had been in the process of reducing the size of her fleet. In 1982 this had totalled 38 vessels, making her the world's eighth largest independent tanker owner, bigger even than Niarchos.

Her holdings in South America included numerous estates in Argentina and mines in Uruguay. There were untold millions of shares in international banks and other major companies, and – a legacy of the founder's obsession with secrecy – several companies in Panama that served as offshore tax havens. Collections of paintings, sculpture and jewellery, which had only ever been valued for insurance purposes, were either in Christina's homes or locked away in vaults.

Eleni Syros and her husband Jorge were each given $200,000, but the largest bequest was the lifetime annuity to Roussel of $1.42 million, although he had not been mentioned in any of the nine previous wills Christina had drawn up since inheriting her fortune. The only other substantial bequests went to long-time Onassis officers Stelio Papadimitriou, Apostolos Zabelas and Paul Ioannides, who each received $2 million. These three men, all directors of the Onassis Foundation, were named as trustees of Athina's inheritance along with the foundation's secretary, Theodore Gabrielides, and Thierry Roussel. The makings of the financial feud that guaranteed her daughter would become an object of curiosity in the eyes of the world were all written down, as Greek law required, in Christina's own hand.

NINETEEN

FEUD OVER THE ONASSIS BILLIONS

FOR A BRIEF moment it appeared as though a truce might be reached between Thierry Roussel and the Greek trustees over Athina's future. Christina's uncle, George Livanos, offered to raise the little girl as a member of his family. Livanos and his wife Lita were in an excellent position to act as adoptive parents. They had five children of their own and, as well as impeccable Greek connections, there were homes in London, New York and St Moritz.

However, Roussel rejected the olive branch. 'The relative Christina really loved was George Livanos, and he and Lita loved the little girl,' said Florence Grinda. 'George was really hurt that he wasn't made a trustee in the will, but there was nothing he could do about it. They see Athina sometimes, but he would have liked to have done more for the child. They are a very good couple, and he was really the last part of Christina's family. It would have been ideal for Athina to live with Greek people. I'm sure that Thierry influenced Christina's decision. He didn't like George; the only one he was afraid of was George.'

From the outset it was clear that Roussel had assumed complete control over Athina, and the trustees and other Onassis associates in

Athens reluctantly accepted the position. 'According to law, he is the only and deciding factor in Athina's upbringing,' said Professor Ioannis Georgakis, who had been appointed president of the Onassis Foundation after Christina's death. 'I don't think this child should undergo some of the bitter experiences that her mother had with her unhappy family life.'

A few days after George Livanos had made his offer, Athina was back in Boislande with Roussel, Gaby, Erik and Sandrine for her fourth birthday. Just a year earlier, Christina had hosted a huge celebration in St Moritz for her third birthday. While Thierry and Gaby prepared a small party in her honour, Athina and the other children drove through the mansion's gates with two nurses, two bodyguards and the family's pet Labrador dog. They travelled five miles along the road to a secluded spot, where they parked the car to enable the children to go for a walk along a public footpath in the forest. Wrapped up against the chill winter air in a white woollen bonnet and boots, Athina lagged behind the rest of the group, lost in a world of her own.

Athina now owned Boislande, as well as the Villa Crystal in St Moritz and the Falcon 50 that Christina had used to commute between the two homes. The first test of strength between her father and the four Greek greybeards came in March when Roussel ordered the Falcon 50 to fly him and Athina from Geneva to spend the weekend in St Moritz as guests of George and Lita Livanos at the Livanos home, the Villa Bambi. The plane's pilot said he had received instructions from the trustees that the plane was no longer available for Roussel's use.

As though reinforcing the point that Athina belonged to him, Roussel took his brood not to Skórpios that summer but to his villa on the Ibizian beach of Malibu. A small fleet of pleasure craft moored at the beach as guests arrived for Erik's fourth birthday. In a white party frock, Athina was presented with a blue musical box to include her in the celebrations.

When reporters caught up with him on a business trip to London, Thierry was asked about his plans for Athina. 'She will be brought up with all the love a father can have for his daughter, and even more because I will try to compensate for what she lost when her mother died,' he said. 'I will bring her up as normally as possible in a family atmosphere with the family principles I have a duty to pass on to my children. I don't want my daughter to be manipulated.'

Roussel wasn't thinking of himself at that moment, but possibly of Luis Basualdo, who had manipulated Christina during their marriage even though he had been banished from her circle of friends. Through a deft manoeuvre in Austria, the Argentinian had appropriated $1.2 million of Christina's money, which, she said, had been intended for her Swiss bank account. When Austrian police interviewed Basualdo, he claimed he had been entitled to the money for services rendered and, anyhow, he had lost it through bad investments. Christina had dropped the charges against him, but it was not a matter that Roussel was prepared to dismiss after her death. He regarded Basualdo's cavalier attitude towards his ex-wife's fortune as a personal insult.

'Thierry had detectives looking for him, but I found him very quickly,' said Kirsten Gille. 'I knew he played polo, so I phoned up the president of the polo club in Paris and got his number. He was in Buenos Aires. I rang him, pretended that my name was something completely different and told him I had seen him and thought he was very charming, a fantastic man, and I would like to meet him. He was very excited, and we made arrangements to meet the next time he came to Paris. I passed that information on to Thierry.' However, Basualdo wisely decided to settle in New York, where he continued to prosper, until his freewheeling lifestyle finally caught up with him. In September 1995 he was back in Buenos Aires, being treated for addiction to alcohol and drugs.

In Switzerland, Roussel moved his family from Boislande into a new £2 million home 30 kilometres further along Route Nationale 1 in the direction of Lausanne. Bois L'Essert was a spacious, low-slung house set in two and a half acres just outside the village of Lussy-sur-Morges with a view of the snow-capped French Alps across Lac Léman. Surrounded by 10ft-high conifers and a green chain-link fence, the only entrance to the property was through TV-supervised gates monogrammed with the initials TGR for Thierry and Gaby Roussel. A picture window in the living room at the rear of the premises overlooked a forest, through which a winding dirt track led to a picnic area for barbecues. For the first time in her life, Athina was living in a home that had no connection with her mother.

Like Gingins, Lussy with its church and cottages, framed by begonias, roses, geraniums and pansies, was the centre of an agricultural district that had attracted a number of rich residents who were prepared to pay high prices for privacy. Small, exclusive housing estates had sprung up amid clumps of forest that dotted the countryside. From the Place de La Fontaine, the Route du Bon led to vineyards, apple orchards and fields of corn, potatoes and poppies, where Athina's horse grazed among haymakers. In one field adjacent to Bois L'Essert, strawberry pickers brought in the harvest, which was sold to passersby from a roadside stall. To wash down the fresh fruit, a fine selection of the region's most palatable vintages were on sale at the Caveau de Lussy in the village centre.

Two miles away on the shores of the lake was the picturesque village of St Prex, where paddle steamers for Geneva, Lausanne-Ouchy and St Gingolph departed from a jetty on the Quai du Suchet. Directly across the lake on the French side was the well-known watering hole of Evian-Les-Bains. Thierry's friend Paul Hagnoer said: 'He has placed Athina in a loving, family environment to protect her.'

Roussel's next move was to legitimize his two love children by taking Gaby as his second wife. His uncle, Jean-Noel Grinda, said: 'Thierry said he would wait 18 months after Christina's death before marrying Gaby, but I said it should be two years.' In fact, Thierry stuck to his original timetable, and he and Gaby were married at Villeny near Bonneville on 12 May 1990. Athina and Sandrine were flower girls, while Erik acted as pageboy. Once again, reporters had the chance to fire some questions at Roussel about his plans for Athina's fortune, but he came up with the stock answers: 'I want Athina to have a happier, calmer life than her mother. We must find a way to bring her up in a normal, everyday way like other children.'

Mrs Thierry Roussel became pregnant in the New Year, and Athina doted on the new baby, a little sister called Johanne, who was born in late summer 1991. 'Every man must rise to two challenges in his life,' declared the new father, 'succeeding in his family life and making the most of his professional life.'

Roussel was often away from Bois L'Essert during 1992, either in Paris or on the Roussel estate in Kenya or in Portugal. He threw his considerable energies into consolidating his businesses, and he was never bashful about asking either Teresa Prater or Kirsten Gille to accompany him on trips to enhance his status as a man of the world. Kirsten went with him on one such jaunt to London. The large apartment in Grosvenor Square had been sold, but they stayed in a splendid town house that bore the Roussel name, in the Little Boltons, South Kensington. In Portugal he had started an experimental farm on 550 hectares he had bought in the Brejao region, 250 kilometres south of Lisbon. A model organic farm had risen on the once arid and infertile fields and was producing 100 tonnes of fruit and vegetables a day.

When his family visited him, they took lunch at tables set up under umbrellas on a terrace with a backdrop of a swimming pool, hothouses and neatly arranged garden beds. Answering charges that he was really a playboy at heart, Roussel said: 'I probably go to a night club once a year, but I spend 200 days here working very hard.' He said he had visited 15 European countries in 16 days to set up a distribution network for the farm's output, which was marketed under his own Cap Verde label. Roussel now piloted a private plane that he could really call his own, a new eight-seater Cessna Citation jet worth $2 million.

One source claimed that he had invested millions in the farming project to grow fresh produce out of season. 'I could lose everything, but I intend to succeed and on my own terms,' Roussel said. 'I want to prove that a business can be profitable at the same time as it respects the environment. In farming, I think it is essential to limit chemical fertilizers and to protect our water resources. Ladybirds, not insecticides, fight pests, bees pollinate the strawberries and computers regulate watering in the greenhouses. I was first taught to love nature at my grandmother's home in the Sologne. I collect books on the environment. In my Swiss home I have about 350 of them, and I've learned the rest by working on the land.

'This year we exported 50 per cent of all Portugal's strawberries, 50 per cent of melons, and we pick 80,000 tomatoes an hour. This is from Brejao. My other property at Mira in north Portugal is a nursery and sales warehouse for ornamental plants, and five million trees are planted there.'

Kirsten Gille described visiting her quixotic lover's model farm at Brejao before it was fully operational. 'He was so excited he was like a kid,' she said. 'He had 300 hectares under cultivation, including 17 hectares of strawberries – that was his big thing, those strawberries. We were walking along and he showed me, "See, strawberries. They're all planted. It's fantastic." It looked awfully dry, and I said, "Where's the water?" "Oh, the water – I forgot the water." There was no irrigation. It was typical of Thierry. He was so excited that he had planted the strawberries, but he had forgotten the water. He said, "Well, we haven't got that far yet." And all 17 hectares of these strawberries went dead.'

However, this problem was overcome, and in no time at all strawberry plants were flourishing in neat green rows. 'When you went in his house there was a big mountain of beautiful strawberries,' said Kirsten. 'I ate some but, God knows, I had stomach ache, and I wasn't the only one.

'He was so sure he knew everything about vegetables. People who had been in vegetables for 50 years – they were idiots. Thierry knew everything although he'd only been in farming for a year. He wanted to write a book on how to save the planet. I said, "You don't know anything about ecology," and he said "I've been reading books about it, and I want you to help me." We had a big fight about this, and we did write quite a bit, but the book was a joke.

'He comes up with the craziest ideas. I spent a year with the horsy set in Belgium, and he called me up and said, "Since you like animals so much, I want you to organize a zoo in Portugal for endangered species."

'I said, "You can't do that!" But he insisted, "It's only because you don't want to work." It was an insane idea, but he insisted I call up zoos, so I did but I didn't give my name. Instead, I said, "I'm calling for Mr Roussel. He wants to know about endangered species," because I knew you couldn't do this.'

In the meantime, the tall, athletic Teresa Prater had been working as a model at PH1, an agency run by Paul Hagnoer in Rue Etienne-Marcel, Paris. 'PH stands for my initials and is nothing to do with Thierry,' he told us. 'Teresa was on my books some time ago – about 80 per cent of my models are American girls.' When Thierry offered Teresa the chance to live in his new Portuguese home, she left Paris and moved to the more Californian climes of Brejao. 'When Thierry was there, he lived with her,' said Kirsten Gille. 'He owned the house, and Teresa's pictures were on the wall. But when Gaby and the children came to stay for a week's holiday she went back to her mother Nancy's home in Burbank, California. She decided to attend an expensive interior-decorating school in Los Angeles, and Thierry helped to pay the fees. She came to the Sologne to see him in 1993 at his expense when she had one more year of tuition to go. Thierry told her, "I don't have any more money – you'll have to go and find a job." I remember very well that she was upset. She said,

"I'm 30, and it's my birthday, and he's announced on the same day that I'll have to work instead of finishing school."

'He sent her back to Los Angeles and gave her money although she never told me how much. At Thierry's suggestion, an agreement was drawn up by her lawyer, and she signed it.'

When we contacted Teresa in California, she said: 'I wouldn't want to say anything without Thierry knowing what's happening. I don't see the advantage to me to tell something he probably wouldn't want me to talk about. All these things are personal. [It] depends on what's in it for me. I'm not going to give out information just for the sake of giving it out. Obviously, if I was giving you information, there would have to be something in it for me.' Teresa accepted that she had met Christina during her relationship with Roussel. Told that this affair was the one that had caused the heiress the greatest heartache, she replied: 'Yes, unfortunately.'

Shortly after *Fortune* magazine had named Athina the 150th richest individual in the world at the age of seven, directors of the Onassis Foundation took the unprecedented step of calling a press conference to repudiate Roussel's claims to her fortune. The foundation had 15 directors, and although only four were involved in administering Athina's share, the two halves of the Onassis estate were effectively under one management at the foundation's headquarters in Amalias Avenue, Athens. The new president, Stelio Papadimitriou, was one of the executives who dealt with both halves. Flanked by the treasurer and other directors, he brought the dispute out into the open by accusing Roussel of trying to get his hands on Athina's money. He said Christina's will allocated money to be paid annually to Roussel. 'But he claims the right to manage all the Onassis assets, something we strongly dispute and an issue which must be resolved before the Greek courts,' said Papadimitriou.

Roussel replied that the dispute should go before the international courts, but the directors maintained that the will was covered only by Greek law. They also claimed that Roussel was distancing his daughter from Greece and her origins. 'Athina must become acquainted with her Greek roots,' said Papadimitriou. 'The child's fortune includes the private Onassis island of Skórpios, resting place of her mother Christina, her uncle Alexander and her grandfather Aristotle, yet she never visits.'

Although the foundation refused to reveal the value of its assets, the treasurer Apostolos Zabelas said the estate had more than doubled since Aristotle's death in 1975. He added that more than $100 million had been allocated to welfare causes from profits earned on the foundation's share of the assets.

The main project had been the construction of an ultra-modern heart surgery hospital in Athens at a cost of $75 million. Gifts of $100,000 had been awarded in the field of 'Man and Mankind' to Bishop Desmond Tutu, the South African civil-rights crusader, the BBC External Services, the American politician Robert McNamara, and Jacques Delors, French president of the European Commission. In the field of 'Man and Culture', prizewinners included Harold Macmillan, the former British prime minister, and Peter Brook, the British theatre director, while Ari's old chum Elizabeth Taylor was among the chosen in the field of 'Man and Society' for her work in AIDS relief. In the arts, a first prize of $250,000 was offered to the winner of an international competition for a play on the theme of 'the problems facing Man on the threshold of the 21st Century'.

However, there had been a major shift in the deployment of the group's assets. Although Olympic Maritime managed all Onassis ships, the foundation had held a larger stake in shipping than Christina had done during much of her lifetime. After her death, the trustees had liquidated the shipping side of Athina's inheritance by selling off older ships, including three of Christina's VLCCs (very large crude carriers) to Shell in 1990 for around $100 million. The trustees said that while Aristotle's will had instructed them to continue an active involvement in shipping, Christina's wish was that the four Greek trustees and her former husband should manage her part of the estate 'prudently and diligently' until her daughter came of age.

'We decided it would not be prudent to continue the involvement of a minor in the shipping business,' said Papadimitriou. Thus the foundation had become the sole shipping operator in the group. In 1991 the foundation had also paid a large cash sum to Athina to take over Olympic Maritime, a move that Christina had foreshadowed during the last months of her life. The name had been changed to Olympic Shipping and Management so that Athina would be able to use the Olympic Maritime title should she choose to go back into shipping in the future.

The foundation had also embarked upon a $350 million tanker-building programme, which climaxed in the delivery of *Olympic Loyalty*, only the third double-hulled VLCC to be built and, at $100 million, the foundation's largest investment. *Olympic Loyalty*, named after the spirit that had guided the foundation since its founder's death, went into service in March 1993 with her profits pledged to philanthropic causes. 'The estate gives about 98 per cent to charity,' said Alecko Papamarkou. 'They have renewed the fleet, and Olympic is still a big name in shipping.'

Athina was becoming aware of the wrangles taking place in her name, and she got an inkling of the interest in her when she acted as a bridesmaid at the wedding of her cousin Arietta Livanos to Giorgios Vardinoyannis at the Aghia Sophia, the Greek Orthodox cathedral in London's Bayswater, in June 1994. The 700 guests included King Constantine, Christina's former stepfather the Duke of Marlborough, and Spyros Niarchos and his wife Daphne, daughter of Guinness chief Lord Moyne. Although 30 minders were hired to keep photographers at bay, a fracas broke out around the child. 'She had been trapped by newsmen at airports before,' said one guest, 'but she had never seen such brute force.'

Although Roussel maintained his charismatic aura in public, his financial state fluctuated alarmingly. In August 1994, he told friends he had lost $15 million on the two innovative farms. 'Thierry makes everything so big, and then it falls apart,' said Kirsten Gille. 'They even took the house in Portugal away because of his financial problems. He used my horse box to move things out. It brought back some horses, including a white one I had given to Thierry and a pony belonging to Athina.' The news only increased Greek anxieties about his suitability to manage Athina's money. 'He's done things so badly,' said Papamarkou. 'All that money, and he'd got next to nothing left! He's a bad businessman.'

On 1 December 1994, the trustees went to court in a bid to take the control of Athina's allowance from her father. They sued in Switzerland, Greece and France over the right to administer her annual 'pocket money', a little matter of £600,000. The trustees claimed that Roussel had used some of the money to take his wife and their three children on holiday with Athina. They alleged that he had included the cost of renovating Bois L'Essert among Athina's expenses. With the dispute between Thierry and the Greeks in the open, Kirsten Gille said: 'They will never, ever, over their dead bodies, let Thierry put a hand on the money. But he will go to the limit.'

Another matter of concern for the Greeks was a suggestion that Athina would convert to Roman Catholicism. 'No matter what the trustees think, Thierry loves his little girl and only wants to do what is best for her,' replied one of his closest friends. 'The whole thing about converting to Catholicism isn't something he's pushing. Athina herself wants to convert because of peer pressure at school.' That was precisely the point, exclaimed the old Greeks, because if she had attended a Greek school, the question would not have arisen.

After Teresa Prater had returned to the West Coast, Roussel faced a new rebellion in his love life from Kirsten Gille. 'The jet set are angels compared with the horsy world,' she said. 'Jetsetters just want to have fun; they're not trying to do business, but the horsy people tried to rip Thierry off, and he got so angry that he sold a lot of our horses. He told me, "Go and work for somebody else because this doesn't amuse me any more." When I'm in love with somebody, I give up everything. I still had some of his horses and some of mine, and I bought ex-racehorses, reworked them and sold them to make enough money to keep going. Thierry had also bought me the horse box, a blue and white Volvo, to drive to competitions, and when somebody asked him at one of the meetings, "Does she cost you a lot?" he replied, "No, she's not expensive at all." I had four horses doing competition, and when they had big health problems, he said to me, "Send them to the butchers."'

After that remark, the relationship was doomed. This had been the final argument, and the Geneva Convention d'Amour was terminated in the summer of 1993. 'Suddenly it just ended when he didn't send me any more money,' said Kirsten. 'I said to him, "You just can't drop me like this. You said you wouldn't." If he hadn't had any money I wouldn't have expected it, but he had money, and I've seen so much of it just thrown away – there is no other word for it.'

Before she packed her Volvo and moved well away from Roussel to a chalet apartment at a ski resort in the Swiss Alps, Kirsten trained a replacement to dance attendance on her lover. 'She was his Moroccan maid Oufa, a very sweet girl,' she said. 'She was not a private secretary, she was more like a private nurse. She came in as a maid and looked very ordinary, but she lost weight and became very pretty, and she really loved Thierry. I taught her how to dress him, and how she was to take care of him. The Moroccan girl really wanted to look after him. He needed to have someone to wash his hair and look after his clothes. She followed Thierry everywhere; if he were in Paris she was with him. She travelled with him a lot. He really needed that.

'She really wanted to learn how to do it, and I showed her. I went out to buy clothes for Thierry at Armani and took photographs of everything so she would know which shirts went with which ties. She adored him, and he needed somebody like her in the world he lives in.'

In an Armani suit and silk shirt and matching tie, with luxurious homes and a private jet at his disposal, Roussel exhibited all the accoutrements of success. However, he was reluctant to speak about himself. 'There are things he doesn't want to talk about,' Roussel's press agent Lionel Lelouch told us in Paris. 'He doesn't want to speak about his private life with his children. He wants to be seen like a family father and someone who takes care of childhood [through the charity Action for Childhood] and, of course, as a businessman. He is a photographer, a boatmaker; he is working in Egypt where he has a factory making household goods, and he is working in collaboration with Roussel Uclaf as a partner. He doesn't stop travelling.'

'People hear the name Onassis and completely lose their brains,' said Kirsten Gille. 'Thierry amuses himself trying to scare them. He blows up and screams or talks very loud and has everybody shaking. He does have a certain charm, which he gets from his mother's side of the family, but he gives the impression that without him you're a dead duck, and he's done it to a lot of people other than me. When Athina is 18 I would like her to turn around and say, "Who *is* my father? What's he really like?"' But Athina for the meantime was still devoted to childhood pursuits.

TWENTY

ATHINA'S DATE WITH DESTINY ON SKÓRPIOS

ATHINA ONASSIS ROUSSEL and her father made an impressive sight out there in the stone-walled cove of Skórpios, the richest girl in the world and the man who was fighting to control her fortune. As a reminder of Athina's status, an armed bodyguard watched from a rocky outcrop and, just off shore, other bulky figures bobbed in powerboats to chase away intruders. Skórpios hadn't seen the like of it in years.

In Greece and Switzerland lawyers still haggled over the billions of dollars that bore the Onassis name. But on Skórpios, in her new blue swimsuit, the sole heiress to this vast legacy was doing something more important to a nine-year-old child. She was taking her father for a ride. Suddenly emboldened, the little girl gunned the Marine Jet 6's powerful engine into life. Straddled behind her, Roussel tensed his muscles as the jetski picked up speed until it was skimming across the turquoise waters of the Ionian Sea. Along the cliffs of this feudal Onassis outpost, the old hands watched in delight: it *was* like old times. They remembered the day Athina's grandfather, Aristotle, had called in the Greek Navy, which threatened to shoot an invading armada of newsmen and photographers out of the water if they persisted in threatening his privacy. That was the image they liked to remember of Onassis: *mangas* – tough, macho.

Ironically, Aristotle was little more to Athina than a face in a photograph and the name on a tombstone. The only man who mattered to her was her father, and in those few moments she had him all to herself on a bucking white seahorse. A man less well prepared than Roussel might have been caught off-guard by the jetski's abrupt departure, but not even the sunglasses framing his plump, clean-shaven cheeks slipped down the length of his rosily tanned nose. The stiff headwind barely ruffled a single blond hair of his neatly coiffed head. As the spray flew in all directions, he looked like a film star who had just stepped on to the set.

At 41, Roussel had long grown accustomed to expect the unexpected from anyone – or anything – associated with the Onassis name. In his experience, there were no exceptions to that rule, not even his eldest daughter. Athina was an Onassis to the very core of her being, no matter how much time and money had been spent protecting her from her tragic past. Black hair tied behind her ears, brow furrowed, lips pursed, dark eyes attentive and alert, Athina was a picture of determination that summer's day in 1994. Concentrating intently, she drove the jetski round and round in large looping circles. While the lawyers argued in three languages and her wealth increased with every loop, Athina was lost in the simple childlike pleasure of showing off to her father.

After 15 minutes, Athina eased up on the throttle, guided the jet-propelled craft into the clear pebbled shallows and deposited Roussel safely back on shore. As she lifted her face to him, she broke into a huge grin, and he kissed her. Whatever the outcome in the courts, Thierry Roussel was certain about one thing: he was never going to let go of his little Grecian daughter. Waiting to greet Athina on the beach were Erik, Sandrine and Johanne. The children chattered in French, the younger ones pleading with their older sister to take them for the next ride. As fishing caiques plied along the coast, eight-year-old Erik announced that he wanted to be a fisherman when he grew up. Not to be upstaged, seven-year-old Sandrine opted for riding instructor, while Johanne, at three the youngest, couldn't make up her mind. Athina, however, was quite sure about her future. 'When I grow up I want to be an acrobat,' said the little girl.

Roussel laughed. 'My role is essentially to prepare Athina to be herself, even if that isn't what people are expecting,' he explained.

'My greatest pride would be for her to be well adjusted like my other children, that she feel part of the family. She calls my wife Mummy and speaks to her in Swedish, like her brother and sisters. She is entitled to a carefree childhood. I don't want her to be treated like a wise monkey. Have you read *The Last Emperor*? That's exactly what I don't want for Athina, that she should become a cult figure. I don't want her to be treated differently from other children.'

Roussel was enormously proud of this high-spirited brood. And protective. 'I suppose I'm a bit like the Mafia when it comes to my family,' he said, 'and that's quite an image.' He added hastily: 'What I mean is, I would be prepared to kill anyone to defend my family if they were attacked.' His attitude was understandable. Kidnapping, hijacking or a terrorist raid were all possibilities, considering the trophies of wealth associated with the Onassis legacy.

It was from Bois L'Essert that Athina and the rest of the Roussel clan had arrived on Skórpios for this important rite of passage into the Greek world. To the island's inhabitants, it was like the fulfilment of a prophecy. Under the terms of Onassis's will, everyone on the Skórpios payroll had to be recruited from Nidri. Their numbers varied between 50 in winter and 100 in summer, so there was a full turn-out to meet their mistress. To their delight, Athina had mastered enough Greek to greet them in their own language. Although she had a picture of Skórpios on her bedroom wall, all she really knew about it was that 'Maman Christina' was buried here.

Inauspiciously for the people of Skórpios, Christina had died just before she could bring her daughter back to this most sacred of all Onassis shrines. They had waited six years to see their new mistress, tending the olive and cypress groves as though she might appear at any time. They rebuilt roads, repaired roofs, kept the houses aired, planted and harvested crops, repainted the boats, all for the Onassis heiress. While *Christina* rusted in a government shipyard, the stone quay built for her was taken over by local fishing boats. The beach where guests had come for lunch at the water's edge became the preserve of seagulls. And when ferryloads of curious tourists approached from Nidri the guards sent them away with a desultory wave. 'They were there to guard the bodies of Aristotle and Alexander from bodysnatchers who would hold the remains to ransom,' said John Politis, an Athenian expert on the Onassis legend.

The villagers worked hard and waited as patiently as they knew they must. In the newspapers, they read that Athina spent her holidays in Marbella, Ibiza or the Sologne. They saw photographs of the little dark-haired girl surrounded by three blond children at her new fortress home near Lausanne and sadly shook their heads. She went to a private school where, apart from her high marks and the presence of a bodyguard, there was little to distinguish her from the other children. They laughed when they read that she had swapped her £1000 Rolex with one of her classmates for a £20 Swatch because she thought it looked more exciting. And they loved the story that, when she had wanted a St Bernard puppy, she couldn't bear to break up the litter – so she had taken all thirteen. Thus was a new legend being grafted on to the old.

But when in high summer the bougainvillaea was in flame and the jasmine gave off its scent, there was also sadness in the air. And when the ouzo flowed more freely than usual, they gave voice to their true feelings. They blamed Thierry Roussel for keeping Athina from them, and they cursed his name. 'He is very badly thought of in Greece,' said John Politis.

Sensing the hostility from his Swiss redoubt, Roussel had felt it was time to make a gesture and planned the holiday. Now, the villagers watched Athina jump in the waves, sunbathe on the beach and tuck into the Greek delicacies they had prepared for her, and they secretly smiled to themselves. The little girl raised by a French father and a Swedish stepmother was still one of their own. Veterans of many years' service, the people of Skórpios were familiar with every twist and turn of the Onassis odyssey. Faithful to the deeper mysteries of mythology, they understood the nature of the hubris that Onassis had brought down upon himself by challenging the gods. The islanders prayed that his only grandchild might at last break the chain of retribution. Perhaps Nemesis had finally drunk her fill of Onassis blood.

'I asked the people in Skórpios not to treat Athina any differently from the other children,' sighed Roussel, knowing he had asked the impossible. 'I am almost satisfied with the result. But the children are overwhelmed by the number of people working for us. Skórpios is very beautiful, but it is also emotionally charged. Several times, Athina has picked some wild flowers to put on "Maman Christina's" grave, although I don't think she remembers her mother.'

Before this visit, Skórpios had been just a name attached to that photograph on Athina's bedroom wall. Now it was a place where real people – her people – lived and worked. She had watched the women, dressed in peasant black, collect olives and bake them into bread, visited the island's farm and followed the fishermen in with the day's catch. And down on the beach, she had listened to the secrets of the murmuring pebbled shore.

No one had minded that Roussel had chosen to move his family into an old fisherman's house rather than the well-appointed villa built for Christina. The house was a four-bedroom residence with a vine-covered verandah overlooking the port. To keep in touch with the latest developments in the drama in which he and his daughter were the key players, Roussel had installed a mobile communications centre. On Skórpios, he knew he was operating behind enemy lines.

Not only was Roussel at the epicentre of ancient Greek culture but he was also surrounded by the advocates of modern Greek aspirations towards his daughter. In this tense atmosphere, it would have been unnatural if he hadn't felt uneasy. Memories seemed to cling to the vine leaves and, in the shadowy groves, restless spirits stirred. But Roussel was not superstitious, and there was ample help available of a less metaphysical kind. His small army of ex-SAS bodyguards was capable of repelling anything from a kidnapping attempt to an invasion of uninvited revellers. In case of emergency, a helicopter stood on a mountain-top landing strip ready for a getaway.

The holiday proved so successful that Roussel repeated the exercise in August 1995 and was back on Skórpios with his family as well as a host of guests. Eleni Syros travelled from Athens to see Athina but soon returned home. 'It was not too bad, not too good,' she told us. 'Athina was very happy – she told me she is going to start at a new school near Geneva. She was a beauty girl, beauty, beauty. I stayed just a couple of days because Mr Thierry had too many visitors. But I was to rejoin them in October when Mr Thierry was taking Athina to Paris to stay at Avenue Foch and to Gothenburg to see Madame Gaby's family.'

No one had loved Christina Onassis more than Eleni Syros, and she was the first to accept that Gaby had turned out to be an excellent mother to Athina. Others among Christina's friends were also willing to concede that this was true. Florence Grinda said: 'It's awful to say this, but maybe Athina has a normal life, and if she had grown up with Christina she would have been spoiled. It's very sad she lost her real mother, it's awful, but at the same time people say Gaby is very nice with her, and Athina always seems very happy, so that makes me happy.' However, she was still highly critical of

Roussel. 'Sometimes I see Thierry when I go to the Avenue Foch to have lunch with my mother,' she said. 'I see him coming out of the house, and we say hello. But I don't want anything to do with the Roussel side of the family because of the way he treated Christina, although he did get her to take a lot fewer sleeping pills. Unfortunately, it didn't save her life.'

If Roussel himself hadn't undergone a substantial change of heart towards things Onassis, he had certainly taken to his role as master of Skórpios. He knew it held a magnetic attraction for people likely to be helpful in business and, once again, an invitation to the island became much sought after. The locals whispered that George Bush, the former US President and director of Onassis's old enemies, the CIA, had been one of the island's holidaymakers. 'It looked like a James Bond villain's hideout,' said a British tourist who got as close as he could to the island at the time.

In this new phase of his career, Roussel knew exactly how Aristotle Onassis had felt all his combative life. In his mind's eye, he pictured the old man, barrel-chested and bandy-legged, dressed only in baggy cotton pants, waving a Montecristo cigar and holding forth in that famous gravelly voice in the mauve light of a Skórpios evening. 'Be rich or be an enemy of the rich,' Onassis liked to say, 'but never envy them or try to please them.' Money was also a favourite topic of Thierry Roussel. 'Fortunes are made and unmade in the wink of an eye,' he said, sending a chill through the greybeards in Athens. But even though Roussel had carved a name for himself, he had to admit that he would be part of the Onassis legend from now on whether he liked it or not. That was the price he had to pay for being the father of Athina.

SOURCES

We are deeply indebted for the generous help we received from many people in researching *Athina: The Last Onassis*. In alphabetical order by place, our special thanks go to the following: Athens: Eleni Syros; Geneva: Kirsten Gille; Gingins: Marianne Fritsch, Tina Schneider; London: Nigel Neilson, Sir Eric Drake, Nadia Stancioff; Melbourne: Bill Green; Miami: Senator George Smathers; New York: Alexander Papamarkou, Frank Monte; Paris: Florence Grinda, Claude Wolfe, Chris Lafaille, Alison James, Graham Tearse; Stockholm: Nicholas George; Sydney: Dimity Torbett, John Jones.

Our gratitude also goes to Doris Lilly, whom Peter Thompson interviewed in New York before her death, Peter Evans for his seminal work, *Ari*, and the *Sunday Times* team led by Nicholas Fraser. We have also quoted from Goronwy Rees in the *Sunday Times* and from *Paris-Match* and *Hello!* The works of Kitty Kelley and C. David Hayman were a great help in understanding Jacqueline Kennedy Onassis.

The books we read included:

Cafarakis, Christian, *The Fabulous Onassis: His Life and Loves*. New York: William Morrow, 1972.

Davis, John H., *The Kennedy Contract*. New York: HarperCollins, 1993.

Davis, L. J., *Onassis & Christina*. London: Gollancz, 1987.

Dedichen, Ingeborg, and Henri Pessar, *Onassis Mon Amour*. Paris: Editions Pygmalion, 1975.

Dempster, Nigel, *Heiress: The Story of Christina Onassis*. London: Weidenfeld & Nicolson, 1989.

DuBois, Diana, *In Her Sister's Shadow: An Intimate Biography of Lee Radziwill*. New York: Little Brown, 1995.

Edwards, Anne, *The Grimaldis of Monaco*. London: HarperCollins, 1992.

Englund, Steven, *Grace of Monaco: An Interpretive Biography*. London: Sphere, 1985.

Evans, Peter, *Ari: The Life and Times of Aristotle Onassis*. London: Jonathan Cape, 1986.

Finley, M. I., *The Ancient Greeks*. New York: Viking, 1963.

Fraser, Nicholas, with Philip Jacobson, Mark Ottaway and Lewis Chester, *Aristotle Onassis*. London: Weidenfeld & Nicolson, 1977.

Frischaeur, Willi, *Onassis*. New York: Meredith, 1968.

Hamilton, Nigel, *JFK: Reckless Youth*. New York: Random House, 1992.

Hayman, C. David, *A Woman Named Jackie*. London: Heinemann, 1989.

Kelley, Kitty, *Jackie Oh!* New York: Ballantine, 1979.

Kesting, Jurgen, *Maria Callas*. Dusseldorf: Claassen, 1990.

Lacey, Robert, *Grace*. London: Sidgwick & Jackson, 1994.

Lilly, Doris, *Those Fabulous Greeks*. New York: Cowles, 1970.

Montague Browne, Anthony, *Long Sunset: Memoirs of Winston Churchill's Last Private Secretary*. London: Cassell, 1995.

Robinson, Jeffrey, *Yamani*. London: Simon & Schuster, 1988.

Sampson, Anthony, *The Seven Sisters*. New York: Viking, 1975.

Summers, Anthony, *Official and Confidential: The Secret Life of J. Edgar Hoover*. London: Gollancz, 1993.

Wright, William, *All the Pain that Money can Buy: The Life of Christina Onassis*. London: Gollancz, 1992.